INSTANT REFERENCE CLASSICAL MUSIC

TEACH YOURSELF®

For UK orders: please contact Bookpoint Ltd, 78 Milton Park, Abingdon, Oxon OX14 4TD. Telephone: (44) 01235 400414, Fax: (44) 01235 400454. Lines are open 9.00–6.00, Monday to Saturday, with a 24-hour message answering service. E-mail address: orders@bookpoint.co.uk

For USA and Canada orders: please contact NTC/Contemporary Publishing, 4255 West Touhy Avenue, Lincolnwood, Illinois 60646-1975, USA. Telephone: (847) 679 5500, Fax: (847) 679 2494.

Long renowned as the authoritative source for self-guided learning – with more than 40 million copies sold worldwide – the *Teach Yourself* series includes over 200 titles in the fields of languages, crafts, hobbies, business, computing and education.

British Library Cataloguing in Publication Data
A catalogue record for this title is available from the British Library.

Library of Congress Catalog Card Number: On file

First published in UK 2000 by Hodder Headline Plc, 338 Euston Road, London NW1 3BH.

First published in US by NTC/Contemporary Publishing, 4255 West Touhy Avenue, Lincolnwood (Chicago), Illinois 60646-1975, USA.

The 'Teach Yourself' name and logo are registered trademarks of Hodder & Stoughton.

Copyright © 2000 Helicon Publishing Ltd

Picture credits:
With special thanks to AKG:
10, 16, 17, 36, 37, 46, 58, 69, 83, 85, 89, 97, 108, 115, 121, 124, 127, 129, 160, 164, 168, 173, 175, 186, 188, 189, 201, 204, 212.

Text editor: Jonathan Powell
Typeset by TechType, Abingdon, Oxon
Printed in Great Britain for Hodder & Stoughton Educational, a division of Hodder Headline Plc, 338 Euston Road, London NW1 3BH, by Cox & Wyman Ltd, Reading, Berkshire

Impression number   10 9 8 7 6 5 4 3 2 1
Year   2006 2005 2004 2003 2002 2001 2000

Contents

Bold type in the text indicates a cross reference. A plural, or possessive, is given as the cross reference, i.e. is in bold type, even if the entry to which it refers is singular.

Abel, Carl Friederich (1723–1787)
German composer whose 40 symphonies and overtures are notable for their advanced harmonic style. He played the harpsichord and viola da gamba, and was a member of the court band at Dresden 1743–58. He wrote a large quantity of instrumental music, of which the works for viola da gamba are perhaps the most notable.

From 1759 Abel lived in London, where he was appointed chamber musician to Queen Charlotte. He promoted, with J C **Bach**, the Bach-Abel Concerts (1765–81).

accent
The stressing of an individual note. Accents can be produced in different ways: by adding loudness; by lengthening a beat (usually the first, as in Viennese waltz rhythm); by shifting the beat, as in syncopation; or by tone quality, where a melody is accented by, say, a crash of cymbals. Strong accents are marked by the sign > or by the abbreviation *sfz* (*sforzando*).

accidental
Signs found in music notation that alter the **pitch** of a note, either up (with a sharp sign ♯), or down (with a flat ♭); a natural sign (♮) returns the pitch back to normal. Music written in **key signatures** that contain many accidentals may require the rarer double sharp (♯♯) and double flat (♭♭) signs, indicating a change in pitch of a full tone.

accompaniment
Music that is provided, frequently by a piano, alongside a solo voice or instruments. It usually furnishes a bass line, chord structure, and rhythmic elements in support of the solo melody. The accompaniment may provide harmonic support (as in the **continuo** playing of the 17th and 18th centuries), melodic imitation and continuation of the solo part (as in many 19th-century songs), atmospheric background (as in orchestral

accompaniments to operatic arias), and so on. In much piano music, the left hand fulfils an accompanimental role.

acoustic
Term describing a musical instrument played without electrical amplification or assistance, for example a classical guitar or a piano. It is also a term used to characterize room response, an important factor in performance. The study of acoustics concerns the science of sound generation and propagation but also embraces psychoacoustics, the psychology of perception.

A so-called 'bright' acoustic provides a lively reverberation, while a 'dry' one is lacking in response.

Adams, John Coolidge (1947–)
US composer whose music relies on the repetition of arpeggio-like structures; he is regarded as a central figure of American **minimalism.** He has gained popularity with his orchestral works *Harmonielehre* (1984–85) and *A Short Ride in a Fast Machine* (1997), while his opera *Nixon in China* (1987) provoked interest with its portrayal of recent political events.

Adès, Thomas (1971–)
English composer whose tartly direct, technically accomplished, and flippantly camp music has wooed the critical establishment and concert-going public alike. He attracted attention with his opera *Powder Her Face* (1994) concerning the decadent Duchess of Argyle; its notoriety, however, stemmed from the fertile imagination of the librettist, Philip Hensher, rather than Adès's conservative score.

Akimenko, Fedir Stepanovych (1876–1945)
Ukrainian composer who studied with **Rimsky-Korsakov** but later developed an impressionistic style and employed delicate textures and unusual harmonies. He was **Stravinsky's** first composition teacher, and settled in France after the Russian Revolution.

Albéniz, Isaac (1860–1909)
Spanish nationalist composer and pianist. His works include numerous **zarzuelas** and orchestral pieces, but his major

Albéniz appeared in public as a pianist at the age of four, then ran away to South America where he played in bars.

achievement lay in the 12-movement piano suite *Iberia* (1906–09). Its highly complex textures, unusual harmonies, and often grandiose manner require a virtuosic technique, while in terms of atmosphere it is unparalleled in its evocation of Spain.

d'Albert, Eugen (Eugène Francis Charles) (1864–1932)

Scottish-born French composer who appeared as a child prodigy. He later became a cornerstone of the German musical establishment and during World War I he repudiated his British birth. His gargantuan piano concertos were recorded in the 1990s after decades of neglect, and his opera *Tiefland* (1903) is still heard sporadically.

> d'Albert was famed for his gargantuan technique as well as his six marriages.

He was greatly admired as an interpreter of the piano works of **Bach**, **Beethoven**, and **Liszt**.

alberti bass

Description of the left-hand **accompaniment** found in much piano writing of Haydn, Mozart, and Beethoven. A broken-chord pattern, it takes its name from Domenico Alberti, who made much use of it.

alberti bass *The typical alberti bass pattern.*

Albinoni, Tomaso (1671–1751)

Italian composer whose music was studied and adapted by J S Bach. He was wealthy and never held a musical appointment, but was a trained musician and wrote over 40 operas and numerous sonatas and concertos in five parts for oboe, trumpet, bassoon, violin, organ, and strings, which helped to establish Baroque orchestral style. His concertos were among the first to be cast in three movements. (*See box on p .4*).

ADAGIO

The popular *Adagio*, often attributed to Albinoni, was actually composed from a fragment of manuscript by his biographer, Giazotto.

---

aleatoric technique

From the Latin word *alea*, meaning 'dice', the term refers to music in which the content is to some extent random, determined by the performer or performance environment. Several post-World War II avant-garde composers allow the performer to choose the order of succession of the composed sections; examples include **Boulez's** *Piano Sonata no. 3* (1956–57), and **Stockhausen's** *Momente* (1961–72). In his *Music of Changes* (1952), **Cage** determined the content of the work by random procedures: by throwing dice according to methods described in the I Ching.

Alkan (Morhange), Charles Valentin (1813–1888)

French pianist and composer of Jewish origin whose formidably difficult piano pieces were neglected until the 1970s. Although he cultivated an advanced, immensely difficult, and often modern technique, he was a follower of Classical formal traditions. As a performer he was ranked with **Liszt**, who was said to

He became a recluse after 1849 and is alleged to have met his death under a collapsing bookcase.

be afraid of playing in his presence. His works were written largely for the piano, and include the *Grande Sonate: Les quatre âges* (1848), in every major and minor key, preludes and studies and the piano Concerto in C sharp minor.

Allegri, Gregorio (1582–1652)

Italian composer who was maestro di cappella of the Sistine Chapel, Rome, 1610–29. His output includes Magnificats, Masses, and motets.

MOZART'S HAND

Allegri's celebrated *Miserere mei* was reserved for performance by the Sistine chapel choir until Mozart, at the age of 14, wrote out the music from memory.

Andriessen, Louis (1939–)

Dutch composer who has questioned many aspects of classical music making, especially through work with his own ensemble, which he performs standing up. His earlier work was influenced by the US composer John **Cage** and is notable for its riotous experimentation (as in *The Nine Symphonies of Beethoven* for promenade orchestra and ice-cream bell of 1970). His later works are notable for a jazz-inspired freeform **minimalism** and vigorously direct form of expression.

Antheil, George (1900–1959)

American composer whose *Ballet mécanique* (1923–25) is scored for anvils, aeroplane propellers, electric bells, car horns, and pianos. This work, along with his aggressive piano sonatas, earned him the reputation of a futurist.

Antheil called himself the 'bad boy of music'.

anthem

An often elaborate religious choral composition, sometimes accompanied by the organ; also a song of loyalty and devotion. English composers of anthems include **Byrd**, **Gibbons**, **Purcell**, **Blow**, and **Handel**.

antiphony

(Greek *anti*, 'against'; *phon*, 'voice') Music that exploits directional opposition of widely spaced choirs or groups of instruments to create perspective in sound. It was developed from Greek models in 17th-century Venice by Giovanni **Gabrieli** and in Germany by his pupil **Schütz**. The practice was revived in the 20th century by **Stockhausen** and **Berio**.

Arcadelt, Jacob (*c.* 1505–*c.* 1567)

Of Dutch or French origin, but particularly noted for his Italian madrigals. He entered the papal chapel in Rome in 1540, and in 1551 he left papal service to go to France, entering the service of Charles, Duke of Guise. Arcadelt wrote Masses and motets and may also have been associated with the royal chapel of France for a time, for he was described as a musician of the king in 1557.

Arensky, Anton Stepanovich (1861–1906)

Russian composer whose elegant but passionate *Piano Trio no. 1* has charmed audiences for over a century. He was originally influenced by nationalist tendencies (he studied with **Rimsky-Korsakov**) but later developed a more eclectic style. He was admired by **Tchaikovsky**, and wrote a set of variations for strings on a theme of his. However, he suffered a major disappointment when Tchaikovsky expressed his dislike for a symphony (based on stories by Dumas) on which Arensky had worked for several years. Mental crisis along with addiction to alcohol and gambling followed.

Argento, Dominick (1927–)
US composer who studied with **Dallapiccola** in Italy. Amidst his modernist colleagues, he employs an agreeably tonal idiom in his lyrical operas, which include *Sicilian Limes* (1954), *The Masque of Angels* (1964), *Miss Havisham's Fire* (1978), *Casanova's Homecoming* (1985), *The Aspern Papers* (1988), and *The Dream of Valentino* (1993).

aria
(Italian 'air') Solo song of reflective character, often with a contrasting middle section, expressing a moment of truth in the action of an **opera** or **oratorio**. Already present in **Peri's** *Euridice* (1600), it reached its more elaborate form in the work of **Handel**, becoming a set piece for virtuoso opera singers. By the early 18th century an aria was a song in three sections, of which the third repeated the first, while the second introduced contrast. This is known more exactly as the 'da capo aria'. Less rigid forms subsequently developed, shaped by the dramatic action of an opera. (**See also** *Beethoven, Weber*, and *Verdi*).

Arne, Thomas (1710–1778)
English composer who introduced Italian-style opera to the London stage with works such as *Artaxerxes* (1762). He is remembered for the songs 'Where the bee sucks' from *The Tempest* (1746), 'Blow, blow thou winter wind' from *As You Like It* (1740), and, above all, 'Rule Britannia!' from the masque *Alfred* (1740).

> ❝ Kept bad company: he had written for vulgar singers and hearers too long to be able to comport himself properly at the opera house. ❞
>
> **C. Burney,** *A General History of Music,* on Thomas Arne

Arnold, Malcolm Henry (1921–)

English composer of traditional inclination whose witty, high-spirited, and well-designed compositions include orchestral, chamber, ballet, and vocal works. His overture *Tam O'Shanter* (1955) is well known. He also wrote music for more than 80 films, including *The Bridge on the River Kwai* (1957), for which he won an Academy Award.

ars antiqua

(Latin 'old art') Music of the Middle Ages including plainsong; generally lacking **counterpoint**.

Ars nova (Latin 'new art') Developed in France and Italy during the 14th century. Originally introduced by Philippe de Vitry, it is distinguished by rhythmic and harmonic variety, and the increased importance of independent voice parts. Machaut mastered the style in France, while in Italy it was developed into the madrigal.

Ars subtilior (Latin 'the more refined art') Describes a late 14th-century style of great notational and rhythmic complexity. Certain works by Philipottus, Senleches, Ciconia, and Asproys include cross-rhythms of a baffling complexity that have no parallels until the 20th century.

atonality

Music in which the sense of **tonality** is distorted or obscured; music of no apparent key. It is used by film and television composers for situations of mystery or horror, exploiting dissonance for its power to disturb.

For **Schoenberg**, pioneer of atonal music from 1909, the intention was to liberate tonal expression, not primarily to disturb, and he rejected the term as misleading. Other exponents of atonality include **Berg**, **Webern**, **Stockhausen**, and **Boulez**.

Auber, Daniel François Esprit (1782–1871)

French composer of nearly 50 operas, including *Fra Diavolo* (1830), and *Manon Lescaut* (1856), 37 years before Puccini's opera of the same name. Born in Normandy, he was sent to London to follow a commercial career. His first opera to be produced in public, *Le Séjour militaire* (1813), failed miserably,

Auber's opera *La muette de Portici* (1828) caused a riot at its first performance.

and he had no success until his father's death in 1819 compelled him to make music his means of livelihood. *La Bergère châtelaine* (1820) was a brilliant success. In 1822 he began his association with the librettist Scribe, and the two began a series of successful and popular productions.

Auric, Georges (1899–1983)
French composer and member of the group 'Les Six', who were influenced by **Satie**. His works include a comic opera, *Sous le masque*, several ballets, and music for films ranging from Cocteau's *Orphée* (1950) to the Ealing comedy *The Lavender Hill Mob*.

authenticity
A trend initiated in Austria and the Netherlands in the 1950s that aimed to reproduce the original conditions of early music performance. Pioneered by performers such as Nikolaus Harnoncourt and Gustav Leonhardt, authenticity stimulated important practical research in manuscript editing and transcription, instrument making, and vocal techniques. The interest in authenticity grew rapidly; there are a number of flourishing 'authentic' ensembles in the USA and in most European countries. Notable UK exponents include the conductors Andrew Parrott and Roger Norrington, and the harpsichordist Trevor Pinnock.

Babbitt, Milton (1916–)

US composer and theorist who pioneered the application of information theory to music in the 1950s, and introduced set theory to musical analysis. His works include four string quartets, works for orchestra, *Philomel* for soprano and tape (1963–64), and *Ensembles for Synthesizer* (1967). The latter two works were both composed using the 1960 RCA Princeton-Columbia Mark II Synthesizer, which he helped to design. He taught at Princeton from 1948 and has influenced many US composers and theoreticians.

Bacewicz, Grazyna (1909–1969)

Polish composer and violinist who studied in Paris with Nadia **Boulanger**. Although most of her work has been described as **Neo-Classical**, her later music also uses techniques associated with her avant-garde compatriots such as **Lutosławski**. She taught at Lódz Conservatory 1934–35, returning to Paris in 1945. She wrote four symphonies (1945–53), seven violin concertos (1937–65), and much chamber music.

Bach family

At least 20 members of this family were active musicians between the 17th and 19th centuries.

- *Johann Christoph Bach* (1642–1703) became organist at Eisenach in 1665 and remained there to the end of his life. He composed motets, church cantatas, chorale preludes for organ, and harpsichord music. His cousin was the father of the most famous member of the family:

- *Johann Sebastian Bach* (1685–1750), the master of **counterpoint**, his music epitomizes the Baroque polyphonic style. His orchestral music includes the six *Brandenburg Concertos* (1721), other concertos for keyboard instrument and violin, four orchestral suites, sonatas for various instruments, three partitas and three sonatas for violin solo, and six unaccompanied cello suites. Bach's keyboard music, for clavier and organ, his **fugues**, and his choral music are of equal importance. Bach married twice and had more than 20 children (although several died in infancy). His second wife, Anna Magdalena Wülkens, was a soprano; she also worked for him when his sight failed in later years. Although he was not always appreciated by his contemporaries, Bach's place in music history has been unassailable since the early 19th century.

Born at Eisenach, Bach came from a distinguished musical family. After his father's death in 1695 he went to Ohrdruf and studied under Johann Christoph Bach (see above). In 1705 he took leave to travel to Lübeck, to hear Dietrich **Buxtehude** play the organ; this had a profound effect on Bach's own writing for the instrument. In 1708 he went to Weimar as court organist, and remained there for nine years; during this time he wrote such famous cantatas as *Christ lag in Todesbanden, Weinen, Klagen, Sorgen, Zagen* (1714), and *Ich hatte viel Bekümmernis* (about 1717). In 1717 Bach was appointed Kapellmeister to the court of Prince Leopold of Anhalt-Cöthen. At Cöthen

Bach family *Johann Sebastian Bach.*

Bach had little opportunity for composing church music and wrote mainly instrumental works, including the *Brandenburg Concertos* (1721), *Orchestral Suites*, and works for solo cello and violin. In these works instrumental music seems for the first time to emerge from private use into the public domain.

In 1723 he returned to church work, succeeding Kühnau as Cantor of St Thomas' in Leipzig. He remained there for the rest of his life and wrote some of his greatest compositions, including the B minor Mass (1724–46), *St Matthew Passion* (1729), and *Goldberg Variations*. In 1749 his eyesight failed; an operation in 1750 was unsuccessful, and he spent his last months totally blind. Although Bach is not credited with revolutionizing musical forms, he invested contemporary models with a unique brand of creative polyphony and intense spirituality: all his works were dedicated 'To the Greater Glory of God'.

> ❝ I have always kept one end in view, namely, with all good will to conduct a well regulated church music to the honour of God. ❞
>
> Johann Sebastian **Bach**, in a letter, 1708

- *Wilhelm Friedemann Bach* (1710–1784) was the eldest son of Johann Sebastian and also an organist. Educated at Leipzig University, he received his musical training from his father. He was appointed organist of St Sophia's, Dresden, in 1723, and in 1746 succeeded Friedrich Zachau as organist of St Mary's, Halle. He did not hold a permanent position after 1748, living an unsettled life and attempting to support his family, mainly by teaching. In 1774 he went to Berlin where his remarkable organ playing could still arouse astonishment, but his last years were spent in increasing poverty. His works include cantatas and other church music; 9 symphonies; keyboard concertos; 9 sonatas, 12 fantasias, and other works for keyboard.

- *Carl Philip Emanuel Bach* (1714–1788) was the third son of Johann Sebastian but next after him in order of significance. He introduced a new 'homophonic' style, light and easy to follow, which influenced **Mozart**, **Haydn**, and **Beethoven**. In the service of Frederick the Great 1740–67, he left to become master of church music at Hamburg in 1768. He wrote over 200 pieces for keyboard instruments, and published a guide to playing the piano. Through his music and concert performances he helped to establish a leading solo role for the piano in Western music.

- *Johann Christoph Friedrich Bach* (1732–1795), the ninth son of JS Bach, wrote mainly choral works: among his most notable are the oratorios *Die Kindheit Jesu* and *Die Auferweckung Lazarus*.

- *Johann Christian Bach* (1735–1782), the eleventh son, became famous in Italy as a composer of operas. In 1762 he was invited to London, where he became music master to the royal family. He remained in England until his death, achieving great popularity both as a composer and a performer.

A musical theme derived from the name BACH in German nomenclature – the notes B♭, A, C, B♮ – has been used by various composers as a reference to Johann Sebastian Bach, who was himself the first to use it. Some examples are:

- Bach, J S   the final unfinished fugue in *The Art of Fugue*
- Bach, J C   Fugue for organ
- Busoni   *Fantasia contrappuntistica* for piano
- Casella   *Ricercari sul nome di Bach* for piano
- Honegger   *Prélude, ariso et Fughette* for piano
- Koechlin   *Offrande musicale* for organ or orchestra
- Liszt   Fantasy and Fugue for organ
- Nielsen   Ricercare, Chorale, and Toccata for piano
- Reger   Fantasy and Fugue for organ
- Rimsky-Korsakov   Fugue in *Chopsticks* Variations
- Schoenberg   Variations for Orchestra
- Schumann   Six Fugues for organ or pedal piano

Badings, Henk (Hendrik Herman) (1907–1987)
Dutch composer who trained as a mining engineer. Although he ran the Hague Conservatory during the Nazi occupation, he was later cleared of collaboration; he struck out in an experimental direction with various pieces involving electronics, including radio operas and the first all-electronic ballet *Kain* (1956). He also devised a 31-note scale of **microtones.**

bagatelle
(French 'trifle'). A short character piece, often for piano.

Balakirev, Mily Alekseyevich (1837–1910)
Russian composer who was leader of the group known as 'The Five' and taught its members, **Mussorgsky**, **Cui**, **Rimsky-Korsakov**, and **Borodin**. His piano fantasy *Islamey* (1869) is a compendium of Romantic virtuosic styles and devices; it also epitomizes the instrumental writing of the Russian nationalists.

Balakirev learnt most of what he knew in the music library and private orchestra of the landowner Aleksandr Ulibishev. At 18 he went to St Petersburg and won the approval of **Glinka**. In 1861 he began to form the group of nationalist musicians, and even influenced **Tchaikovsky** to some extent. In 1862 he helped to establish the Free School of Music and conducted its progressive symphonic concerts. However, in 1871 he had a grave nervous breakdown and withdrew from public life; he was forced to resort to becoming a railway official and turned to religious mysticism. Not until 1876 did he begin to compose again, and only in 1883, when he was appointed director of the Imperial Chapel, did he emerge once more. He retired in 1895 with a pension and composed with renewed energy, but was almost forgotten by his former friends. His works include two symphonies, symphonic poems *Russia* and *Tamara*, two piano concertos (the second finished by Lyapunov), many piano works including two sonatas, *Reminiscences of Glinka's* and *A Life for the* Tsar, numerous shorter pieces, and 43 songs.

ballad

Originally the music for a dancing song, but by the 14th century the term had lost its connection to dance and later became a simple, narrative song. The related *ballade* was a poetic form developed in France in the later Middle Ages. In music, a ballade is an instrumental piece based on a story real or imaginary; it was a term used for piano works by **Chopin, Liszt,** and **Fauré**.

ballet

(Italian *balletto* 'a little dance') Theatrical representation in dance form in which music also plays a major part in telling a story or conveying a mood. Some such form of entertainment existed in ancient Greece, but Western ballet as we know it today first appeared in Renaissance Italy, where it was a court entertainment. From there it was brought by Catherine de' Medici to France in the form of a spectacle combining singing, dancing, and declamation. There was not always a clear distinction between opera and ballet, since ballet during this period often included singing, and vice versa, but during the 18th century, ballet gradually emerged as an art form in its own right.

Carlo Blasis is regarded as the founder of Classical ballet, since he defined the standard conventional steps and accompanying gestures. Characteristics of the Romantic era were the new calf-length white dress and the introduction of dancing on the toes, *sur les pointes*. The technique of the female dancer was developed, but the role of the male dancer was reduced to that of being her partner. Important choreographers of the period were Jules Joseph Perrot (1810–1894) and Arthur Saint-Léon (1821–1871). From 1860 ballet declined rapidly in popular favour in Europe, but its importance was maintained in St Petersburg under Marius Petipa (1818–1910).

Russian ballet was introduced to the West by Diaghilev, who set out for Paris in 1909 and founded the Ballets Russes (Russian Ballet). Ballets presented by Diaghilev's company included *Les Sylphides*, *Schéhérazade*, *Petrushka*, *The Rite of Spring*, and *Les noces*. With the founding of the Ballets Russes, innovative choreography transformed the visual aspects of ballet and striking new compositions by **Debussy**, **Ravel**, and especially **Stravinsky** left their mark, not only on the ballet composers who followed, but on the course of music history itself. In the 20th century Russian ballet has had a vital influence on the Classical tradition in the West, and ballet developed further in the USA through the work of Balanchine (who had danced in the Ballets Russes), and in the UK through the influence of Marie Rambert. She launched the careers of choreographers such as Frederick Ashton, who helped found the National Ballet in 1928.

Banchieri, Adriano (1568–1634)

Italian organist, theorist, and composer whose theoretical works, especially on **figured bass** (*L'organo suonarino*, 1605) and vocal ornamentation (*Cartella musicale*, 1614) has done much to help the understanding of performance practice in the pre-Classical era. A Benedictine monk, he helped to found the Accademia dei Floridi at Bologna in 1615.

Banchieri's sequence of madrigals *La pazzia senile* (1595) has been described as the first comic opera.

Barber, Samuel (1910–1981)

US composer who wrote his famous *Adagio* for strings at the age of 25. This lyrical and fastidiously worked composition hung like an albatross around Barber's neck for the duration of his career; many of his subsequent works are in a **Neo-Classical**, astringent style. His opera *Antony and Cleopatra* (1966) was commissioned for the opening of the new Metropolitan Opera House at the Lincoln Center, New York City. Owing to an over-elaborate staging, the opera was a failure at its premiere, although it had some success in a revised version in 1974. His Piano Sonata was championed by Vladimir Horowitz

barcarolle

Song of the type sung by Venetian gondoliers. The barcarolle is always in moderate duple time (6/8 or 12/8), with a swaying rhythm. Instrumental barcarolles also exist, for example Chopin's *Barcarolle* (1846).

Baroque music

Music of the period following the Renaissance and preceding the Classical period, lasting from about 1600 to the deaths of **Bach** and **Handel** in the 1750s. It is characterized by independent voices and instrumental parts, as epitomized by the **fugue**, which flourished during these years; the development of continuo writing, specifically the **figured bass**, as an accompaniment to a melody line or orchestral parts; the use of contrasting effects, both instrumental (groups are opposed in the **concerto grosso**) and dynamic (for example, from *forte* (loud) to *piano* (soft), in the manner of an echo), and the importance of **ornamentation**. The most important Baroque composers include **Bach, Handel, Frescobaldi, Monteverdi** (in his later works), and **Vivaldi**.

Barraqué, Jean (1928–1973)
French composer whose disciplined technique was well suited to serialism, which formed a cornerstone of his compositions. His first compositions were the Piano Sonata, begun in 1950 and subsequently established as a classic of its time, and *Séquence*, revised in 1955. In 1955 he began work on a series of major compositions collectively entitled *La mort de Virgile*, based on the book by Hermann Broch, but never completed it. His highly eloquent and dramatic voice has, since his early death, emerged as one of the most singular of the post-World War II era. His last completed work was the clarinet concerto (1962–68). He also wrote a short book on **Debussy**.

Barry, Gerald (1952–)
Highly original Irish composer influenced somewhat by composers with whom he has studied, including **Stockhausen, Kagel**, and Friedrich Cerha. His *Cheveux-de-frise* caused a stir at the 1988 London Promenade Concerts; other works include the operas *The Intelligence Park* (1987) and *The Triumph of Beauty and Deceit* (1993), a piano concerto (1977), and *Handel's Favourite Song* for clarinet and ensemble (1981).

Bartók, Béla (1881–1945)
Hungarian composer, much influenced by Hungarian folk music. He incorporated its rhythms and melodic characteristics into complex, subtle, and effective forms. A child prodigy, he studied music at the Budapest Conservatory, having appeared in public as a pianist at the age of ten. Initially influenced by **Liszt**, he wrote the symphonic poem *Kossuth* (1903), which was conducted by Hans Richter in Manchester in 1904. About 1905 he began to collect folk tunes, often with **Kodály**, and they discovered that the true Magyar music differed greatly from that of the Hungarian gypsies, whose music had been regarded as the only Hungarian folk music.

After World War I Bartók began to be known in Europe and the USA, and in 1922 was made an honorary member of the International Society for Contemporary Music. Some of his most demanding music was written in the years 1917–34: *The Miraculous Mandarin*, his first two piano concertos, and string quartets nos. 2–5. Increasing political isolation in his homeland (Hungary became Fascist before Germany) encouraged Bartók to pursue a career abroad. A more accessible idiom, with longer melodic lines and less astringent harmony, was in evidence by

Bartók, *A caricature of Béla Bartók by Aline Fruhauf.*

1938, with the *Music for Strings, Percussion and Celesta* and the second violin concerto.

In 1940 Bartók emigrated to the USA. He was already suffering from leukaemia and was not in demand as a pianist or, initially, as a composer. A 1943 commission from the Koussevitzky Foundation for the *Concerto for Orchestra* helped to alleviate his financial hardship. The third piano concerto was written when Bartók was terminally ill; the central adagio religioso pays direct tribute to Beethoven's 'Song of Thanksgiving' from the A minor quartet, although Bartók must have known that in his case there was to be no recovery from illness. Bartók's orchestral music has become relatively popular, although his genius is more fully revealed in his innovative approach to the keyboard and especially the six string quartets, which are widely regarded as the best since Beethoven's.

BARTÓK'S BANNED BALLET

The lurid *Miraculous Mandarin* ballet was written under the influence of Stravinsky and Schoenberg; it was banned after a single performance in Cologne.

Bax, Arnold Edward Trevor (1883–1953)

English composer whose sumptuous, late-Romantic style found little favour from the modernist 1920s onwards. His Second Piano Sonata was admired by **Rachmaninov** and was written, as were many other of his pieces for the instrument, for Harriet Cohen. Other works, often based on Celtic legends, include seven symphonies and the tone poems *The Garden of Fand* (1913–16) and *Tintagel* (1917–19). He was Master of the King's Musick (1942–53).

Bax was noted for his passions for women, alcohol, and Ireland, and suggested that:

> ❝ One should try everything once, except incest and folk-dancing. ❞
>
> Arnold **Bax** in *Farewell, my Youth*, 1943

Beethoven, Ludwig van (1770–1827)

Beethoven's mastery of musical expression in every genre made him the dominant influence on 19th-century music. Born in Bonn, the son and grandson of musicians, Beethoven became deputy organist at the court of the Elector of Cologne at Bonn before he was 12; he then studied under **Haydn** and for a short while **Mozart**, whose influence dominated his early work. After returning to Vienna in 1792 he lived there for the rest of his life, scarcely leaving the city or its suburbs. In 1795 Beethoven published his Op.1, three piano trios, and made his first public appearance in Vienna as a pianist and composer. He lived by playing and teaching, and later increasingly by the

Beethoven *He began to free music from its religious and courtly contexts and establish it as an art in its own right*

publication of his works. The set of six string quartets Op.18 (1798–1800), though Classical in form and influenced by Haydn, are strongly expressive in content. The deafness that had threatened from as early as about 1795 increased, and his despair gave rise to the suicidal '*Heiligenstadt Testament*' in 1802; Beethoven's musical response, however, was the radiant and untroubled Second Symphony. His Third Symphony (*Eroica*) was dedicated to Napoleon, but Beethoven changed the dedication when Napoleon proclaimed himself Emperor. The symphony was highly influential in driving music towards the Romantic style asserted later in the century – the very concept of symphonic form was hugely extended.

Beethoven conducted his only opera, *Fidelio*, in 1805; the difficulties he faced in reaching a final version are typical of his painstaking working methods. He refused to accept regular employment, but in 1808 Archduke Rudolph agreed to pay him an unconditional annuity; the Fifth Symphony dates from the same year, and is seen to proclaim the individual's sense of worth and identity. By 1806 deafness forced him to abandon performance, leaving time for composition: there followed the piano concertos 4 and 5, the Rasumovsky quartets, and symphonies 6–8. By turns lyrical, expansive, serene, and dynamic, the music of this middle period gained Beethoven further public recognition as the leading composer of the day. The last great piano works were initiated in 1818 by the *Hammerklavier* sonata; these pieces extended instrumental technique to new limits, but at the same time combine the intellectual and expressive in a way not achieved by other composers. By 1819 Beethoven was totally deaf; he had begun work on the Ninth Symphony in 1817, this was followed by the *Missa solemnis* (1819–22) and the last five quartets (1822–26). In 1826 he caught an infection from which he never recovered, and his death the following year was due to dropsy.

- *Beethoven's Symphonies*

  no. 1 in C, Op.21 (1800); no. 2 in D, Op.36 (1802); no. 3 in E♭ (*Eroica*), Op.55 (1803); no. 4 in B , Op.60 (1806); no. 5 in C minor, Op.67 (1808); no. 6 in F (*Pastoral*); Op.68 (1808); no. 7 in A, Op.92 (1812); no. 8 in F, Op.93 (1812); no. 9 in D minor (*Choral*); Op.125 (1817–24).

- *Beethoven's Quartets*

  Op.18 nos. 1–6, in F, G, D, C minor, A, and B♭ (1798–1800); Op.59 nos. 1–3, *Rasumovsky*, in F, E minor, and C (1806); Op.74 in E♭ *Harp*, (1809); Op.95 in F minor (1810); Op.127 in E♭ (1825); Op.130 in B♭ (1826; present rondo finale replaces original *Grosse Fuge*, Op.133); Op.131 in C♯ minor (1826); Op.132 in A minor (1825); Op.135 in F (1826).

- *Beethoven's Piano Sonatas*

  Op.2 nos. 1–3, in F minor, A, and C (1795); Op.7 in E♭ (1796); Op.10 nos. 1–3, in C minor, F, and D (1798); Op.13 in C minor (*Pathétique*) (1799); Op.14 nos. 1 and 2 in E and G (1799); Op.22 in B♭ (1800); Op.26 in A♭ (1801); Op.27 nos. 1 and 2, in E♭ and C♯ minor (*Moonlight*) (1801); Op.28 in D (*Pastoral*) (1801); Op.31 nos. 1–3, in G, D minor, and E♭ (1802); Op.49 nos. 1 and 2, in G minor and G (1802); Op.53 in C (*Waldstein*) (1804); Op.54 in F (1804); Op.57 in F minor (*Appassionata*) (1805); Op.78 in F♯ (1809); Op.79 in G (1809); Op.81a in E♭ (*Les Adieux*) (1801); Op.90 in E minor (1814); Op.101 in A (1816); Op.106 in B♭ (*Hammerklavier*) (1818); Op.109 in E (1820); Op.110 in A♭ (1821); Op.111 in C minor (1822).

Other works include the opera, *Fidelio*, (1805, revised twice); the Mass in C, Op.86 (1807); *Choral Fantasia*, for piano, chorus, and orchestra, Op.80 (1808); Mass in D, (*Missa solemnis*), Op.123 (1819–22); 5 piano concertos; Violin Concerto, Op.61 (1806); Triple Concerto for piano, violin, and cello, Op.56, (1804); 3 *Leonora* overtures (1805, 1806); *Coriolan* overture, Op.62 (1807); 6 piano trios; 10 sonatas for violin and piano; 5 sonatas for cello and piano; sets of smaller pieces and variations for piano; and numerous songs, including *An die ferne Geliebte* for tenor and piano (1816).

> ❝ Prince, what you are, you are by the accident of your birth; what I am, I am of myself. ❞
>
> Ludwig Van **Beethoven**, in a letter to Prince Lichnowsky, 1806

bel canto
(Italian 'beautiful song') An 18th-century Italian style of singing, with emphasis on perfect technique and beautiful tone. The style reached its peak in the operas of **Rossini**, **Donizetti**, and **Bellini**.

Bellini, Vincenzo (1801–1835)
Italian composer of operas who developed a simplicity of melodic expression in his Romantic evocations, as in *La Sonnambula/The Sleepwalker* and *Norma*, both of 1831. His first opera, *Adelson e Salvini*, was produced in 1825, while still a student; it attracted the attention of Domenico Barbaia, who commissioned him to write a second, *Bianca e Gernando*, produced

at the Teatro San Carlo in 1826. *Norma* followed in 1831: this opera marks the culmination of Bellini's style, with its long and elegiac melodic line and superbly crafted dramatic tension. In *I Puritani* (1835), his last work, he discovered a new boldness and vigour of orchestral effect. His popularity after his death was enormous, but his operas later fell into neglect. Since World War II, however, singers including Maria Callas, Joan Sutherland, and Montserrat Caballé, have helped to restore their popularity.

> ❦ Carve in your head by letters of brass: an opera must draw tears, cause horror, bring death, by means of song. ❧
>
> **Bellini**, in a letter, 1834

Benda, Jiři or Georg (1722–1795)
Member of a noted Czech musical family whose three melodramas for narrator accompanied by an orchestra are the first of their kind. His other works include church music, cantatas, chamber music, and works for the stage.

Benjamin, George William John (1960–)
English composer who, as a teenager, studied with **Messiaen** who, along with the younger **Murail,** has influenced his work. He then went to Cambridge to study with Alexander **Goehr**, later returning to France to work at the electronic studios IRCAM. His elegant and colourful compositions also incorporate elements of the British mainstream as represented by **Knussen**. His works include *At First Light,* for chamber orchestra (1982); *A Mind of Winter,* for soprano and ensemble; *Antara* for chamber orchestra with electronics (1985–87); and *Sudden Time* for orchestra (1993).

See also: *electronic music.*

Bennett, William Sterndale (1816–1875)
English composer and friend of **Schumann** who dedicated his *Etudes symphoniques* to him. A chorister at King's, Cambridge, he later conducted the first English performance of Bach's *St Matthew Passion* in 1854. He was professor of music at Cambridge University (1856–75) and principal of the Royal Academy of Music (1866–75). His works include incidental music to Sophocles' *Ajax* (1872), the cantata *The May Queen* (1858), six symphonies (1832–64), and five piano concertos (1832–38).

berceuse

Lullaby, usually in the form of an instrumental piece in moderately relaxed duple time (6/8). The most famous example is Chopin's *Berceuse* (1844).

Berezovsky, Maksym Sosnovych (1745–1777)

Ukrainian composer who, in 1765, went to Italy to study under Martini. Returning to Russia, he was unable to secure an appointment and finally committed suicide. His most important contribution was to church music, especially in his choral concertos; he also wrote an opera, *Demofoonte* (1773), the first by a Russian to be heard in Italy.

Berg, Alban (1885–1935)

Austrian composer whose music has become far more widely appreciated than that of the two other composers of the Second Viennese School, **Webern** and **Schoenberg**. The latter's influence on him was profound, and may be seen as Berg passed from the extended tonality of his early works to atonality and, later, serialism. Berg developed a personal twelve-tone idiom of great emotional and stylistic versatility. His music was known only to a small circle until the 1925 production of the opera *Wozzeck*. The Chamber Concerto and *Lyric Suite*, which followed shortly after, incorporate complex formal patterns, numerical puzzles, and autobiographical allusions. He was a friend of Alma Mahler, and the death of her daughter, Manon, inspired his last completed work, the Violin Concerto. Dedicated 'To the Memory of an Angel', Berg wrote the concerto as a Requiem for Manon, yet in its poignant lyricism, quoting a Bach chorale, it is the composer's own last testament. His second opera, *Lulu*, was begun in 1929 but left unfinished after his death and not performed in the full, three-act version until 1979. Other works include a large number of songs, some with orchestra, the *Lyric Suite* for string quartet (1925–26), and the Piano Sonata (1907–08).

> ❝ *Wozzeck* ... marks the summing up of opera, and perhaps Berg has finally written 'finis' to the history of opera. ❞
>
> Pierre **Boulez**, in his notes to his production of Berg's *Wozzeck*

Berio, Luciano (1925–)

Italian composer whose lyrical manner and theatricality have confused the public who wish to see him as a modernist. He attended the Darmstadt courses in the 1950s and mastered serial techniques; his virtuosic handling of the human voice soon became apparent with the series of works he wrote for his wife, Cathy Berberian. Chief among these is *Sequenza III* (1966) in which the expression of almost every conceivable human emotion is crammed into seven minutes' of music. His friendship with Italian writer Umberto Eco propelled him towards James Joyce, who was one of the writers (along with Russian Poet Vladimir Mayakovsky and others) whose work provided the impetus for the splendidly zany *Sinfonia* (1969). Subsequent works such as *Formazioni* (1987) for orchestra, and the opera *Un ré in ascolto/A King in Waiting* (1984) have seen him experiment with **antiphonal** techniques and the aesthetic of the commedia dell'arte.

Berkeley, Lennox Randal Francis (1903–1989)

English composer whose training under Nadia **Boulanger** left a strong French imprint on his style. Much of his work is distinguished by elegance and neatness, but he also developed a more powerful style, especially in his opera *Nelson* (1954). Works of his were heard at the International Society for Contemporary Music festivals at Barcelona and London in 1936 and 1938, and at the Leeds and Worcester festivals (1937–38). Other works include the operas *A Dinner Engagement* (1954), and *Ruth* (1956); the ballet *The Judgement of Paris* (1938); four symphonies (1940–78); a piano concerto (1947); and numerous others.

Berlioz, (Louis) Hector (1803–1869)

French Romantic composer, noted as the founder of modern orchestration. Much of his music was inspired by drama and literature and has a theatrical quality. Berlioz was sent to Paris to study medicine but entered the Conservatory and won the Prix de Rome in 1830. In the meantime he had fallen in love with Harriet Smithson, whom he eventually married in 1833. To supplement his income he became a critic, writing witty dissections of the idiocies of Parisian musical life. His *Messe des morts*, commissioned by the French Government in 1836, was performed the following year at a memorial service for soldiers who had fallen in Algeria. In 1838 **Paganini** sent him 20,000 francs to enable him to devote all his time to composition; the Paganini-inspired *Harold en Italie* had been written in 1834 and was followed by *Roméo et Juliette* (1838–39) and *Benvenuto Cellini* (1834–37).

Berlioz travelled much during the next few years, and conducted in Germany, Vienna, Prague, Budapest, Russia, and London. His brilliant 'légende dramatique' *La Damnation de Faust* was premiered in 1846 and the massive *Te Deum* in 1855, but Berlioz continued to suffer throughout his life from lack of public recognition. He composed his masterpiece, the vast opera *Les Troyens*, in the late 1850s. For many years Berlioz's reputation rested on his *Symphonie fantastique*. It was not until his operas and other large-scale works were widely performed in the 1960s that his true genius was fully revealed. He wrote seven books, including *Treatise on Orchestration* (1844) and his not always reliable *Mémoires*. His works also include the cantata *L'enfance du Christ* (1854) and the opera *Béatrice et Bénédict* (1862).

> ❧ Time is a great teacher, but unfortunately
> it kills all its pupils. ❧
>
> Hector **Berlioz**, *Almanach des lettres françaises*

Berners, Lord (Gerald Hugh Tyrwhitt-Wilson) (1883–1950)
Eccentric English composer, painter, and author. He studied music at Vienna, and also sought the advice of **Stravinsky** and **Casella**. His opera *Le carrosse du Saint-Sacrement* was produced in Paris in 1924, and the ballet *The Triumph of Neptune* in London in 1926; another, with words by Gertrude Stein, *The Wedding Bouquet*, was produced at Sadlers Wells, London, in 1937, with settings he designed himself. He also published two popular autobiographical works, *First Childhood* (1934) and *A Distant Prospect* (1945).

Lord Berners was famed for dyeing the pigeons on his lawns different colours to match his mood.

Bernstein, Leonard (1918–1990)
US conductor and composer whose works established a vogue for realistic, contemporary themes; they include symphonies such as *The Age of Anxiety* (1949), ballets such as *Fancy Free* (1944), and scores for musicals, including *Wonderful Town* (1953) and *West Side Story* (1957). In 1943 he made his debut as a conductor, beginning a highly successful international career:

from 1958 to 1970 he was musical director of the New York Philharmonic. Among his other works are *Jeremiah* (1944), *Facsimile* (1946), *Candide* (1956), and the *Chichester Psalms* (1965).

Berwald, Franz Adolf (1796–1868)
Swedish violinist and composer whose music was largely unplayed in his own lifetime. His symphonies of the 1840s, with titles such as *Capricieuse* and *Singulière*, are highly original: they show a fertile and unusual harmonic imagination as well as an original approach to questions of form. He also wrote operas, a piano concerto, symphonic poems, and some distinguished chamber music. His music is an individual product of the early Romantic period. He settled in Stockholm in 1849 as director of music at the university and court *kapellmästare*; later he managed a sawmill and glassworks.

Biber, Heinrich Ignaz Franz von (1644–1704)
Bohemian composer and virtuoso violinist whose brilliant technique is best heard in the solo sonatas with **continuo** of 1681 and the 16 *Mystery* or *Rosary* sonatas of 1676. Spatial effects are created in the *Vesperae* (1693), the *Missa Sancti Henrici* (1701), and Mass in F minor. He also wrote an opera, *Chi la dura, la vince* (1687), and the *Nightwatchman Serenade*. He is also the probable author of the 53-part *Missa salisburgensis*, performed in Salzburg Cathedral in 1682.

Birtwistle, Harrison (1934–)
English composer who has been misguidedly appointed by the public as an unapologetic avant-gardist. However, he has never been a serialist, nor has he employed any of the other trappings of the avant garde. His early music was influenced by **Stravinsky**, and it may well have been the prominent temporal aspects of that composer's style that attracted Birtwistle, whose own works are often propelled by insistent, if unexpected, rhythms. His first opera, *Punch and Judy* (1967), terrified **Britten** at its first performance, while his masterpiece, *The Mask of Orpheus* (1986), with **electronic music** by Barry Anderson, is a powerful and multi-faceted retelling of the myth central to music. The issue of large-scale form was resolved in his later works by the evolution of a captivatingly organic technique, in which the problems of form find their solution in the musical material itself rather than relying on pre-existent models. Orchestral works include *The Triumph of Time* (1972), *Earth Dances* (1985), and *Panic*.

Bizet, Georges Alexandre César Léopold (1838–1875)

French composer whose operas include *Les Pêcheurs des perles/The Pearl Fishers* (1863) and the immensely popular *Carmen*, produced a few months before his death in 1875. Born near Paris, his abilities developed quickly and his Symphony in C, written when he was 17, is one of the finest pieces written by an adolescent; the score, however, was not performed until 1935 and is now well-known. In 1857 he won the Prix de Rome; he wrote several works in that city and on his return to Paris in 1860 he set out to capture the operatic stage; but although the Opéra-Comique accepted his one-act opera, *La Guzla de l'Emir*, he withdrew it, destroying it later. The Théâtre Lyrique produced his next work, *Les Pêcheurs de perles*, in 1863; *Ivan le Terrible*, written in 1865, said to have been burnt by him, was recovered in 1944 and performed in Germany. In 1872 he was commissioned to write incidental music for Daudet's play, *L'Arlésienne*, produced at the Vaudeville in October. In 1874 Bizet set to work on *Carmen*, which was premiered at the Opéra-Comique, with spoken dialogue, in March 1875. At first it scandalized audiences by its realism, and did not achieve its great popularity until after Bizet's death. His reputation has become hostage to his best-loved work; the passion and melody of *Carmen* should not obscure the same qualities to be found in the Symphony in C, *Les Pêcheurs de perles*, and even *La Jolie Fille de Perth* (1866).

> ❝ As a musician I tell you that if you were to suppress adultery, fanaticism, crime, evil, the supernatural, there would no longer be the means for writing one note. ❞
>
> Georges **Bizet**, in a letter to Edmond Galabert, October 1866

Blacher, Boris (1903–1975)

German modernist composer who encountered difficulties during the Nazi regime. But he later became successful, developing a system of variable metres following arithmetical progressions, upon which many of his works are based. In 1953 he became director of the Berlin Hochschule für Musik. His works include the operas *Fürstin Tarakanova* (1940), *Preussisches Märchen* (1949), *Abstrakte Oper no.1* (1953), *200,000 Taler* (1969), *Das Geheimnis* (1975), and numerous chamber works and songs.

Bliss, Arthur Edward Drummond (1891–1975)
English composer who wrote *A Colour Symphony* (1922) and conducted the first performance of Stravinsky's *Ragtime* in 1918. Educated at Rugby and Cambridge, he served in the army throughout World War I. Early experiments with unusual musical media, as in a concerto for tenor, piano, strings, and percussion, and *Rout* for soprano and chamber orchestra to a text constructed of nonsense syllables, gained him a reputation as an *enfant terrible*. His early compositions were miniaturist but he later embraced larger forms. He published his memoirs, *As I Remember*, in 1970.

Bloch, Ernest (1880–1959)
Swiss-born composer whose highly coloured music often draws on elements of Jewish folk music. Among his finest works are the lyrical drama *Macbeth* (1910), *Schelomo* for cello and orchestra (1916), five string quartets, and *Suite Hébraique* for viola and orchestra (1953). After living in Paris, he went to the USA in 1916 and settled in New York as professor at the David Mannes School of Music. In 1920 Bloch founded the Cleveland Institute of Music, and in 1930 he retired to Europe where some interest was shown in his work: his *Sacred Service* was produced at Turin and *Macbeth* was revived in Naples in 1938. But the anti-Semitic movement encouraged by the Fascists put an end to this appreciation and he returned to live in retirement in the USA at the end of 1938.

Blomdahl, Karl-Birger (1916–1968)
Swedish composer who combined expressionist leanings with **electronic music** in his operas and ballets. In 1960 he was appointed professor at the Stockholm Conservatory. His other works include three symphonies (1943, 1947, 1950), symphonic dances, concert overture, *Concerto grosso* for orchestra; violin concerto (1946), viola concerto, chamber concerto for piano, wind, and percussion, and two string quartets.

Blomdahl's opera *Aniara* (1957–59) concerns a spaceship fleeing Earth after nuclear war.

Blow, John (1648–1708)
English composer who taught **Purcell**. He wrote church music including the anthem 'I Was Glad When They Said Unto Me' (1697). He became one of the children in the Chapel Royal in London as soon as it was re-established after the Restoration in 1660. In 1668 he succeeded Albert Bryne as

organist at Westminster Abbey; in March 1674 he was sworn a Gentleman of the Chapel Royal. In 1679 he was followed in the Westminster organist's post by

Blow's masque *Venus and Adonis* (1685) is sometimes called the first English opera.

Purcell, but returned as organist after Purcell's death in 1695. In 1687 he succeeded Michael Wise as almoner and choirmaster at St Paul's Cathedral (at that time unfinished). He wrote a great deal of effective harpsichord music as well as contributing a significant body of sacred works.

Boccherini, (Ridolfo) Luigi (1743–1805)
The most important Italian representative of the Viennese Classical style. He travelled much and was particularly successful in Paris, where he published his first chamber music. In 1769 he went to Madrid and settled there, being first in the service of the king's brother. In 1787 Boccherini was appointed court composer to Frederick William II of Prussia, who had the exclusive right to his works, but he seems to have maintained his residence in Madrid. After the king's death in 1797 he spent his last years in increasing poverty, largely owing to inconsiderate treatment by his publishers. He composed some 350 instrumental works, an opera, and oratorios.

Boieldieu, François Adrien (1775–1834)
French composer whose first opera, *La Fille coupable*, was produced at Rouen when he was 18. He moved to Paris in 1797, producing his first opera away from home, *La Famille Suisse*, which was so successful that he brought out four more within two years. Being reproached by **Cherubini** for having attained too easy a success on very slender gifts, he studied with him for a while. In 1803 he left for St Petersburg as conductor of the Imperial Opera. There he wrote nine operas 1804–10. In 1811 he returned to Paris, where he had greater success than previously; probably due to there being less competition and an improvement in his work. But he began to suffer from tuberculosis contracted in Russia, and his fortune declined until he was granted a state pension. His works include the operas *Le Calife de Bagdad* (1800), *Ma tante Aurore* (1803), *Aline, Reine de Golconde* (1804), *Rien de trop, Jean de Paris* (1812), *La dame blanche* (1825), and *Les deux nuits*; also a piano concerto (1792), harp concerto (1801), and chamber music.

Boismortier, Joseph Bodin de (1689–1755)
French composer who is reputed to have written the first French concerto in 1729. He wrote three opera-ballets, *Les voyages de l'amour* (1736), *Don*

Quichote (1743), and *Daphnis et Chloé* (1747); eight cantatas, in two books (1724 and 1737), and over 50 instrumental works.

Borodin, Aleksandr Porfirevich (1833–1887)

Russian composer whose principal work is the opera *Prince Igor*, left unfinished and completed by **Rimsky-Korsakov** and **Glazunov**; it includes the famous Polovtsian Dances. His other works include symphonies, songs, and chamber music, all using traditional Russian themes. His father, Prince Gedeanov, registered Borodin as the son of one of his serfs. In 1862 he began to take lessons from **Balakirev**, who conducted his First Symphony in 1869. In the same year, he began his opera *Prince Igor*, working on it at irregular intervals. He lectured on chemistry at the School of Medicine for Women from 1872 to his death and wrote

By profession, Borodin was an expert in medical chemistry.

important treatises on his subject. His best work is highly charged and colourful, without being lurid or melancholy in the manner of some of his contemporaries. Other works include three symphonies (third unfinished); *In the Steppes of Central Asia* for orchestra (1880); two string quartets (1874–79, 1881), and the *Little Suite* for piano.

> ❦ The supreme justification of the amateur in music. ❧
>
> Gerald **Abraham** on Borodin, in *Borodin*

Bortnyansky, Dmytro Stepanovych (1752–1825)

Ukrainian composer who with **Berezovsky** established the choral concerto in Russia and the Ukraine. He studied in Moscow and St Petersburg under the Italian **Galuppi**, whom he followed to Italy in 1768. After further studies at Bologna and Naples, he wrote motets and operas at Venice in 1776. In 1779 he returned to Russia and became director of the Imperial church choir, which he reformed and turned into the Imperial Chapel in 1796.

Böse, Hans-Jurgen von (1953–)

German composer best known for his stage compositions: operas *Die Leiden des jungen Werthers*, after Goethe (1986), *63: Dream Palace* (1990), introducing some popular music elements) and *Slaughterhouse Five* (1995); ballets *Die Nacht aus Blei* (1981) and *Werther Szenen* (1989). Other pieces include Symphony (1976), *Sappho-Gesänge* for mezzo and ensemble (1983), and three string quartets (1973, 1977, 1987).

Boulanger sisters
Nadia Boulanger (1887–1979) taught at the Paris Conservatory and the American Conservatory at Fontainebleau. Many distinguished composers were her pupils, including **Berkeley, Copland, Françaix, Harris, Piston**, and **Glass**. She was the first woman to conduct the Royal Philharmonic, London, in 1937, and the New York Philharmonic. She also taught her sister:
Lili Boulanger (1893–1918), who, at the age of 19, won the Prix de Rome with the cantata *Faust et Hélène* (1913), after Goethe, for voices and orchestra. Her other works include incidental music for Maeterlinck's *La Princesse Maleine* (1918); two poems for orchestra; psalms with orchestra.

Boulez, Pierre (1925–)
French composer and conductor who founded IRCAM, an **electronic music** research studio in Paris 1977. His music is serial in technique but often delicate and sonically beautiful. His style was initially expressionistic, and *Le marteau sans maître* (1955) and the Second Piano Sonata established him early in his career, but as his reputation as a composer grew, so did his desire to become enmeshed in polemics, politics, and administration. His most successful works, which include *Pli selon pli* (1962) for soprano and orchestra, *Rituel* (1974), *Répons* (1981), and *Dérive* for small ensemble (1984), reflect his interests in **Debussy** and **Webern** and also in Joyce and Mallarmé. Boulez is also a leading conductor of 20th-century music: he was principal conductor of the BBC Symphony Orchestra 1971–75 and of the New York Philharmonic Orchestra 1971–77. Many of his major works, such as *...explosante-fixe...*, and his Third Piano Sonata are still incomplete.

❦ Just listen with the vastness of the world in mind.
You can't fail to get the message. ❧

Pierre **Boulez**, quoted in Jacobson, *Reverberations*

Boyce, William (1710–1779)

English composer and organist, best known for his song 'Heart of Oak' (1759). Much of his music exhibits a fresh liveliness, particularly his many dance movements. He was appointed Master of the King's Musick in 1755 and from 1758 organist of the Chapel Royal until deafness forced him to give up. He wrote the stage entertainments *The Chaplet* (1749) and *The Shepherd's Lottery* (1751); **masques** *Peleus and Thetis* (1740) and Dryden's *Secular Masque* (about 1746); incidental music for Shakespeare's *Tempest*, *Cymbeline* (1746), and *Romeo and Juliet* (1750); and the pantomime *Harlequin's Invasion* (with M Arne and Aylward, and containing the song 'Heart of Oak').

Brahms, Johannes (1833–1897)

German musician, considered one of the greatest composers of symphonic music and of songs. Although intended for a career as an orchestral player, he made such progress on the piano that his parents decided to make a prodigy performer of him when he was about 11, but his teachers wisely opposed this. Soon afterwards he began to compose, and in 1853 met Robert and Clara **Schumann**, who took much interest in him. At Hanover in 1859 he premiered his first piano concerto, which, although one of the masterpieces

Brahms, although conservative in taste, had a profound influence on **Mahler** and **Schoenberg**.

of the genre, was poorly received. He first visited Vienna in 1862 and settled there the following year. From 1864 he devoted his time entirely to composition, except for some concert tours on which he played mainly his own works. At Bremen in 1868 he conducted the premiere of his most profound vocal work, *A German Requiem*. His success as a composer was firmly established during the 1860s, and he became known abroad. He did not complete his First Symphony until 1876. It had taken him 15 years and

❝ The metronome has no value ... for I myself have never believed that my blood and a mechanical instrument go well together. ❞

Johannes **Brahms**, in a letter to George Henschel

was written in **Beethoven's** shadow. But after its premiere Brahms was established as the foremost composer of instrumental music of his time. In 1896 he began to suffer from cancer of

As a boy, Brahms had to play in sailors' taverns and dancing-saloons at night to supplement his parents' earnings.

the liver, the disease from which he died. His other works include four symphonies, two piano concertos, a violin concerto, a double concerto for violin, cello and orchestra, three string quartets, three piano quartets, much piano music, and more than 200 songs.

brass family

Musical instruments made of brass or other metal, including trumpets, trombones, and horns. The player's lips, shaped and tensed by the mouthpiece, act as a valve releasing pressurized air into the tube. They are powerful instruments and produce tones of great depth and resonance. In the symphony orchestra the brass instruments are the French horn, trumpet, trombone, and tuba. The *cornet* has its own repertoire of virtuoso pieces; a famous early exponent was the Frenchman Arban, for whom **Berlioz** wrote a part in his *Symphonie fantastique*.

The *horn* family were originally used for signalling and ritual, and share a generally conical bore and curved shape. The hunting horn was adapted and enlarged in the 18th century to become an orchestral instrument. The modern valve horn is a 19th-century hybrid Bb/F instrument; the name *French horn* strictly applies to the earlier *cor à pistons* which uses lever-action rotary valves and produces a lighter tone. The *Wagner tuba* is a horn variant in tenor and bass versions devised by Wagner to provide a fuller horn tone in the lower range.

The *trumpet* is member of an ancient family of instruments existing worldwide in a variety of forms and materials. Valve trumpets were introduced around 1820, giving access to a full range of pitches. Today's orchestral trumpet is valued for its clearly focused, brilliant tone, and variants of the normal trumpet include the soprano in D, and piccolo trumpet.

The *trombone* is a descendant of the Renaissance sackbut and incorporates a movable slide that allows a continuous glissando (slide) in pitch over a span of half an octave. The longer the tube length, the lower the note, so all the notes of the scale are therefore available by placing the slide in any of seven basic positions.

The *tuba* was introduced around 1830 and is surprisingly agile and delicate for its size and pitch, qualities exploited by Berlioz, **Ravel**, and

Vaughan Williams. Different shapes of tuba exist, including the circular or helicon sousaphone that wraps around the player.

See also: *woodwind family*.

Bridge, Frank (1879–1941)

English composer who taught **Britten**. He played the viola and gained experience as an operatic and concert conductor, but later devoted his time to composition, under the patronage of Elizabeth Sprague Coolidge. Starting with the Piano Sonata (1924), his music explores modernist harmonies; his third and fourth string quartets (1927, 1937) show an advanced idiom, not far removed from that of **Berg**. He possessed a formidably polished technique, and is now recognized as one of the finest composers of his generation, particularly in the field of chamber music.

Britten, (Edward) Benjamin, Baron Britten (1913–1976)

English composer whose Sinfonietta was published when he was 19 years old. His first international success was the *Variations on a Theme of Frank Bridge*, played at the Salzburg Festival in 1937. This was followed by a number of works that established him as the leading English composer of the day, especially the stark *Sinfonia da Requiem* (1940) and the *Serenade* (1943). In 1945 his second opera, *Peter Grimes*, established him as a dramatist; it was succeeded by further operas, including the chamber opera *The Turn of the Screw* (1954). Other large-scale operas are *The Rape of Lucretia*, *Albert Herring* (after Maupassant 1947), *Billy Budd* (1951), *Gloriana* (1953), *Noyes Fludde* (1958) and *The Little Sweep* for children (1949), *A Midsummer Night's Dream* (1960), *Owen Wingrave* (after Henry James, 1971, commissioned for television), and *Death in Venice* (1973).

> ❝ There are many dangers which hedge around the unfortunate composer: pressure groups which demand true proletarian music; snobs who demand the latest avant-garde tricks; critics who are already trying to document today for tomorrow, to be the first to find the correct pigeonhole definition. ❞
>
> Benjamin **Britten**, on receiving the first Aspen Award, 1964

Much of his music is inspired by words, as shown by the many song cycles, the *Spring Symphony* (1949), and the *Nocturne* (1958); most of his tenor songs and roles were written for the tenor Peter Pears. He had a close artistic association with **Shostakovich** and Russian cellist Mstislav Rostropovich (1927–) from 1960.

By intellectual conviction and personal disposition (as a homosexual) Britten was an outsider; the themes of lost innocence, persecution, and isolation are constantly repeated in his music, especially the operas. Once treated with caution by both conservatives and the avant garde, he has now reached a wider acceptance.

Brown, Earle (1926–)
US composer who pioneered graph notation (a method of notating controlled improvisation by graphical means) and mobile form during the 1950s, as in *Available Forms II* (1962) for ensemble and two conductors. He was an associate of **Cage** and was influenced by the visual arts, especially the work of Calder and Pollock.

Bruch, Max (1838–1920)
German composer whose G minor Violin Concerto has all but eclipsed his other works which include three operas, including *Hermione* (1872), and many choral pieces. Bruch studied with **Reinecke**, and in 1863 produced his opera *Die Loreley* at Mannheim, having obtained permission from its writer, Geibel, to use a libretto originally intended for Mendelssohn. From 1880 he was conductor of the Liverpool Philharmonic Society, and in 1891 became professor of composition in Berlin. Recent revivals of such works as the oratorio *Odysseus* (1872), the opera *Loreley*, and chamber music such as the Septet have allowed a more balanced view of the composer.

Bruckner, (Josef) Anton (1824–1896)
Austrian Romantic composer whose extraordinary symphonies reflect his naive but profound religious outlook and devotion to **Wagner**. The son of a country schoolmaster, he became an organist in 1845. By this time he had begun to compose, but was dissatisfied with his poor technique and went to study in Vienna in 1855. He was cathedral organist at Linz (1855–68), and on visiting Munich for the production of *Tristan* (1865), he became an ardent Wagnerian. The progress of his work was hindered by his identification by critics with Wagner. Bruckner's music, however, is imbued with a kind of spirituality; this is illustrated by the abundance of

early religious works, and the late *Te Deum* (1882–84). Wide success came after the first performance of the Seventh Symphony in 1884. In 1891 he received an honorary doctorate from the University of Vienna. His Ninth Symphony remained incomplete at his death. Bruckner's symphonies went through several editions and revisions, first through well-meaning cuts and alterations made by the conductor Franz Schalk and then by Bruckner himself. Later editions by Haas and Novak attempt to return to Bruckner's original thoughts.

> ❖ When God finally calls me and asks "What have you done with the talent I gave you, my lad?", I will present to him the score of my *Te Deum* and I hope he will judge me mercifully. ❖
>
> Anton **Bruckner**, quoted in Sutton, *Introduction to the Te Deum*

Bryars, (Richard) Gavin (1943–)

English experimental composer influenced by **Satie** and **Cage**. He studied music privately and has been professor of music at De Montfort University from 1985. Chief among his earlier compositions is *The Sinking of the Titanic* (1969); while he scored a success with the later opera *Doctor Ox's Experiment*.

Bull, John (*c.* 1562–1628)

English composer and keyboard virtuoso. He gained music doctorates at both Cambridge (1589) and Oxford (1592) but in 1613 left England, apparently to escape punishment for adultery, and became organist at the archducal chapel in Brussels. In 1617 he was appointed organist at Antwerp Cathedral, where he remained to his death. Much of his technically brilliant keyboard music is found in the collection *Parthenia* (1613).

Bülow, Hans Guido Freiherr von (1830–1894)

German conductor and pianist who in 1857 married **Liszt's** daughter Cosima. From 1864 he served Ludwig II of Bavaria, conducting first performances of **Wagner's** *Tristan und Isolde* and *Die Meistersinger*. His wife left him and married Wagner in 1870, after which he became more enthusiastic about **Brahms**, conducting the first performance of his Fourth Symphony in 1885.

Burrell, Diana (1948–)
English composer and viola player who was a member of various orchestras after studying at Cambridge. Her music is lyrical, skilfully crafted, and often reflects themes related to nature. Her works include *Symphonies of Flocks, Herds and Shoals* (1995–96), *Scene with Birds* (1989) for orchestra, choral works *Missa Endeliente* (1980), and *Creator of the Stars of Night* (1989), and a singular Viola Concerto (1994).

Bush, Alan Dudley (1900–1995)
English composer who forged his compositions in line with his Marxist beliefs. He wrote a large number of works for orchestra, voice, and chamber groups. His operas include *Wat Tyler* (1948–51) and *Men of Blackmoor* (1955), both had their first performances in East Germany. Bush studied composition with John **Ireland** and piano with Artur Schnabel. He became professor at the Royal Academy of Music, conductor of the London Labour Choral Union, and in 1936 chairman of the Workers' Music Association.

Busnois, Antoine (c. 1430–1492)
Early French composer who was a pupil of **Okeghem**. He served in the Burgundian court until 1482, when he became music director at the church of Saint-Sauveur at Bruges. His works include two Masses, a Magnificat, hymns, 61 songs for three or four voices; motets, including *Fortunata desperata*, used later by **Josquin Desprez**.

Busoni, Ferruccio Dante Benvenuto (1866–1924)
Italian pianist and composer whose visionary composition and playing caused him to be revered by many in his lifetime and beyond. Born in Empoli, near Pisa, he appeared as a pianist in public at the age of seven. He taught in Helsinki, Moscow, Boston, Berlin, Bologna, and Zürich. Extremely prolific in his youth, in 1900 he rejected his previous works and embarked on a highly singular stylistic journey that incorporated Italianate (in the monumental Piano Concerto, with chorus), occult (*Sonatina seconda*), virtuoso (*Toccata*), post-Bachian polyphonic (*Fantasia contrappuntistica*), and Mozartian (the opera *Arlecchino*) elements. His masterpiece, the opera *Doktor Faust*, rejects Wagnerian music-drama in favour of a highly humanist, warmly lyrical, and profoundly visionary aesthetic. His ideas, distilled

in his *Sketch of a New Aesthetic of Music* (1907), were attacked by conservatives such as **Pfitzner**, and lead many to associate Busoni with the futurist movement. As a pianist Busoni was considered to have the most powerful individuality and greatest technical mastery since **Liszt** and **Rubinstein**. As a composer he was admired by **Mahler** and **Schoenberg** alike (one premiered his *Berceuse élégiaque* 1909, and the other arranged it).

Busoni *Italian pianist and composer Ferruccio Busoni.*

❝ I want to attain the unknown. What I already know is boundless. But I want to go even further. The final word still eludes me. ❞

Ferruccio **Busoni**, *Der mächtige Zauberer*

Bussotti, Sylvano (1931–)

Italian composer who embraced the decadent and erotic with the 'chamber mystery play' *La passion selon Sade*. Although associated with the avant garde (mostly because of his early use of graphic notation) his music is almost unfailingly beautiful and rooted in Italian traditions. His interests lie equally in painting, music, and the theatre; he designs the costumes and sets for his many stage works. His most important works include the *Rara Requiem* (1969), the *Lorenzaccio Symphony* (1972), and the ballet *Bergkristall*.

Butterworth, George (Sainton Kaye) (1885–1916)

English composer killed at Pozières in the Battle of the Somme, shortly after being awarded the Military Cross. He collected folk songs, and cultivated folk dancing and composition, and suggested to **Vaughan Williams**' the idea for his *London Symphony* (1911–13); the work is dedicated to his memory. His songs, 'A Shropshire Lad' and 'Bredon Hill', are regarded as among the finest in English music.

Buxtehude, Dietrich (1637–1707)

Danish composer whose fame as an organist awed **Bach** and **Handel**. He is remembered for his elaborate and virtuosic organ works and cantatas, written for his evening concerts (*Abendmusiken*); he also wrote numerous trio sonatas for two violins, viola da gamba, and harpsichord. He was the greatest organ composer of the period preceding Bach.

> Bach is alleged to have walked 200 miles to hear Buxtehude play the organ.

Byrd, William (1543–1623)

English composer whose choral music, including over 200 motets and Masses for three, four, and five voices, exemplifies the English polyphonic style. Probably born in Lincoln, Byrd studied under **Tallis** as one of the children of the Chapel Royal. He became organist at Lincoln Cathedral in 1563 and was elected a Gentleman of the Chapel Royal in 1569, but continued his duties at Lincoln until 1572, when he became organist of Queen Elizabeth's Chapel Royal jointly with Tallis. In 1575 Queen Elizabeth granted Byrd and Tallis an exclusive licence for printing and selling music and they dedicated to her their *Cantiones sacrae* published that year. In 1593 he bought Stondon Place near Stapleford-Abbott, Essex, where he remained for the rest of his life, as far as his duties in London would let him. He was frequently involved in litigation and was several times prosecuted for recusancy

Byrd *The Elizabethan composer William Byrd.*

as a Roman Catholic, but remained in favour with the Queen. Byrd's reputation rests with his three great Masses, in three, four, and five parts, in which his contrapuntal mastery is most fully displayed. Other aspects of his genius are found in the ornate *Cantiones sacrae* and the large body of consort songs and instrumental music.

Caccini, Giulio (c. 1545–1618)

Italian singer, lutenist, and composer of one the first operas. He attended Count Bardi's salon in Florence, and was credited with the invention of a new style of song, the *stile recitativo*, which developed there. In 1600 he was appointed musical director at the court of the Medici family, and remained in their service until his death. He wrote short vocal pieces in recitative style and sang them to the theorbo, which led to Rinuccini's libretto for the opera *Euridice*, first set by **Peri** and by Caccini in 1602. In 1604–05 he visited Paris with his daughter, Francesca Caccini, who was herself a composer as well as a singer.

cadence

Closing progression of chords, usually of two chords linked by a note in common. A cadence defines the completion of a phrase in relation to its starting **key**. A perfect cadence (V–I) corresponds to a full close, a

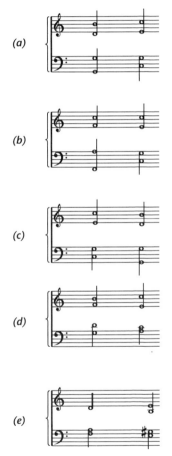

(a)

(b)

(c)

(d)

(e)

cadence *Traditional forms, in the key of C major:*
(a) perfect: dominant to tonic; (b) plagal: subdominant to tonic; (c) imperfect: tonic to dominant; (d) interrupted: dominant to a chord other than the tonic (usually the submediant or subdominant); (e) the so-called Phrygian cadence, where the fall is in the lowest voice. Apart from these traditional forms any harmonic progression which suggests finality, if only temporarily, is technically a cadence.

plagal cadence (IV–I) corresponds to a weak close, and an imperfect cadence (I–V) corresponds to a half close. Other transitional cadences are also found, including the interrupted cadence (V–VI), resolving on a minor chord, and the Phrygian cadence.

cadenza
A solo passage in the style of an improvisation, often found the climax of a **concerto** movement. The practice of actually improvising a cadenza largely ceased around 1780; composers thereafter supplied their own in written form. In the 20th century, however, the practice of the interpreter composing a cadenza re-emerged, with Busoni and Stockhausen writing new cadenzas for Mozart concertos.

Cage, John (1912–1992)
US composer whose interest in Indian classical music led him to the view that the purpose of music was to change the way people listen. From 1948 he experimented with instruments, graphics, and methods of random selection in an effort to generate a music of pure incident. For example, he used 24 radios, tuned to different and changing stations, in *Imaginary Landscape No 4* (1951). Cage studied briefly with **Schoenberg**, and also with **Cowell**, but joined others in reacting against the European music tradition in favour of a freer idiom open to non-Western attitudes. During the 1930s, Cage assembled and toured a percussion orchestra incorporating ethnic instruments and noisemakers, for which *Double Music* (1941) was composed in collaboration with Lou Harrison. He invented the prepared piano, in which different objects are inserted between the strings, altering the tone and the sound produced, to tour as accompanist with the dancer Merce Cunningham, a lifelong collaborator.

Cage was the most prominent pioneer and exponent of experimental concepts as indeterminacy, **aleatoric** music, and silence, his ideas having had a very considerable influence in both the USA and Europe. He sometimes worked to reduce the control of the composer over the music, introducing random elements and allowing sounds to exist independently. In one work, *4 Minutes and 33 Seconds* (1952), the pianist sits at the piano reading a score for that length of time but does not play. He also explored **electronic music**, multimedia (in *Roaratorio*), and published a large quantity of essays and writings that were collected in, for example, *Silence* (1961) and *For the Birds* (1981). Other works include *Europeras I–IV* (1987–91), ballet *The Seasons* (1947), concerto for prepared piano and chamber orchestra (1951), *Construction I in Metal* for percussion sextet (1939), *Fontana Mix* for tape or instruments (1958), *HPSCHD* for seven harpsichords, or tape machines (1970), 30 pieces for string quartet (1984), *Sonatas and Interludes* for prepared piano (1946–48), and *Music of Changes* (1951) for piano.

> ❦ He is not a composer, but an
> inventor – of genius. ❧
>
> **Schoenberg** on Cage, quoted in Yates, *Twentieth Century Music*

camerata
(Italian 'society') A group of intellectuals meeting for cultural exchanges, in particular one at Florence under Count de' Bardi (*c.* 1573–87) who were strongly influenced by Girolamo Mei's research into ancient Greek music. The earliest operas seem to have emerged from their deliberations.

See also: *Caccini, opera, Peri.*

Campion, Thomas (1567–1620)
English poet and musician who wrote four books of *Ayres* (1601–17), for which he composed both words and music. The *Art of English Poesie* is an attack on the use of rhyme and a plea for the adoption of unrhymed metres formed on classical models, such as are used in Campion's own 'Rose-cheeked Laura, Come'. His songs are verbally delicate, and he composed most of his own settings for them; the balance between the lyrics and the music is sensitive and satisfying.

canon
An echo form in which the same melody is played by two instruments or voices with a lapse of time between their starting points. Canonic variations may also introduce a difference in starting pitch between the voices; the highest expression of canonic writing is the **fugue**. A cryptic form of canon cultivated as a form of calling card by composers requires the same fragment of music to be performed by different players in different clefs, for example **Schoenberg's** 'Legitimation als Canon/Canonic Licence' (1925). *Cancrizans* is a term used for the device of repeating a musical phrase or theme backwards, note for note; thus, a canon cancrizans is a canon in

(a) 'standard'

(b) by inversion

(c) by diminution

canon *Canons: (a) standard; (b) by inversion; and (c) by diminution.*

which one part or more proceed normally while another one or more go backwards.

cantata

An extended work for voices; from the Italian, meaning 'sung', as opposed to **sonata**, meaning 'sounded' (for instruments). A cantata can be sacred or secular, sometimes uses solo voices, and usually has orchestral accompaniment. The first printed collection of sacred cantata texts dates from 1670.

Canteloube (de Malaret), (Marie) Joseph (1879–1957)

French composer. In 1900 he began to collect and study French folk song, particularly of the Auvergne region, of which he published several collections. He is best known for his four volumes of folk-song arrangements *Chants d'Auvergne* (1923–30). Other works include the operas *Le Mas* (1910–13) and *Vercingetorix* (produced 1933); the symphonic poems *Vers la princesse lointaine* and *Lauriers*; *Pièces françaises* for piano and orchestra; and the *Poème* for violin and orchestra.

canticle
A hymn or song of praise based on scripture and similar to a psalm, but whose text does not originate in the Book of Psalms. An example of a canticle is the Magnificat of Anglican evensong.

cantus firmus
(Latin 'fixed song') Any melody employed in counterpoint as a reference for the invention of an accompanying melody. In early music, multiple parts were composed one at a time, each referring to the cantus firmus, but not to any other, with sometimes unusual harmonic results.

Cardew, Cornelius (1936–1981)
English composer and pianist who switched from avant-garde aesthetics (which he later attacked as imperialist) to Marxist oversimplification. In 1969 he founded the Scratch Orchestra for non-professional performers, who are free to produce any sounds or no sounds on conventional or improvised instruments. He is most famous for his 193-page graphic score *Treatise* (1967), and the Mao-inspired *The Great Learning* (1970).

Carissimi, Giacomo (1605–1674)
Italian composer famous for his reform of the recitative, and for being practically the inventor of the cantata. He wrote sacred and secular cantatas and motets. His music is distinguished by its pure style and its exquisite melodies, and his followers included the elder **Bononcini** and Alessandro **Scarlatti**. He pioneered the use of expressive solo aria as a commentary on the Latin biblical text. He wrote five oratorios, including *Jephtha* (1650).

carol
Song that in medieval times was associated with a round dance; Christmas carols were common as early as the 15th century. The custom of singing carols from house to house, collecting gifts, is called wassailing.

Carter, Elliott Cook (1908–)
US composer whose creative career has spanned eight decades. He created intricately structured works in a post-Schoenbergian serial idiom, incorporating 'metrical modulation', an adaptation of standard notation allowing different instruments or groups to remain synchronized while playing at changing speeds. This practice was first employed in his *String Quartet No 1* (1950–51), and to dense effect in *Double Concerto* (1961) for harpsichord

and piano. His later music has shown a new tautness and vitality, as in *Three Occasions for Orchestra* (1986–89); he turned again to writing operas (in conjunction with the English writer Paul Griffiths) in the mid-1990s. His most important works include the Piano Concerto (1965), *Concerto for Orchestra* (1969), *A Symphony of Three Orchestras* (1976), and five string quartets (1951, 1959, 1971, 1986, 1995).

Casella, Alfredo (1883–1947)
Italian composer who reacted strongly against the melodramatic operatic tendencies in the Italy of his time and aimed at reviving the Classical Italian, predominantly instrumental music. His own work moved from the influence of **Debussy** and **Mahler** through atonality and towards **Neo-Classicism**. In 1924 he founded, with d'Annunzio and **Malipiero**, an association for the propagation of modern Italian music. His works include the operas *La donna serpente* (after Gozzi, 1928–31), *La favola d'Orfeo* (1932), *Il deserto tentato*; ballets *Il convento veneziano* and *La giara* (after Pirandello); three symphonies, suite *Italia*, *Elegia eroica*, *Pagine di guerra*, *Introduzione, aria e toccata* (1933), concerto for orchestra; *A notte alta*, *Partita*, and *Scarlattiana* for piano and orchestra, and much chamber music.

Castiglioni, Niccolo (1932–1997)
Italian composer whose music is eclectic in style, reflecting the influences of **Debussy, Messiaen, Webern**, and **Cage**, and remarkable for its delicate but precise textures. He has also pursued a career as a concert pianist. His works include *Impromptus I–IV*, and *Rondels* for orchestra; *Movimento continuato* for piano and small ensemble (1959), and *A Solemn Music I* for soprano and chamber orchestra (after Milton, 1963).

Cavalieri, Emilio de' (c. 1550–1602)
Italian composer, long in the service of Ferdinando de' Medici at Florence, and in close touch with the **camerata**. In 1589 he oversaw the production of a lavish series of *intermedi* ('interludes'), to celebrate the marriage of Ferdinando to Christine of Lorraine. His own works were dramatic pieces to be performed in concert form. They include the following, all set to words by Lelio Guidiccioni: *Il satiro*, *La disperazione di Fileno*, and *Il giuoco della cieca* (all lost), and *La rappresentatione di Anima, et di Corpo*, an allegory produced in 1600 and the first play set throughout to music.

celesta
A keyboard glockenspiel producing high-pitched sounds of glistening purity. It was invented by Auguste Mustel of Paris in 1886 and first used to effect by **Tchaikovsky** in the 'Dance of the Sugar Plum Fairy' from his *The Nutcracker* ballet (1890).

Chabrier, (Alexis) Emmanuel (1841–1894)
French composer who was initially employed at the Ministry of the Interior, but cultivated music as an amateur. Having produced two operettas in 1877 and 1879, he devoted himself entirely to composition. After the production of *Le roi malgré lui* (1887), which was interrupted by a fire at the Opéra-Comique, Paris, he came under the influence of **Wagner**. A colourful and ebullient figure (characteristics reflected in his music), Chabrier was one of the most entertaining letter-writers among French composers. His other works include the operas *Gwendoline* (1885), the orchestral rhapsody *España* (1883), and ten *Pièces pittoresques*, *Habanera* and *Bourrée fantasque* for piano.

chamber music
Music originally intended for performance in a small room rather than in the concert hall, and usually written for instrumental combinations, played with one instrument to a part, as in the string quartet. At first a purely instrumental style, it developed through **Haydn** and **Beethoven** into a private and often experimental medium, making demands on players and audiences alike. By the 19th century chamber music had found its way into the concert hall, sometimes taking on a quasi-orchestral quality, as in the work of **Brahms**. During the 20th century, the financial limitations encouraged many composers to scale down their orchestras (these are called chamber orchestras), as in Alban **Berg's** *Chamber Concerto* (1923–25) and **Stravinsky's** ballet *Agon* (1953–57).

chant
Ritual incantation by an individual or a group.
- *Ambrosian chant* developed as a result of reforms introduced by St Ambrose in the 4th century. It retains many features of Middle Eastern religious chant.
- *Byzantine chant* is used by the Greek-speaking Orthodox Church. Byzantine **liturgy**, art, and music began to gain supremacy in the 6th century. Byzantine music, notated in neumes, is based on a system of

eight modes (*echoi*), defined by characteristic melodic formulas as well as by tonality. The comparative simplicity of earlier and middle Byzantine music gave way, at the end of the period, to a highly embellished style in which the balance between verse and music tended to be destroyed.

• *Plainchant* or *plainsong* is medieval church music still surviving in some services of the Roman Catholic Church, properly sung in unison, without harmony and with no definitely measured rhythms. The old notation on a stave of four lines, with square or diamond-shaped notes and ligatures, is still used for plainsong.

• *Gregorian chant* is any plainsong associated with Pope Gregory the Great (540–604) that became standard in the Roman Catholic Church.

Chausson, Ernest (1855–1899)
French composer who combined Wagnerian harmonic experiment with French melodic and atmospheric sensibilities. A fastidious, perhaps too self-critical artist, Chausson was one of the most important successors of **Franck**. His admirable Symphony (1890), *Poème*, for violin and orchestra, and the concerto for violin and piano with string quartet (1891) all demonstrate his genius.

It is claimed that Chausson was one of the first people to be killed in a bicycle accident.

Chávez, Carlos Antonio de Padua (1899–1978)
Mexican composer who incorporated national and pre-Columbian folk elements into his ballets, seven symphonies, and concertos for both violin and piano. He was founder-director of the Mexico Symphony Orchestra (he later became its conductor), and director of the National Conservatory (1928–34). He was a leading figure in the cultural life of his country, doing much to explore Mexican folk music.

Cherubini, Luigi (Carlo Zanobi Salvadore Maria) (1760–1842)
Italian composer, greatly admired by **Beethoven**. Following his appointment as court composer to King George III of England in 1784, he settled in Paris, where he produced a number of dramatic works including *Médée* (1797), *Les Deux Journées* (1800), and the ballet *Anacréon* (1803). In 1815 he composed an overture and a symphony for the Philharmonic Society, London. In 1816 he became attached to the royal chapel gaining a large salary and in 1822 he became director of the Conservatory, where he often confronted

the precocious **Berlioz**. In 1833 he produced his last work for the theatre, *Ali Baba, ou les quarante voleurs*. Henceforward he devoted himself to church music, and his Requiem in D minor (1836) is one of his finest works. In his last years he was affected by depression and unsettled by an uneasy relationship with the authorities. He is, with **Gluck**, an austere representative of a nobler Classical style in French opera; as a teacher his influence was harmful in restricting his pupils by the narrow rules of an earlier age. **Mendelssohn** was the only young composer whom he openly praised.

choir
Group of singers, usually of sacred music, and of more than one voice to a part. A traditional cathedral choir of male voices is required to sing responses, **hymns**, and psalms appropriate to the church calendar. During the 19th century, choir festivals became a popular feature of British musical life, promoting mixed-voice choral singing by amateur groups.

Chopin, Frédéric François (1810–1849)
Polish composer and pianist who revolutionized piano-playing and the style of composition for the instrument. He went to Paris in October 1831 and decided to remain there. He appeared frequently in public and gave private lessons, especially in aristocratic circles. In 1838 he visited George Sand (the penname of Madame Dudevant) at Nohant; his relationship with her lasted several years. The last ten years of his life were a continual struggle against illness, and he gave his last public concert in February 1848. His pupil Jane Stirling took him to Scotland in August 1848 for a rest at the country house of her brother-in-law, Lord Torphichen. Chopin afterwards played at Manchester, Glasgow, and Edinburgh, and went to London in

Chopin *Self-taught on the piano, Chopin was able to earn high fees teaching and composing in 1830s Paris.*

November. In January 1849 he was back in Paris in a critical state of health and finance, but was supported by wealthy friends until his death. Chopin's music, written almost exclusively for solo piano, was (along with **Liszt's)** the most important of the 19th century in the development and perfection of a Romantic style. It is entirely original, with an apparent melodic simplicity that usually masks a variety of more complex undercurrents of harmony and rhythm. His works include two piano concertos, 52 mazurkas, 27 études, 26 preludes, 19 nocturnes, 17 waltzes, 16 polonaises, 4 ballades, 3 sonatas, and many other miscellaneous pieces.

chord

The simultaneous sounding of three or more pitches; the resultant combination can be described as consonant (harmonious) or dissonant, but these are coming to be seen as relative terms. The chords most commonly found in tonal music are major and minor triads ('a' and 'b'), dominant and diminished seventh ('c' and 'd'), augmented triads ('e') and French sixths ('f').
See also: *harmony.*

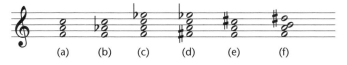

(a)   (b)   (c)   (d)   (e)   (f)

chord *Examples of different types of chord, namely (a) major; (b) minor; (c) dominant seventh (d) diminished seventh; (e) augmented triad; and (f) French sixth, a type of augmented sixth chord.*

Cimarosa, Domenico (1749–1801)

Italian composer of more than 60 operas. He studied at Naples, and produced his first opera there in 1772. Later he lived by turns in Rome and Naples, and in 1787 went to the court of Catherine II at St Petersburg, Russia. In 1791 the Emperor Leopold II invited him to Vienna to succeed Antonio **Salieri** as court Kapellmeister. There he produced his most successful opera, *Il matrimonio segreto* (1792), based on *The Clandestine Marriage* by Colman and Garrick; it was encored in its entirety at its premiere. His engagement in Vienna ended the same year; Cimarosa returned to Naples, where he became maestro di cappella to the king.

Cimarosa was imprisoned because of his involvement in the Neapolitan rising of 1799 and on his release he set out for St Petersburg, but died at Venice on the way, allegedly by poison.

cimbalom
Instrument common in Hungary, modernized during the 19th century from a gypsy instrument. It consists of a box-shaped resonator over which strings are stretched laterally, the performer playing front to back rather than across, using light beaters. The sound is brittle but exotic. **Stravinsky** used it in his *Renard* (1922) and **Kodály** in the orchestral suite *Háry János* (1927).

cipher
Coded reference to a name using the letter-names of notes to form a motif. The most widely quoted is BACH (**see** *Bach family*); **Schumann's** *Abegg Variations* (1830) is dedicated to his friend Meta Abegg; **Berg's** *Chamber Concerto* (1923–25) includes motivic references to himself and **Schoenberg**. DSCH is the acronym for Dmitry **Shostakovich** (using German spelling again, S being 'Es' or E♭), the basis of a monumental *Passacaglia on DSCH* by Stevenson. **Boulez's** tribute to Paul Sacher *Messagesquisse* (1977) incorporates the French 'Re' (the note D in English).

Čiurlionis, Mikolajus Konstantinas (1875–1911)
Lithuanian composer and painter. After studying in Warsaw and Leipzig, he returned to Lithuania, where he instigated the development of national art and music, collecting folksongs, organizing exhibitions, and conducting choirs. During his time in St Petersburg he exhibited with the *World of Art* group of painters and sold a canvas to **Stravinsky**. He became mentally ill and died in a Polish asylum. His music is mostly for the piano and contains harmonic innovations; it frequently recalls folksong. He also composed two symphonic poems, *In the Forest* and *The Sea*.

Clarke, Jeremiah (c. 1674–1707)
English composer of *The Prince of Denmark's March*, a harpsichord piece that was arranged by Henry Wood as a *Trumpet Voluntary* and wrongly attributed to **Purcell**. In 1699 he was appointed organist at St Paul's Cathedral in London. He was sworn Gentleman-extraordinary of the Chapel Royal in 1700 and organist in 1704. He committed suicide, supposedly after an unhappy love affair.

Clarke, Rebecca (1886–1979)
English viola player and composer. In a US competition in 1919 she won a prize with a viola sonata, settling there at the outbreak of war in 1939. Her other works include *Psalm* for chorus, a piano trio (1921), *Rhapsody* for cello and piano (1923).

Classical era
The period between approximately 1750 and 1830, in which composers' concerns for form and symmetry were thought analogous to those of classical Greek and Roman art and philosophy. As epitomized by the Viennese Classical school of **Haydn**, **Mozart**, and **Beethoven**, Classical music is characterized by the growth of clear formal and sectional elements, especially in **sonata form**.

clavichord
Small keyboard instrument developed in the 16th century and common until around 1760. Notes are sounded by a metal blade striking the string. The sound is clear and precise, and a form of vibrato (bebung) is possible by varying finger pressure on the key. The first clavichords had few strings, using an array of metal tangents combining the function of plectrum and bridge.

clef
A symbol prefixed to a five-line stave indicating the pitch range to which the written notes apply. The treble (G) and bass (F) clefs are most commonly used. The C clef is now comparatively rare, except for viola, cello, and bassoon; for most other instruments the G and F clefs are standard.

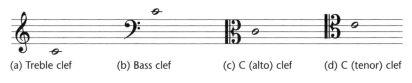

(a) Treble clef   (b) Bass clef   (c) C (alto) clef   (d) C (tenor) clef

clef

Clementi, Aldo (1925–)
Italian composer much influenced by the 'informal' art movement. He studied with **Petrassi** and **Maderna**, who propelled him towards twelve-note serialism. His works are densely structured and include *Informels* (1961–63), concerto for wind orchestra and two pianos (1967), the stage series *Blitz* (1973), and *Collage 4* (1979).

Clementi, Muzio (1752–1832)
Italian pianist and composer who settled in London in 1782 and founded the present-day technique of piano playing. His series of studies, *Gradus ad*

parnassum (1817), is still in use. In 1773 he published the first (of about 70) piano sonatas and appeared with spectacular success as a virtuoso pianist and composer. He was associated with the publishers and piano manufacturers Longman & Broderip, upon whose bankruptcy in 1798 he re-established the firm in partnership with Longman. He was again on tour in Europe 1802–10, taking his pupil **Field** with him to St Petersburg, and in 1807 met Beethoven in Vienna.

cluster
Effect of simultaneously playing all the notes within a chosen interval. It was introduced by US composer **Ives** in his *Concord Sonata* (*c*.1912–18), for which using a ruler on the piano keys is recommended. The effect is also used in Stockhausen's *Piano Piece X* (1961), and Ligeti's *Volumina* (1962) for organ, using the player's forearms. Cluster writing for strings features in **Penderecki's** *Threnody for the Victims of Hiroshima* (1960), and for voices in Ligeti's *Lux aeterna* (1966).

(a)   (b)   (c)

cluster   *To avoid writing out all the notes in a cluster, a special type of notation has developed. This is usually a solid bar showing where the cluster starts and ends. Sometimes large accidentals are placed before or above the bar to show whether black notes, white notes, or both are to be played.*
- *a) is all black and white notes between G and G sharp*
- *b) is all white notes between F and C*
- *c) is all black notes between E flat and B flat.*

Coleridge-Taylor, Samuel (1875–1912)
English composer famous in his lifetime for the cantata *Hiawatha's Wedding Feast* (1898), a setting in three parts of Longfellow's poem. The son of a West African doctor and an English mother, he had works performed while still at college. He was appointed conductor of the Handel Society in 1904, and visited the USA that year, as well as in 1906 and 1910; but otherwise devoted all his time to composition and teaching. His Violin Concerto and chamber works were also highly regarded.

concerto

Composition for solo instrument (or instruments) and orchestra. It developed during the 18th century from the *concerto grosso* in which a group of solo instruments (concerto) is contrasted with a full orchestra (ripieno). The form blossomed first in the 18th century – **Mozart** wrote about 40 concertos – and often served as a vehicle for virtuosic display in the next. The genre was not subsequently abandoned, with later notable examples produced by **Berg, Ligeti**, and many others.

conducting

The direction of a performance by visual gestures. Groups of more than about eight performers have nearly always needed someone to ensure ensemble and consistency of interpretation, and there is iconographic evidence of conductors in Egypt and Sumeria from the third millennium BC. Direction originally lay in the hands of a leading performer – in the **Baroque** era, often controlling the ensemble from an organ, harpsichord, or (particularly in **Classical** music) from the violin. Conducting with a baton as an independent activity arose mainly in the 19th century, particularly with **Spontini, Spohr**, and **Mendelssohn**; and the earliest professional career conductor seems to have been Otto Nicolai (1810–1849). But the 20th century saw a further rise of the status of the conductors, with the appearance of figures such as Furtwängler, Toscanini, Boult, Svetlanov, Karajan, Abbado, Rattle, and others.

> ❝ There are two kinds [of conductors]: one takes the music too fast, and the other too slow. There is no third. ❞
>
> Camille **Saint-Saëns**, on conducting quoted in Beecham, *A Mingled Chime*

continuo

In much music of the Renaissance and Baroque eras, the keyboard and a bass string instrument formed the continuo; they were provided with a bass line onto which the keyboard built up a fuller harmonic accompaniment through the interpretation of numbers placed above notes on the bass line according to the rules of figured bass.

Copland, Aaron (1900–1990)

US composer whose early works, such as his Piano Concerto (1926), incorporate jazz and modernist idioms. Copland studied in France with Nadia **Boulanger**, and taught from 1940 at the Berkshire Music Center (now the Tanglewood Music Center). He took avant-garde European styles and gave them a distinctive American pitch. His eight film scores, including *The Heiress* (1949), set new standards for Hollywood. He later assimilated local American styles, notably in the ballets *Billy the Kid* (1938) and *Appalachian Spring* (1943–44) based on a poem by Hart Crane. His chamber music is more introspective and complex in character. He did much to promote American music, and also wrote and lectured extensively. He also toured widely as a conductor of his own and other American music. Among his orchestral works are three symphonies, (1925, 1933, 1946), *Music for the Theatre, Symphonic Ode, A Dance Symphony, Statements, El Salón México* (1933–36), *Music for the Radio, An Outdoor Overture, Quiet City* (1939), *Letter from Home, Danzón Cubano; Lincoln Portrait* for orator and orchestra (1942), piano concerto (1926), and a clarinet concerto (1948).

> ❝ Most people use music as a couch ... But serious music was never meant to be used as a soporific. ❞
>
> Aaron **Copland,** quoted in the *New York Times*, 1949

Corelli, Arcangelo (1653–1713)

Italian composer and one of the first virtuoso exponents of the Baroque violin. His music, marked by graceful melody, includes a set of *concerti grossi* and five sets of chamber sonatas. Born at Fusignano, in about 1685 he settled in Rome, where he lived at the palace of his patron, and published his first violin sonatas. He visited Modena and Naples, conducted at the Roman residence of Queen Christina of Sweden, collected pictures, and taught many pupils including **Geminiani**. Corelli's music is richer in contrapuntal and harmonic interest than that of any other Italian Baroque master, and has been admired for the poise, balance, and brilliance of its style.

Cornyshe, William (died 1523)

English composer, actor, and producer of interludes and pageants, attached to the courts of Henry VII and VIII. He was made a Gentleman of the Chapel Royal in about 1496, and succeeded William Newark as Master of the Children in 1509. He wrote music for the court banquets and masques, and officiated in France at the Field of the Cloth of Gold in 1520. His father, William Cornyshe (died *c.* 1502), was the first recorded master of the choristers at Westminster Abbey, about 1480–90, and wrote much church music and secular songs, some with satirical words.

counterpoint

(Latin *punctus contra punctum* 'note against note') The art of combining different forms of an original melody with apparent freedom while preserving a harmonious effect. **Palestrina** and **Bach** were masters of counterpoint.

Couperin, François le Grand (1668–1733)

French composer for organ and harpsichord. A favoured composer of Louis XIV, he composed numerous chamber concertos and harpsichord suites, and published a standard keyboard tutor *The Art of Playing the Harpsichord* (1716), in which he laid down guidelines for fingering, phrasing, and ornamentation. His uncle, Louis (*c.* 1626–1661), was regarded as one of the finest keyboard composers of the 17th century; among his 215 surviving pieces are allemandes, courantes, sarabandes, chaconnes, and pasacailles for harpsichord.

Cowell, Henry Dixon (1897–1965)

US experimental composer whose *New Musical Resources* (1930) sought to establish a rationale for modern music. He worked with **Grainger** (1941) and **Cage**, and although remembered as a discoverer of piano effects such as strumming the strings in *Aeolian Harp* (1923), and for introducing **clusters**, he was also an astute observer and writer of new music developments. He later developed an interest in the folk music of many countries.

Crawford (Seeger), Ruth (Porter) (1901–1953)

US composer whose 1931 String Quartet was published by **Cowell** and is regarded as revolutionary in its static harmony. She also compiled many folksong anthologies, including *American Folk Songs for Children,*

(1948). She married the composer Charles Seeger, whose son Pete became a well-known known folk singer.

Crotch, William (1775–1847)
English composer who played the organ at the age of four, went to Cambridge at the age of eleven to assist at the organ of King's College, and produced an oratorio *The Captivity of Judah* there in 1789. In 1790 he began to study music and was appointed organist at Christ Church, Oxford, succeeding Philip Hayes as professor in 1798. On the establishment of the Royal Academy of Music in London in 1822 he became its first principal.

Crumb, George Henry (1929–)
US composer of so-called 'imagist' works employing unusual graphics and imaginative sonorities, such as the musical saw in *Ancient Voices of Children* (1970), settings of poems by Lorca. His often spec-

Crumb's *Dark Angels* for amplified string quartet was prompted by his despair at the state of the US during the Vietnam War.

trally beautiful works include *A Haunted Landscape* for instrumental ensemble (1984), *Vox balanae*, instruments with electronics (1972), and the remarkable four books of *Makrokosmos* for amplified piano (1972–79).

Cui, César Antonovich (1835–1918)
Russian composer and writer who is remembered mainly for his astringent criticism. An army engineer by profession, he became a member of 'The Five' group of composers, studied with **Balakirev** and was an enthusiastic proponent of Russian nationalist music in the press. He composed some attractive vocal and piano miniatures, and ten operas, including *A Prisoner in the Caucasus* (1857–58), first performed 1883, and *William Ratcliff* (1861–68), first performed 1869. He completed **Mussorgsky's** opera *Sorochintsy Fair*.

Czerny, Carl (1791–1857)
Austrian pianist and teacher whose technical exercises, including the *Complete Theoretical and Practical Pianoforte School* (1839), are still in

widespread use. He became a pupil of **Beethoven** at about the age of ten but, not liking to appear in public, he took to teaching and soon attracted an enormous following of pupils. This left him enough leisure for composition, which he cultivated so assiduously as to produce almost 1,000 works.

Dallapiccola, Luigi (1904–1975)

Italian composer who adopted a lyrical twelve-tone style around 1945 after **Neo-Classical** beginnings. He studied at the Florence Conservatory and in 1931 became professor. His mature music, while using serial techniques, did not avoid tonal references, thematic structures, and harmonic progressions. His *Songs of Captivity* were prompted by the Fascist racial laws of 1938, and represent the expression in music of an imprisonment that was as much mental as physical. This 'protest music' was continued in his later opera *Il prigionero* (1944–48). He had great influence in post-war Italy, and played a dominant part in the cultural renaissance of that country.

dance

Dance has formed an integral part of formal music composition. Its many forms appear either undisguised (often as suites, especially in **Baroque music**) or as the rhythmic inspiration behind a more abstract composition. The most common dances found in the concert repertoire are as follows:

name	speed	metre	origin	used by
allemande	medium	4	Germany	Bach
bolero	moderate	3	Spain	Ravel, Chopin
branle	slow	2 or 3	France	Couperin
fandango	moderate	3	Spain	Granados
forlana	moderate	3	Italy	Bach, Ravel
galliard	fast	3	Italy	Byrd
gavotte	fastish	4	France	Prokofiev, Schoenberg
gigue	fast	3	Italy	Bach, Schoenberg
habañera	slow	2	Spain	Debussy
hopak	fast	4	Ukraine	Mussorgsky
jota	quick	3	Spain	Albéniz
krakowiak	quick	2	Poland	Chopin, Paderewski
malagueña	moderate	3	Spain	Albéniz
mazurka	any	3	Poland	Chopin, Tchaikovsky
minuet	moderate	3	France	Haydn, Mozart

name	speed	metre	origin	used by
pavan	slow	2	Italy	Byrd, Ravel
polka	fast	2	Bohemia	Smetana
polonaise	moderate	3	Poland	Chopin, Lyadov
saltarello	fast	3	Italy	Mendelssohn
seguillidas	fast	3	Spain	Albéniz
tango	slow	2	Argentina	Piazzolla
verbunkos	slow/fast	2	Hungary	Liszt
waltz	any	3	Austria	Johann Strauss

Daquin, Louis Claude (1694–1772)

French keyboard virtuoso appointed aged 12 as organist of Petit Saint-Antoine in Paris. In 1727 he was **Rameau's** successful rival for the post of organist at Saint-Paul, and in 1739 succeeded Dandrieu at the Chapel Royal. He is especially remembered as one of the great French representatives of harpsichord music; his many pieces for the instrument include *Le coucou*.

Dargomïzhsky, Aleksandr Sergeyevich (1813–1869)

Russian composer whose songs, many of a satirical nature, anticipate those of **Mussorgsky**. In 1864 he visited western Europe, and on his return he associated himself with **Balakirev's** nationalist group, without actually joining it. He set Pushkin's poem '*The Stone Guest*', based on the story of Don Juan, as an opera word for word. It was left unfinished at his death, but was completed, on his directions, by **Cui** and orchestrated by **Rimsky-Korsakov** in 1872. Though inferior to **Glinka**, Dargomïzhsky is a figure of some importance in the history of Russian opera.

David, Félicien-(César) (1810–1876)

French composer who scored a great success with his oriental descriptive symphony *Le désert* (1844), inspired by his travels in Palestine. He was one of the first Western composers to introduce oriental scales and melodies into his music. He also wrote operas, four symphonies, and 24 string quintets.

Davies, Peter Maxwell (1934–)

English composer who combined medieval and serial codes of practice with expressionism, as in his opera *Taverner* (1972), based on the life and works of the 16th-century composer John **Taverner**. Born in Manchester, after training at the Royal Manchester College of Music alongside composers **Goehr** and **Birtwistle**, he studied with **Petrassi**. Since 1970 he has been based in Orkney. Other works include the opera *The Lighthouse* (1980), the chamber work *Vesalii icones* (1969), and the highly dramatic *Eight Songs for a Mad King* (1969). More recently, he has turned to the composition of symphonies and concertos.

Debussy, (Achille-) Claude (1862–1918)

French composer whose orchestral work *L'après-midi d'une faune* (1894) has been described as the beginning of modern music. He broke with German **Romanticism** and introduced new ideas about melody and harmony. His use of the pentatonic and whole-tone **scales** often evoke oriental music. The son of a shopkeeper, he was taught the piano by a former pupil of Chopin, and was later domestic musician to Nadezhda von Meck, **Tchaikovsky's** former patroness. During the late 1880s he began to reject the prevalent Wagnerian ideas; his first mature work was a setting of Rossetti's *Blessed Damozel*, in 1888. In 1902 his only completed opera, *Pelléas et Mélisande*, was pro-

duced; it was described by its conductor, André Messager, as opening a window on the whole world of modern music. Only during his last decade did he achieve general acclaim, but he was also suffering from terminal cancer.

Debussy's approach to certain chords as 'sound-events' in themselves, important for their own colour and sensuous qualities even more than as stages in a harmonic progression, indicated a new path for Western music. He influenced composers as diverse as **Ravel**, **Stravinsky**, **Bartók**, **Varèse**, **Messiaen**, and **Boulez**. Among his other works are numerous piano pieces, songs, orchestral pieces such as *La Mer* (1903–05) and *Trois nocturnes* (1899), and the ballet *Jeux* (1910–13).

Debussy *A drawing of Claude Debussy by D Lindloff, 1913.*

Delibes, (Clément Philibert) Léo (1836–1891)
French composer whose lightweight, perfectly judged works include the ballets *Coppélia* (1870) and *Sylvia* (1876), and the opera *Lakmé* (1883).

Delius, Frederick Theodore Albert (1862–1934)
English composer of northern European origin who spent much of his life in France. His meeting with **Grieg** influenced his Romantic approach to composition; he had little systematic teaching. He assimilated influences of **Wagner** and **Debussy**, and found his own voice in *Paris: Song of a Great City* (1899). From 1907 important first performances were given in England: Thomas Beecham conducted his masterpiece, *A Mass of Life*, in 1909. He contracted syphilis and by 1926 was totally blind. He continued to compose, however, with the assistance of Eric Fenby, who acted as his amanuensis from 1928. His haunting, richly harmonious works also include the opera *A Village Romeo and Juliet* (1901); the choral pieces *Appalachia* (1903), and *Sea Drift* (1904); orchestral works such as *In a Summer Garden* (1908) and *A Song of the High Hills* (1911); chamber music, and songs.

Del Tredici, David (1937–)
US composer obsessed with Lewis Carroll's 'Alice' stories. Among his compositions on this theme are *Pop-Pourri*, for voices, rock group, and orchestra (1968), *The Lobster Quadrille* for soprano, folk music ensemble, and orchestra (1969, revised 1974), *Vintage Alice* (1971, same forces), *An Alice Symphony* (1976), and *Final Alice*, for orchestra (1976). His early music, however, includes several settings of Joyce.

Denisov, Edison (1929–1997)
Russian composer who, along with **Gubaydulina** and **Schnittke**, formed the second Soviet avant garde and courted controversy by allowing his works (such as *The Sun of the Incas* (1964) to be performed in the West. Initially influenced by **Prokofiev**, after contacts with the **Webern** pupil Herschkowitz he wrote a number of works suggested by the writing of Boris Vian, including the opera *L'écume des jours* (1977–80). He did much to encourage experiment in younger Russian composers and also resurrected 1920s modernists **Mosolov** and **Roslavets**, banned under Stalinism.

Desprez, Josquin
See **Josquin Desprez**.

Diabelli, Anton (1781–1858)

Austrian composer who was the original publisher of **Beethoven**, **Haydn**, and **Schubert**. He is most famous today for appearing in the title of Beethoven's *Diabelli Variations* (1823). He studied music with Michael Haydn and went to Vienna as piano and guitar teacher in 1818; his publishing firm became Diabelli & Co. in 1824.

Dieren, Bernard van (1887–1936)

Dutch-born British composer of eclectic tastes who was widely admired in early 20th-century Britain. A scientist by training, in 1909 he settled in London as correspondent to foreign newspapers. His real creative career began after making serious music studies in Germany in 1912. His *Chinese Symphony*, songs, and six string quartets are considered to be among his finest works. He wrote a book on the sculptor Jacob Epstein and a volume of musical essays, *Down Among the Dead Men* (1935).

Dillon, James (1950–)

Scottish composer influenced by Renaissance music, the writing of, among others, Hölderlin (*Helle nacht* for orchestra, 1986) and Baudelaire (*Spleen* for piano, 1980), and non-Western cultures. His music initially met with bafflement – especially in Britain – for its uncompromising and often virtuosic nature, but his works were subsequently widely performed, especially in Europe. Many of his pieces are notable for their sensuality (*Vernal Showers* for violin and ensemble) and intricate but immediate textures (three string quartets).

Dittersdorf, Karl Ditters von (1739–1799)

Austrian composer and violinist who played in string quartets with **Haydn** and **Mozart**. He travelled in 1764 to Italy with **Gluck**, and was ennobled in 1773; his autobiography, dictated shortly before his death, was published in 1801. His works include over 40 operas (including *Amore in musica*, *Betrug durch Aberglauben*, *Doktor und Apotheker* (1786), *Hieronimus Knicker* (1789), *Das rothe Kaeppchen*, and *Die Hochzeit des Figaro*), and others; over 100 symphonies, including 21 on Ovid's *Metamorphoses*, and chamber music.

Dohnányi, Ernö (Ernst von) (1877–1960)

Hungarian pianist and composer who drew upon the Classical German tradition, especially **Brahms**. Born in Poszony (modern-day Bratislava), he attended the Academy at Budapest, where he met **Bartók**. He visited England in 1898

and the USA in 1899, and made many more tours, but eventually became bet-
ter known as a composer. He premiered Bartók's *Four Orchestral Pieces* in
Budapest 1922. He left Hungary in 1944 and subsequently settled in the USA.
His works include three symphonies, two piano concertos, *Variations on a
Nursery Song* for piano and orchestra (1913); two violin concertos, much
chamber music, and many piano pieces.

Donatoni, Franco (1927–)
Italian composer for whom composition appears to be a game or puzzle.
One work for string quartet reaches a central point and then plays itself
backwards, while some compositions consist of parts of other pieces filtered
through various procedures. He originally used serial techniques but abandoned the strict application of these in the 1970s, producing works of direct
simplicity, often relying on the almost mechanical repetition and variation
of small thematic gestures. He returned to using the voice with the stunning
Arias in which he confounded critics with its great lyrical warmth. His best
work includes *Refrain* for eight instruments (1986), *Le ruisseau sur l'escalier*
for cello and ensemble, and *Arias* for soprano and orchestra (1978).

Donizetti, (Domenico) Gaetano (Maria) (1797–1848)
Italian composer of more than 60 operas including *Lucrezia Borgia* (1833),
Lucia di Lammermoor (1835), *La fille du régiment* (1840), *La favorite*
(1840), and *Don Pasquale* (1843). They employ the **bel canto** style at its
most effective and are filled to the brim with a flow of expressive melodies.
The opera which made his name widely known was *Anna Bolena*, produced in 1830 at Milan, although by this time he had already produced
over 30 operas. His *Lucia di Lammermoor*, produced at Naples in 1835,
was his greatest success. He excelled not only in serious operas, where he
showed a gift for melody and mastery of dramatic ensembles, but also in
comic operas, such as *L'elisir d'amore* (1832). In 1839–40 and 1843 he visited Paris and produced operas there. At about this time, his physical and
mental health began to fail, and he became paralysed in 1845.

> ❝ While his magical tunes bring joy to the world, while
> everyone sings them and trills them, he himself sits, a
> terrible picture of insanity, in a lunatic asylum near Paris. ❞
>
> Heinrich **Heine** on Donizetti, in *Letters on the French Stage*

Dowland, John (c. 1563–c. 1626)

English composer of lute songs who introduced daring expressive refinements of harmony and ornamentation to English Renaissance. His style is rooted in an elevated aesthetic of melancholy, as in the masterly *Lachrymae* (1605).

Dukas, Paul Abraham (1865–1935)

French composer and teacher whose scrupulous orchestration and chromatically enriched harmonies were admired by **Debussy** and his own pupil **Messiaen**. Plagued by doubt in his powers as a composer, his small output includes the opera *Ariane and Bluebeard* (1907), the ballet *La Péri* (1912), and the animated orchestral scherzo *The Sorcerer's Apprentice* (1897).

Duparc, (Marie Eugène) Henri Fouques (1848–1933)

French composer remembered for his beautifully lyrical songs, of which only 16 survive. He was taught the piano by **Franck**, and also took private lessons in composition from him. His few works include the symphonic poem *Lenore* (1875), and a nocturne, *Aux étoiles*. He was a fierce critic of his own work and destroyed a number of compositions. He never took any share in official musical life, but continued to compose at intervals until 1885, when he began to suffer from an incurable nervous complaint and retired to Switzerland.

Dussek, Jan Ladislav (1760–1812)

Bohemian (Czech) composer and virtuoso pianist whose works, which include over 40 piano sonatas and 15 piano concertos, often display technically challenging passages by the standard of his day. Composing more fully textured (and often more harmonically adventurous) music than most of his contemporaries, Dussek foreshadowed many of the musical developments of the 19th century. He was one of a group of composers known as the London Pianoforte School.

Dutilleux, Henri (1916–)

French composer whose work represents a link between the worlds of **Debussy** and **Messiaen**. He combines modernist and Neo-Romantic trends in works such as *Métaboles* (1962–65) for orchestra and *Thus the Night* (1975–76) for string quartet.

Dvořák, Antonín Leopold (1841–1904)

Czech composer who combined the Classical tradition of **Beethoven** and **Brahms** with the influence of Czech folk music. He heard only popular and simple church music as a child, but later played viola in the orchestra of the Bohemian Provisional Theatre at Prague, conducted by **Wagner**, who influenced his early compositions. In 1874 he received the Austrian state prize for composition; one member of the committee was the composer Brahms, who befriended Dvořák and introduced him to his publisher, Simrock. The *Slavonic Rhapsodies* and *Dances* of 1878 brought an essentially nationalist character to his music, and their publication brought him international fame. In the powerful Sixth Symphony, the presence of Brahms is felt. He was director of the new National Conservatory in New York 1892–95; the premiere of the *New World* Symphony at Carnegie Hall was one of the greatest successes of his career. The cello concerto was written in 1895; Josefina, his first love, died during its composition, and in memory of her the slow section of the finale quotes her favourite song from *Cypresses*. His later **tone poems** suggest he was experimenting until the very end of his career. His son-in-law Josef **Suk** was also a famous Czech composer.

Dvořák wrote nine symphonies; tone poems; operas, including *Rusalka* (1900); large-scale choral works; the *Carnival* (1891–92) and other overtures; violin and cello concertos; chamber music; piano pieces; and songs.

> ❛ Why on earth didn't I know that one could write a violoncello concerto like this? If I had only known, I would have written one long ago. ❜
>
> **Brahms** on Dvořák's Cello Concerto, quoted in Robertson *Dvořák*

dynamics

Symbols indicating relative loudness, changes in loudness such as **crescendo** and **diminuendo**, or loudness in accentuation such as **rinforzando**. Dynamic expression emerged slowly during the 18th century, coinciding with the coming of age of the fortepiano (an early pianoforte), named to advertise its expressive advantages over the dynamically fixed harpsichord.

See also: *accent.*

Eben, Petr (1929–)
Czech composer who suffered at the hands of both Nazis and Communists. His many organ, chamber, and vocal pieces reflect his interest in religion and myth.

Einem, Gottfried von (1918–1996)
Austrian composer who, with his mother, was arrested and held by the Gestapo. After his release he studied with Boris **Blacher**, with whom he wrote the libretto for his first opera and secured a post at the Dresden Staasoper. In 1948, after the success of *Dantons Tod,* he was invited to help to direct the festival at Salzburg, where he later lived. His style has been criticized for its eclecticism, but he is regarded as a fine writer of songs. His opera *Der Besuch der alten Dame* 1971 was based on a stage vehicle for the actress Ingrid Bergman, while his 1980 opera *Jesus' Wedding* caused a scandal through its depiction of its protagonist as married.

Eisler, Hanns (1898–1962)
Schoenberg's pupil who collaborated with the playwright Bertolt Brecht; both men fled Nazi Germany for the USA. Eisler returned to East Berlin in 1950. The music he wrote for the new Communist state consisted chiefly of songs and music for stage and films. His works include the operas *Galileo* (1947) and *Johannes Faustus* (1953), didactic plays *Mother* (after Gorky's novel, 1931), *Hangmen Also Die, For Whom the Bell Tolls; The Roundheads and the Pointedheads* and others; other works include *Die Massnahme* (1930), *Lenin-Requiem* (1937), *Solidaritätslied* (1930), *Kinderlieder* (1951), and *Schweyk in Zweiten Weltkrieg* (1957), all to texts by Brecht.

electronic music
Music composed mainly of electronically generated and modified sounds. The term was first used in 1954 to describe music made up of synthesized sounds recorded on tape, to distinguish it from *musique concrète* (concrete music). This latter type was a reworking of natural recorded sounds; but both

types were soon combined in electronic pieces such as **Stockhausen's** *Gesang der Jünglinge/Song of the Youths* (1955–56), for modified boy's voice and electronic sounds, the first important electronic piece. Since the early 1920s efforts had been made to produce portable electronic instruments; early examples include the croix sonore, the theremin, the trautonium, and the ondes martenot. Computer technology has also greatly improved the range and versatility of electronic instruments: the 4X system installed at the Institut de Recherche et de Coordination Acoustique-Musique (IRCAM) in Paris allowed greater flexibility into the application of computers to electronic music. With the onset of digital recording, whole compositions can be programmed and stored in memory banks. The computer can be used to control and sequence the sounds and their characteristics, and also to synthesize any desired wave form. This has made it possible to produce complex electronic music live in the concert hall, without the necessity of recording it on tape first, and even to manipulate the sounds of the various instruments during the performance, as in **Boulez's** *Répons* (1981).

Elgar, Edward (William) (1857–1934)
English composer who virtually stopped writing after completing his most successful work, the Cello Concerto (1919). Elgar was the son of a music dealer and was self-taught as a composer. In 1890 the Three Choirs Festival included his *Froissart* overture, the first work in which Elgar reveals his characteristic confidence of manner and mastery of orchestration. He will perhaps be best remembered for his *Enigma Variations* (first performed under Hans Richter in 1899). *The Dream of Gerontius* was produced at the Birmingham Festival in 1900 and at the Lower Rhine Festival, Düsseldorf, Germany, in 1901 and 1902. An Elgar Festival at the Covent Garden Theatre, London, in 1904 brought him greater recognition, and he was knighted that year. His First Symphony was performed by Richter in Manchester and London in 1908, and its immense success led to 100 further performances throughout Europe. Fritz **Kreisler** premiered the Violin Concerto in 1910. At his death he left unfinished a Third Symphony, later re-composed by Anthony Payne from sketches.

❝ Music in England was ruined by *Hymns Ancient and Modern*. ❞

Elgar, quoted in Redwood, *An Elgar Companion*

étude

(French 'study') Originally, a musical exercise designed to develop technique but with the works of **Chopin**, **Liszt**, **Rachmaninov**, and **Skryabin** the genre outgrew this pedagogic designation and developed into a miniature **tone poem**.

expression

Signs or words providing a dramatic context for the effective interpretation of more or less neutral performance indicators for **tempo**, **dynamics**, phrasing, and so on.

extended technique

Non-traditional methods of obtaining sounds from musical instruments. Many 20th-century composers have experimented with extended techniques of various sorts, particularly for wind instruments. An early example is the use of percussive keystrokes in **Varèse's** *Density 21.5* for solo flute (1930), in which the performer makes an audible sound by hitting the keys of the flute hard when changing note. Other examples of extended technique for **woodwind** include multiphonics (splitting the note so that two separate harmonics are heard; a technique often achieved accidentally by beginners, but extremely difficult to control deliberately), humming into the mouthpiece, and so forth.

Falla (y Matheu), Manuel (Maria) de (1876–1946)

Spanish composer whose style is deeply affected by the folk idiom of southern Spain and Andalusia in particular. He was born in Cádiz, and in 1902 he produced a **zarzuela**, *Los amores de Inés*, written with very little tuition in composition. He lived in Paris 1907–14, where he was influenced by **Debussy**, **Ravel**, and **Dukas**, but returned to Spain and settled in Madrid on the outbreak of World War I. The production of *La vida breve* at Nice and Paris in 1913 and of the ballet *The Three-Cornered Hat* in London in 1919 spread his reputation. With the rise of the Fascists in Spain in 1939 he moved to Argentina, where he died leaving unfinished his most ambitious work, the cantata *L'Atlantida*. Other works include the opera *Brief Life* (1905), the ballet *El amor brujo/Love the Magician* (1915), his most ambitious concert work, *Nights in the Gardens of Spain* (1916), as well as songs and pieces for piano and guitar.

fanfare

Ceremonial short and brilliant tune for trumpets, or a piece for other instruments imitating the effect of trumpets. Written traditionally for valveless (natural) instruments, an example of a fanfare is the introduction to Act II of Wagner's *Tristan und Isolde*.

fantasia or fantasy, phantasy, fancy

A free-form instrumental composition for keyboard or chamber ensemble, originating in the late Renaissance, and much favoured by English composers such as **Byrd**. It implies the free manipulation of musical figures without regard to models of form. Later composers include **Bach**, **Mozart**, **Liszt**, and **Busoni**.

Farnaby, Giles (c. 1563–1640)

English composer, 50 of whose keyboard works are represented in the 17th-century manuscript collection the *Fitzwilliam Virginal Book*. He also wrote madrigals, and psalms for the *Whole Booke of Psalms* (1621).

Fauré, Gabriel (Urbain) (1845–1924)

French composer whose popular *Requiem* has overshadowed his arguably greater accomplishments in the fields of **chamber music** and song. His early works, notably the song cycle *La bonne chanson* (1892–94), 1st violin sonata (1875–76) and 1st piano quartet (1876–79), were lyrical and contemplative in nature. He adopted a terser, more rigorous but essentially far more refined style at the turn of the century and demonstrated this manner with the piano quintets and cello sonatas. He had many distinguished composition pupils, including **Ravel**, **Enescu**, and **Koechlin**.

> ❝ For me ... music exists to elevate us as far as possible above everyday existence. ❞
>
> Gabriel **Fauré**, in a letter to his son, Philippe, 1908

fauxbourdon

('False bass'). Name given to a wide variety of technical procedures in the 15th–16th centuries, usually involving improvisation. Originally used by **Dufay**, the English used their version of the word for a similar process, with parts being improvised straight from plainsong (at first in the middle, later in the top part). The fauxbourdon itself (that is, the lowest part) was also used as the basis of entirely new compositions.

Fayrfax, Robert (1464–1521)

English choral composer who was a Gentleman of the Chapel Royal on the accession of Henry VIII, with whom he attended the Field of the Cloth of Gold in 1520. He became organist and choirmaster at St Albans Cathedral before 1502. He gained a degree in music at Cambridge University in 1501 (for his Mass *O quam glorifica*), other works include five more cyclic Masses, motets, a *Stabat Mater*, and songs for several voices.

Feldman, Morton (1926–1987)

US composer associated with **Cage** and **Brown** in the 1950s, devising an indeterminate notation based on high, middle, and low instrumental registers and time cells of fixed duration for his *Projection* series. He later returned to conventional notation with *Madame Press Died Last Week at 90* (1970). This elegant, slight work was followed by a series of extended, meditative works that are associated by many with the paintings of Guston, Rothko, and the like. His two string quartets are highly impressive for their vastness and expansive nature; throughout their several hours' duration, they are almost exclusively played extremely quietly.

Ferneyhough, Brian John Peter (1943–)

English composer of international reputation initially shunned by an uncomprehending (and often jealous) British establishment. He went first to Germany and then the USA to teach a growing number of acolytes. His often uncompromising, detailed compositions include *Carceri d'invenzione* (1981–86), a cycle of seven works inspired by the engravings of Piranesi, *Time and Motion Studies* (1974–77), and four string quartets. He is regarded as the most important composer of the so-called New Complexity.

Ferneyhough *The English composer Brian Ferneyhough has received worldwide acclaim.*

Ferrabosco, Alfonso (1543–1588)

Italian composer, later active in England. He wrote madrigals, lute pieces, and motets. He was born at Bologna, son of the singer and composer Domenico Ferrabosco, and settled in London before 1562. Returning to Italy in 1578 he entered the service of the Duke of Savoy at Turin, leaving

> Ferrabosco left the service of Queen Elizabeth I in 1569 after becoming involved in a murder case.

his children in England. One of these, Alfonso Ferrabosco (*c.* 1575–1628), later became court musician to James I.

Fibich, Ždenek (1850–1900)

Czech composer whose 350 *Nalády/Moods* for the piano are personal rather than national, and considerably advanced for their time. After studying in France and Germany, he returned to Czechoslovakia in 1874 and conducted at the National Theatre in Prague. He retired in 1881 to devote himself entirely to composition, and wrote over 600 works of various kinds. He wrote seven operas and a trilogy of melodramas (spoken text accompanied by music) entitled *Hippodamia* (1891), the most ambitious work of the kind ever produced; his three symphonies are exceptionally lyrical.

Field, John (1782–1837)

Irish-born composer and pianist regarded as one of a group of composers known as the London Pianoforte School. He travelled throughout Europe demonstrating **Clementi's** pianos. In 1803 he settled in St Petersburg, where he composed most of his mature music; he moved to Moscow in 1822 and is regarded as exerting a profound influence on Russian composers such as **Glinka**. He also wrote seven piano concertos (1799–1822).

FIELD'S NOCTURNES

All of Field's works include the piano, reaching their peak artistically with his **nocturnes**, a genre he named and devised. These anticipate **Chopin's** nocturnes by 20 years, especially regarding their forward-looking textures and passage work.

---

film score

Music written to accompany a film on the soundtrack. In the early days of cinema, music was composed as a loosely-aligned accompaniment to a major silent film, or was improvised. With the arrival of sound on film came the synchronized film score. Composers in the European Romantic tradition, including **Korngold**, Tiomkin (a pupil of **Glazunov**), and Waxman initially tried to adapt the symphonic style to the faster-moving screen action; a more successful transition was made by animated film music specialists, such as Scott Bradley.

Finnissy, Michael Peter (1946–)

English composer and pianist. He studied at the Royal College of Music with **Stevens** and has taught at the Royal Academy of Music and at Southampton University. His direct manner encompasses the lyrical, violently virtuosic, religious, dramatic, and ecstatic, while his outspokenness on gay issues (in the opera *Tchaikovsky's Last Days*), his promotion of avant-garde US and European composers, and his extravagant pianism have assured him outsider status in his native country. His piano works are numerous and highly varied; they represent his most outstanding contribution.

Flotow, Friedrich Adolf Ferdinand, Freiherr von (1812–1883)
German composer who wrote 18 operas, including *Martha* (1847). He began to produce operas at aristocratic houses; in 1839 he gained his public success with *Le naufrage de la Méduse*, based on an incident in 1816 involving a French ship whose crew were left adrift on a raft while the officers escaped in lifeboats. His greatest success came with *Martha*, produced at Vienna in 1847; its blend of German sentiment and Italian ardour made it popular for many years in Europe and at the New York Metropolitan Opera House.

Foerster, Josef Bohuslav (1859–1951)
Czech composer of operas *Deborah* (1893), *Jessica* (on Shakespeare's *Merchant of Venice*, 1905), and *The Invincibles*, five symphonies (1887–1929), and much else. He held various appointments as organist, teacher, and critic. He favoured a Romantic style; a pupil of **Dvořák**, he later became a friend of **Mahler**.

form
The structure and overall design of a composition, providing a coherent framework for the effective presentation of musical ideas. The simplest forms are:

- *binary form*, which consists of two sections often separated by a double bar (marking off a section)
- *ternary form*, which consists of one section followed by a contrasting section, followed by the return of the first section.

Most larger-scale forms are developments of these two basic types, carefully using a balance of thematic development and transformation, repetition, variation, and contrast; these include **sonata form** and rondo form. During the 19th century, when Romantic composers such as **Liszt** fought against Classical forms, the alternative structure of a literary text or idea often came to replace the traditional forms.

Foss, (born Fuchs) Lukas (1922–)

US composer whose stylistically varied works, including the cantata *The Prairie* (1942) and *Time Cycle* for soprano and orchestra (1960), express an ironic view of tradition. Born in Germany, Foss studied in Berlin and Paris before moving in 1937 to the USA. He became professor of composition at California University in 1953. He has composed much: in the 1940s he wrote vocal music in **Neo-Classical** style; in the mid-1950s he began increasingly to employ improvisation. He has also written chamber and orchestral music in which the players reproduce tape-recorded effects.

Françaix, Jean (1912–)

French Provençale composer whose music is noted for its wit and brilliance, and shows the influence of **Satie** and 'Les Six'. Françaix studied with Nadia **Boulanger** in Paris and showed at an early age great facility in his writing. His works include the operas *Le diable boiteux* (1938), *Paris à nous deux* (1954), ballets *Beach* and *Le Roi nu* (after Hans Andersen); two symphonies (1932, 1953), and much chamber music.

Franck, César Auguste (1822–1890)

Belgian composer who pioneered cyclic form. His music, Romantic in style, includes the *Symphony in D Minor* (1866–68), *Symphonic Variations* (1885) for piano and orchestra, and many organ pieces. He made a concert tour in Belgium at the age of 11. He entered the Paris Conservatory in 1837, winning prizes each year until he left in 1842. In 1853 he became choirmaster and in 1858 organist at Sainte-Clotilde in Paris. He gathered a circle of young, eager students, including **d'Indy**, **Chausson**, **Lekeu**, and **Duparc**; he was the founder of particular branch of French music, one that absorbed the innovations of Wagner without loss of individuality.

Frescobaldi, Girolamo (1583–1643)

Italian composer and virtuoso keyboard player, he was organist at St Peter's, Rome 1608–28. His compositions included various forms of both instrumental and vocal music, and his fame rests on numerous keyboard toccatas, fugues, and capriccios in which he advanced keyboard technique and exploited ingenious changes of key. He studied at Ferrara under **Luzzaschi** and it was reported that 20,000 people came to hear his first recital at St Peter's. Bach owned a copy of his *Fiori musicali* (1635).

fugue

(Latin 'flight') Contrapuntal form with two or more subjects (principal melodies) for a number of parts, which enter in succession in direct imitation of each other or transposed to a higher or lower key, and may be combined in augmented form (larger note values). It represents the highest form of contrapuntal ingenuity in works such as **Bach's** *The Musical Offering*, and *The Art of the Fugue*, and **Beethoven's** *Grosse Fuge*.

Fux, Johann Joseph (1660–1741)

Austrian composer and theorist whose rules of **counterpoint**, compiled in his *Gradus ad Parnassum* (1725), were studied by **Haydn** and **Beethoven**, and are still used as a teaching formula by many music schools. He also wrote a considerable quantity of sacred music, including 50 masses and 10 oratorios.

Gabrieli, Andrea (c. 1533–1585)
Italian composer and organist at St Mark's, Venice, from 1566. He consolidated a Venetian school that cultivated an **antiphonal** style suited to the two choir galleries and two organs of St Mark's. His many distinguished pupils, Italian and foreign, included his nephew Giovanni **Gabrieli**, and **Hassler**.

Gabrieli, Giovanni (c. 1555–1612)
Italian composer who succeeded his uncle Andrea as organist of St Mark's, Venice. His sacred and secular works include numerous madrigals, motets, and the **antiphonal** *Sacrae symphoniae* (1597), sacred canzonas and sonatas for brass choirs, strings, and organ, in spatial **counterpoint**.

VENETIAN ANTIPHONY

Gabrieli's concerti (1587) make much use of the spatial effects possible within St Mark's, with vocal and instrumental groups separated in contrasting ensembles.

Gade, Niels Vilhelm (1817–1890)
The most important Danish composer of the 19th century. He studied in Leipzig where he met **Mendelssohn**, who produced his First Symphony in 1843 and engaged him to conduct the Gewandhaus concerts in his absence. After returning to Denmark he established a permanent orchestra; he wrote the opera *Mariotta* (1849), eight symphonies, and much chamber music.

Gagliano, Marco da (1582–1643)
Italian composer whose opera *Dafne* (1608) followed **Monteverdi's** epoch-making *Orfeo* by one year; it also developed early operatic form, with its inclusion of airs and choruses as well as recitative. He also founded the Accademia dell' Elevati for the cultivation of music (1607).

Galuppi, Baldassare (1706–1785)

Italian composer noted for his comic operas, the most famous being *Il filosofo di campagna* (1754). He visited London (1741–43), and produced several operas there. He was appointed second maestro di cappella at St Mark's, Venice, in 1748, and was subsequently director of Catherine the Great's chapel at St Petersburg, writing operas and Russian sacred music.

Geminiani, Francesco (1687–1762)

Italian violinist and composer whose treatise *The Art of Playing the Violin* (1751) was the first violin tutor ever published. His music – which includes concerti grossi and trio sonatas – was influenced by **Corelli** and is typically brilliant in fast movements and expressive in slow movements. He lived in London, Paris, and Dublin.

Gerhard, Roberto (1896–1970)

Spanish-born composer who studied with **Granados** and **Schoenberg**, settling in England in 1939 after the rise of Fascism in Spain. He united atonal methods with the colours and rhythms of his native Spain; some of his later music, notably the Third Symphony (*Collages*, 1960) employs avant-garde techniques. He lived in Cambridge, first on a research studentship at King's College, then for the rest of his life from composing.

Gershwin, George (1898–1937)

US composer whose musical comedies, mostly to lyrics by his brother Ira Gershwin (1896–1983), were among Broadway's most successful in the 1920s and 1930s, including *Strike up the Band* (1927), *Funny Face* (1927), and *Girl Crazy* (1930). His opera *Porgy and Bess* (1935) uniquely incorporated jazz rhythms and popular song styles in an operatic format. Although his scores to musicals made him famous, his concert works, including *Rhapsody in Blue* (1924) and *Piano Concerto in F* (1925), earned him much critical acclaim.

Gesualdo, Carlo (*c.* 1561–1613)

Prince of Venosa, Italian composer whose compositions are noted for their complex harmonic structure, most unlike the work of his contemporaries. His highly chromatic madrigals (in six books, 1594–1611), set to emotional, passionate texts, have been admired in the 20th century by **Stravinsky**, among others. He married into the Este family, and lived at the court in Ferrara until 1596. He is the subject of **Schnittke's** second opera, *Gesualdo*, and of a theatre piece by **Sciarrino**. (*See box on p. 76*)

GESUALDO'S CRIME

Gesualdo married Maria d'Avalos, a Neapolitan noblewoman, in 1586.
Though only 21, she had already been married twice and had children.
She bore him a son, but became the lover of Fabrizio Caraffa, 3rd Duke
of Andria; Gesualdo had them both murdered on the night of 16
October 1590.

Gibbons, Orlando (1583–1625)

One of the most important Tudor English composers. He wrote sacred
anthems, instrumental fantasias, and madrigals including *The Silver Swan*
for five voices (1612). From a family of musicians, he became organist at
Westminster Abbey, London, in
1623. His contribution to church
music was outstanding, while his
instrumental works, which
include 30 fantasies for strings
and 16 keyboard fantasies, are
most notable.

Gibbons died suddenly at Canterbury
while waiting to officiate at Charles I's
marriage service, for which he had
written music.

Ginastera, Alberto Evaristo (1916–1983)

Argentine composer who initially wrote in a nationalistic style, but after
1958 turned to serialism, **aleatoric techniques**, and the use of **microtones**.
He is best known for his operas *Don Rodrigo* (1964), *Bomarzo* (1967), and
Beatrix Cenci (1971), and his piano music (3 sonatas and two concertos) is
still played.

Glass, Philip (1937–)

US composer who studied with Nadia **Boulanger**, was strongly influenced
by Indian music, and became a central **minimalist** figure. His work is characterized by almost endlessly repeated rhythmic figures that are expanded
and modified. His compositions include the operas *Einstein on the Beach*
(1976), *Akhnaten* (1984), *The Making of the Representative for Planet 8*
(1988), and the *Low Symphony* (1992) on themes from David Bowie's *Low*
album. Later works seemed to have lacked fresh musical ideas, but creative
renewal came with an opera for Columbus Day, given at the New York
Metropolitan Opera House in 1992.

Glazunov, Aleksandr Konstantinovich (1865–1936)

Russian composer who achieved fame with his first symphony, which was written when he was only 17. He absorbed a range of influences, from his teacher **Rimsky-Korsakov's** orchestrational skill to **Tchaikovsky's** lyricism. He made a significant impact as a teacher on the following generation of composers, including **Prokofiev** and **Shostakovich**. His works include the ballets *Raymonda* (1897) and *The Seasons* (1899), eight symphonies (1881–1906), and many chamber and piano works.

GLAZUNOV'S WEAKNESS

In later years, Glazunov became known for his drinking: in 1897 he is thought to have ruined the première of Rachmaninov's First Symphony through his errant conducting; years later, as teacher of Shostakovich, he is reputed to have drunk from a (not very well) concealed bottle of vodka during his classes.

Glière, Reinhold Moritsovich (1875–1956)

Russian composer of Belgian descent whose third symphony *Ilya Muromets* (1909–11) combines influences of **Rimsky-Korsakov**, **Skryabin**, and **Sibelius** to form an epic, grandiose account of legendary exploits. Soviet dictates veered him towards researching Azerbaijani and Ukrainian folksong and he based some of his later works on it. His pupils include **Lyatoshynsky**, **Prokofiev**, and **Mosolov**.

Glinka, Mikhail Ivanovich (1804–1857)

Often regarded as the founder of Russian music, he broke away from Italian influences and turned to Russian folk music for inspiration for revolutionary works such as the opera *A Life for the Tsar* (1836) and the orchestral fantasia *Kamarinskaya* (1848). He exerted a strong influence on several generations of composers, from **Mussorgsky** to **Stravinsky** and beyond. Glinka studied music casually, taking some piano lessons from **Field**. He visited Italy (1830–33) and Berlin, but returned to Russia to work on *A Life for the Tsar* and succeeded in having it produced in 1836; it was an immediate success, combining nationalist musical elements with a patriotic tale composed at a time of unrest. *Ruslan and Ludmilla* was delayed by domestic troubles but was eventually produced in 1842. He later visited Spain (his impressions are demonstrated in the orchestral pieces *Jota aragonesa* and *A Night in Madrid* (1848); he died during a visit to Berlin (1856–57). He also introduced harmonic innovations that were to bear fruit in the work of nearly all later Russian composers.

RUSSIAN ROOTS

In *Kamarinskaya* Glinka established formal procedures based on endless variation that were essentially Russian and, as such, set the seal for much subsequent Russian developments.

Gluck, Christoph Willibald von (1714–1787)

Bohemian–German composer whose series of 'reform' operas moved away from the formal conventions of the day, in which the interests of singers predominated; in particular, endless recitative was replaced by orchestral accompaniments, which improved dramatic flow. In 1762 his *Orfeo ed Euridice* revolutionized the 18th-century conception of opera by giving free scope to dramatic effect. It was followed by *Alceste* (1767) and *Paride ed Elena* (1770). In 1774 his *Iphigénie en Aulide* brought to a head the fierce debate over the future of opera in which Gluck's French style had the support of Marie Antoinette, while his Italian rival **Piccinni** had the support of Madame du Barry. With *Armide* (1777) and *Iphigénie en Tauride* (1779), Gluck won a complete victory over Piccinni.

Gnesin, Mikhail Fabianovich (1883–1957)

Russian Jewish composer who studied with **Rimsky-Korsakov** and **Lyadov** and then in Germany. He was at first attracted to Russian Symbolism and is said to have exerted influence over **Stravinsky** in his early years. His works of the 1920s demonstrate an intense interest in Jewish folk music; he visited Palestine during these years. His chamber works, such as the *Requiem* for piano quintet, and his *Piano Trio* 'in memory of our lost children' (1944) are particularly fine.

Godowsky, Leopold (1870–1938)

Polish-born pianist and composer who appeared in public at the age of nine. He first visited the USA in 1884, settled there in 1901, and later became director of the Chicago Conservatory. He taught many leading pianists including Heinrich Neuhaus. His compositions – which are attracting a growing number of pianists – are notable for their often dense, intricate, and polyphonic textures and luxuriant harmonies. They include 50 studies based on **Chopin's** études, a sonata, a passacaglia (based on a theme from **Schubert's** Unfinished Symphony), and numerous arrangements and transcriptions.

Goehr, (Peter) Alexander (1932–)

German-born English composer who was professor of music at Cambridge (1976–99). A lyrical but often hard-edged serialist, he nevertheless used traditional forms such as the symphony, and more recently turned to tonal and even Baroque models. His output includes orchestral works, four string quartets, the opera *Arianna* (1995), and *The Mouse Metamorphosed into a Maid* (1991) for solo soprano. His writings are notable for their lucidity and warmth.

Goldmark, Karoly (Carl) (1830–1915)

Austro-Hungarian composer whose best-known work today is the *Rustic Wedding Symphony*, although he established his reputation with the Wagner-influenced opera *Die Königin von Saba/The Queen of Sheba* (1875). The son of a Jewish cantor, he studied in Vienna where he eventually settled as a teacher. His other works include the operas *Merlin* (1886), *Das Heimchen am Herd* (after Dickens's *Cricket on the Hearth*, 1896), and *Ein Wintermärchen* (after Shakespeare's *Winter's Tale*, 1908), two violin concertos, and much chamber music.

> During the 1848 Revolution he played at the theatre at Györ in Hungary and was nearly shot as a rebel.

Goldschmidt, Berthold (1903–1996)

Composer who left Nazi Germany in 1935 and settled in England. He did not compose for many years; however, following a revival of his music in the mid-1980s, he returned to composing and produced several notable chamber works before his death. His works include the operas *Der gewaltige Hahnrei* (after Crommelynck, produced by Mannheim, 1932) and *Beatrice Cenci* (after Shelley, 1949–50), *Ciaconna sinfonica* (1936, premiered in Vienna 1960, performed under Simon Rattle in Berlin 1987), and numerous chamber works.

Górecki, Henryk Mikolaj (1933–)

Polish composer whose study with **Messiaen** and exposure to avant-garde influences after 1956 led him to abandon a politically sanctioned style and seek out new sonorities. He later adopted a slow-moving tonal idiom appealing to revived religious tradition, often on tragic themes from Polish history, as in *Old Polish Music* for orchestra (1969), and his Third Symphony, *Sorrowful Songs* (1976), which propelled him to fame in the West in 1992.

Gottschalk, Louis Moreau (1829–1869)

US composer and pianist who adopted Creole and American folk music, Latin American rhythms, and dance forms. The striking colouristic effects of his music won the admiration of **Berlioz**, **Liszt**, **Offenbach**, and others. His compositions include *Souvenir d'Andalousie* (1851) for piano and orchestra, and numerous piano pieces, among which are *La gallina: danse cubaine* and *Le Banjo – esquisse américaine.*

Gottschalk died of yellow fever while on tour in Brazil.

Gounod, Charles François (1818–1893)

French composer whose operas, notably *Faust* (1859) and *Roméo et Juliette* (1867), and church music, including *Messe solennelle* (1849), combine graceful melody and elegant harmonization. His *Meditation on Bach's Prelude* (1889) achieved popularity as 'Gounod's *Ave Maria*'. Intending to become a priest, he did not produce any important music until his opera *Sappho* appeared in 1851. His five-act setting of *Faust* for the Paris Opéra in 1859 brought his melodic gift before a huge public; his success was consolidated by a saccharine but effective version of *Roméo and Juliet* (1867).

grace note

An ornamental note written in small type. They are usually either a slower *appoggiatura* ('leaning note') or a faster *acciaccatura* ('crushed' note). When appearing in a large group, as in a **cadenza** by **Beethoven** or a melody by **Chopin**, the grace notes usually fill in the duration of a single note in the melody, and may (if time permits) be played with greater rhythmic flexibility than in standard notation.

grace note *How grace notes are notated on a stave.*

Grainger, Percy Aldridge (1882–1961)

Australian-born experimental composer and pianist. He is remembered for piano transcriptions, songs, and short instrumental pieces drawing on folk idioms, including *Country Gardens* (1925), and for his settings of folk songs, such as *Molly on the Shore* (1921). Grainger shared with his friend **Busoni** a vision of a free music, devising a synthesizer and composing machine far ahead of its time. He lived in London 1900–14 and became interested in folk music. He toured Scandinavia in 1909, and later settled in the USA.

GRAINGER'S ECCENTRICITIES

Grainger married Ella Viola Ström at the Hollywood Bowl in 1928, conducting his *To a Nordic Princess* in honour of the occasion. In 1938 he founded a museum at Melbourne, to house his manuscripts and souvenirs, but his request for the museum to display his skeleton after his death was declined.

Granados, Enrique (1867–1916)

Spanish composer and pianist best known for his piano work *Goyescas* (1911), inspired by the work of the artist Goya, and converted to an opera in 1916. He became a well-known pianist and in 1900 founded the Sociedad de Conciertos Clásicos in Madrid, which he conducted. His other works include the **zarzuelas** *Maria del Carmen* (1898), and *Gaziel* (1906), orchestral pieces, and numerous songs.

A TRAGIC DEATH

After a visit to New York for the production of the operatic version of *Goyescas* in January 1916, Granados went down in the *Sussex* when it was torpedoed by a German submarine in the English Channel. He had swum to rescue his wife, but was weighed down with the gold that the New York Metropolitan Opera had paid him for *Goyescas*.

Grechaninov, Aleksandr Tikhonovich (1864–1956)

Russian composer who wrote for the Russian Orthodox Church; he left Russia after the Revolution and settled in Paris and later in the USA.

Although the son of a semi-literate small shopkeeper, Grechaninov studied composition with **Rimsky-Korsakov** in St Petersburg. He also wrote two operas, five symphonies, and various concertos.

Grétry, André Ernest Modeste (1741–1813)
Belgian-born composer of about 40 operas; a leading figure in the development of *opéras-comiques*. By 1759 he had already composed some symphonies and church music, which won him a scholarship to study in Rome, where he produced the intermezzo *La vendemmiatrice*. Back in Paris, he produced a stream of *opéras-comiques*, the most popular being *Richard Cœur-de-Lion* (1784), an early example of a rescue opera. He published his memoirs in three volumes (1789–97).

Grieg, Edvard (Hagerup) (1843–1907)
Norwegian composer of Scottish descent. Born in Bergen, the son of a merchant; he studied in Leipzig, and in 1863 he went to live in Copenhagen and studied with **Gade**. In 1864 he met Rikard Nordaak, who fired his enthusiasm for Norwegian national music, and then settled as a teacher and conductor at Christiania. He played a part in the formation of the Norwegian Academy of Music.

In 1869, at Copenhagen, he premiered his most enduring work, the Piano Concerto in A minor. The premiere of Ibsen's *Peer Gynt* in February 1876 secured Grieg's reputation as the leading Scandinavian composer of the day; the work's colourful and evocative vignettes represent his talent at its best.

Grieg repeatedly tried to write a second piano concerto after his first was so succesful, but never got beyond preliminary sketches.

He developed a style that was characterized partly by Norwegian folksong and more by his own harmonic experiments; this combination produced music of great strength and individuality. His works include three sonatas for violin and piano, ten volumes of *Lyric Pieces* for piano, and 143 songs, including the *Haugtussa* cycle (1895).

Gubaidulina, Sofia (1931–)
Russian composer who, along with **Denisov** and **Schnittke**, was the most important representative of the Soviet avant garde that emerged in the 1960s. Her individuality resides in her frequent recourse to the sounds of Asian instruments, an interest in spiritual matters, and the reconciliation of

opposites. She studied with **Shebalin** at the Moscow Conservatory and then privately with Herschkowitz. She has lived in Germany since 1991. Her works include *Offertorium*, a violin concerto (1980–86), *Seven Words* for cello, bayan, and strings (1982), and *Pro et contra* for orchestra (1989).

Guido d'Arezzo (*c.* 990– *c.* 1050)

Italian Benedictine monk and music theorist. He greatly advanced **solmization** and mutation by adapting the syllables ut, re, mi, fa, sol, and la to the **hexachord** and by demonstrating the hexachordal positions on the fingers by the use of the 'Guidonian hand'. He lived in Pomposa and Arezzo, and visited Rome. His chief theoretical work, written about 1026, is entitled *Micrologus de musica*.

d'Arezzo *Music theorist and monk Guido d'Arezzo.*

guitar

Flat-bodied musical instrument with six or twelve strings that are plucked or strummed with the fingers. The fingerboard is usually fretted, although some modern electric guitars are fretless. Derived from a Moorish original, the guitar spread throughout Europe in medieval times, becoming firmly established in Italy, Spain, and the Spanish American colonies. Its 20th-century revival owes much to Segovia, Bream, and Williams. The electric guitar, developed in the 1950s by Les Paul and Leo Fender, amplifies vibrations from electromagnetic pick-ups to produce a range of tone qualities.

Hába, Alois (1893–1973)

Czech **microtonal** composer who also wrote some twelve-tone music, for example *Fantasia* for nonet (1932). He later became a pupil of **Schreker** in Vienna and Berlin; while working for Universal Edition in Vienna he gained a close acquaintance with **Schoenberg's** music. His works include the opera *Mother* (produced 1931).

DIVIDED TONES

Hába pioneered the use of quarter-tones. He later employed sixth-tones (as in the Fifth Quartet 1923), and fifth-tones (as in the 16th Quartet 1967).

Hahn, Reynaldo (1874–1947)

French composer popular in Parisian salons as a performer of his own songs. In 1934 he was appointed music critic of *Le Figaro*, and in 1945 became

Hahn's music was admired by French writer Marcel Proust.

music director of the Paris Opéra. As a conductor he specialized in **Mozart** and as a composer he wrote much incidental music for plays, two ballets, operas, and operettas.

Halffter, Cristóbal (1930–)

Spanish composer initially influenced by **Falla** but who turned to serialism. In 1962 he became professor of composition at the Madrid Conservatory, and has also taught in Navarra and Freiburg. He has appeared as a conductor of several German orchestras. His works include the operas *Don Quichotte* (produced Düsseldorf, 1970), *Cantata in expectatione resurrectionis domini* (1962), *Sinfonia* for three instrumental groups (1963), and much other instrumental music.

Handel, George Frederic (1685–1759)

German composer who became a British subject in 1726. Handel initially studied law, but abandoned it to become a violinist, and later a harpsichordist, at a Hamburg opera house. He travelled in Italy; *Agrippina* was successfully produced at Venice in 1709. In 1710 he was appointed Kapellmeister to the elector of Hanover (the future George I of England). In 1711 his opera *Rinaldo* was performed in London and in 1712 he settled in England, where he established his popularity with such works as the *Water Music* (1717), written for George I. With the founding of the

Handel *German-born British composer Handel who is perhaps best known for his* Messiah.

Royal Academy of Music in 1720 began Handel's most prolific period as an opera composer, and over the next 20 years he wrote more than 30 works. But the rivalry of fashionable Italian opera composers led him to abandon Italianate opera for English oratorio. *Messiah* was the summation of his life's work, composed in a single burst of inspiration but including some elements from earlier music. Its success encouraged him to write 12 more oratorios,

HANDEL'S OPERAS AND ORATORIOS

Handel's operas include *Agrippina* (1710), *Rinaldo* (1711), *Radamisto* (1720), *Giulio Cesare* (1724), *Tamerlano* (1724), *Rodelinda* (1725), *Scipione, Alessandro* (1726), *Orlando* (1733), *Ariodante* (1735), *Alcina* (1735), *Giustino, Berenice* (1737), *Serse* (1735), *Imeneo* (1740), *Deidamia* (1741)

His oratorios include *Athalia* (1733), *Saul* (1739), *Israel in Egypt* (1739), *Messiah* (1742), *Samson* (1743), *Belshazzar* (1745), *Judas Maccabaeus* (1747), *Joshua, Susanna* (1749), *Solomon* (1749), *Theodora* (1750), *Jephtha* (1752)

some on Old Testament texts (*Samson, Solomon*) others on classical mythology (*Semele*). His health declined and in 1751, despite receiving treatment for cataracts, he became totally blind. His last major public success came in 1749 with the suite for wind instruments, to accompany the Royal Fireworks in Green Park.

> ❝ My Lord, I should be sorry if I only entertained them; I wished to make them better. ❞
>
> **Handel**, speaking to Lord Kinnol after a performance of *Messiah*, quoted in Young, *Handel*

harmony

Any simultaneous combination of **pitches**, as opposed to melody, which is a succession of single notes. Although the term suggests a pleasant or agreeable sound, it is applied to any combination of notes, whether consonant or dissonant. The theory of harmony deals with the formation of **chords** and their interrelation and logical progression. Chromatic harmony is produced when a progression from one chord to another is achieved when the movement of the respective **voices** occurs by degrees of the chromatic, twelve-note scale; equally, it can result from unusual modifications of common chords. It is found in the works of **Liszt**, **Wagner**, **Strauss**, **Rimsky-Korsakov**, and others. Atonal harmony ignores (or appears to ignore) usual chordal progressions and is usually dissonant in nature. It was first used rigorously from around 1909 onwards by **Schoenberg** and **Roslavets**.

harp

Plucked string instrument, with the strings stretched vertically and parallel to one side of a triangular framework. A second side of the triangle is a wood and brass soundbox of triangular shape; the third contains pegs that maintain tension of the strings. The orchestral harp is the largest instrument of its type. It evolved in size because of a need for increased volume, following its introduction into the orchestra in the 19th century. It has up to 47 diatonically tuned strings; all the notes of the chromatic scale are made

Recorded from biblical times, the harp existed in the West as early as the 9th century, and was common among medieval minstrels.

available by the depression of a combination of seven pedals (one to raise or lower each note of the major scale).

harpsichord

The largest and grandest of 18th-century keyboard string instruments, used in orchestras and as a solo instrument. The strings are plucked by 'jacks' made of leather or quill, and multiple keyboards offering variation in tone are common. However, unlike the piano, the tone cannot be greatly varied by the player's touch. The revival of the harpsichord repertoire in the 20th century owes much to Wanda Landowska and Ralph Kirkpatrick (1911–1984). A modern repertoire has developed for the harpsichord, with concertos by Carter, de Falla, and Martinu, and solo works by **Ligeti**, **Sciarrino**, and **Xenakis**.

See also: *spinet.*

Harris, Roy (Leroy Ellsworth) (1898–1979)

US composer who used American folk tunes in the *Symphony No 10* (1965, also known as 'Abraham Lincoln'), and the orchestral *When Johnny Comes Marching Home* (1935). His father was a farmer who migrated to California during Harris's boyhood, and at 18 Harris had a farm of his own. After two years spent in Paris studying with Nadia **Boulanger**, he returned to the USA in 1929; his most successful work was his Third Symphony, declaring American ruggedness at the onset of war. It was premiered under Koussevitsky in Boston in 1939.

Harrison, Lou (1917–)

US composer who has experimented with new sonorities, including novel scales and methods of tuning. He helped promote the music of **Varèse**, **Ruggles**, and **Cowell**, and conducted the first performance of **Ives**' Third Symphony in 1946. A visit to the Far East in 1961 inspired much music for the gamelan. His music, like the man, is charming, intelligent, and warm. His works include the opera *Rapunzel* (1959), ballets *The Perilous Chapel* (1949), *Almanac of the Seasons*, and others; a piano concerto (1985), *Ariadne* for flute and percussion (1987); and much else.

Hartmann, Karl Amadeus (1905–1963)

German composer who composed late in life, having destroyed his early works and turned to serialism under the influence of **Webern**. After World War II he organized the important 'Musica Viva' concerts in Munich to propagate new music, and in 1953 he became president of the German section of the International Society for Contemporary Music. His works include the chamber opera *Des Simplicius simplicissimus Jugend* (1934), and eight symphonies (1936–62).

Harvey, Jonathan Dean (1939–)

English composer whose use of avant-garde and computer synthesis techniques is allied to a tradition of visionary **Romanticism** in works such as *Inner Light II* (1977) for voices, instruments, and tape, and the evocative *Mortuos plango, vivos voco* (1980) for computer-manipulated concrete sounds, realized at IRCAM. He studied at Cambridge and Glasgow Universities, and was appointed professor at Sussex University in 1980.

Hassler, Hans Leo (1564–1612)

One of the first Germans to study in Italy, and the polychoral techniques and rich sonorities of his Masses and motets show the influence of the Venetians. After an appointment at Nuremberg he was sent to Venice for further study under Andrea **Gabrieli**. Although Hassler was a Protestant, his early works are all for the Catholic Church. He wrote considerable quantities of church music in Latin and German, in addition to many secular songs.

> The tune of Hassler's love song, 'Mein G'müt ist mir verwirret' (1601), was used in Bach's *St Matthew Passion*.

Hauer, Josef Matthias (1883–1959)

Austrian composer who published pamphlets about his own 12-note system, which was different from **Schoenberg's**. All his works use this system, which is based on groups of notes he called *Tropen*, derived from the combinations of the 12 notes of the chromatic scale allowed by the agreement of their overtones. His works include the opera *Salammbô* (after Flaubert, 1929; performed Vienna, 1983), 7 *Dance Fantasies* (1928), an *Apocalyptic Fantasy* (1913), and about 87 *Zwölftonspiele* for various instruments.

Haydn, (Franz) Joseph (1732–1809)

Austrian composer whose music, along with that of his pupil **Mozart**, epitomized the early **Classical era**. He was a major exponent of **sonata form** in his numerous chamber and orchestral works (he wrote more than 100 symphonies). He was also the first great master of the string quartet, and was a teacher of **Beethoven**.

Born in Lower Austria, the son of a wheelwright, Haydn went as a chorister to St Stephen's Cathedral in Vienna. In composition he was largely self-taught, studying the works of C P E **Bach**, and **Fux's** *Gradus ad Parnassum*. His first string quartets were written about 1755; in 1761 he took employment with the Esterházy family, a post he held for the rest of his life. Beginning with symphony no. 22 (the *'Philosopher'*, 1764) and continuing through the 1760s to no. 49 (*'La passione'*), Haydn gained his maturity as a composer, showing inventiveness in each work. In the set of quartets Op.50 (1787), Haydn repaid the debt that Mozart had acknowledged when dedicating his own quartets to the older composer. Though he was isolated in Eszterháza, his fame spread; he received invitations to travel, which, however, his duties obliged him to refuse.

Haydn *Austrian composer Joseph Haydn.*

On the death of Prince Nikolaus in 1790 he was free to accept an invitation from the impresario Salomon to go to England. His first visit to London (1791–92), for which he composed an opera (not produced) and six symphonies, was a great success, and was followed by another for which a further six symphonies were written. These works confirmed his reputation as the most original composer of the genre during his time. The wit, melodic inventiveness, and densely woven developments of these works were matched in the great sets of string quartets written during the 1790s.

> ❝ It is the melody which is the charm of music, and it is that which is most difficult to produce. ❞
>
> Joseph **Haydn**, quoted in Machlis, *Introduction to Contemporary Music*

Inspired by **Handel's** oratorios he had heard in London, he composed *The Creation* and *The Seasons*. From 1803 he lived in retirement in Vienna.

In spite of huge advances made in the knowledge and performance of Haydn's music in recent years, the sheer range and quantity of his output is so intimidating that he still awaits wide recognition, and some of his works are still unpublished. His works also include 20 operas (of which 7 are lost); 14 Masses; cantatas and oratorios including *Seven Last Words* (1796), 32 piano trios, and about 60 piano sonatas.

HAYDN'S SYMPHONIES

Haydn's symphonies include nos. 1–5 (1758–60); nos. 6–8, *Le matin, Le midi, Le soir* (1761); nos. 9–21 (about 1762); no. 22 in E♭, *The Philosopher* (1764); nos. 23–25 (1764); no. 26 in D minor, *Lamentatione* (1770); nos. 27–29 (1765); no. 30 in C, *Alleluja* (1765); no. 31 in D, *Hornsignal* (1765); nos. 32–42 (about 1768) no. 43 in E♭, *Mercury* (1772); no. 44 in E minor, *Trauersinfonie* (1772); no. 45 in F♯ minor, *Farewell* (1772); no. 46 in B and no. 47 in G (1772); no. 48 in C, *Maria Theresa*, and no. 49 in F minor, *La passione* (about 1768); nos. 50–52 (1773); no. 53 in D, *The Imperial* (1778); nos. 54–59 (1774); no. 60 in C, *Il distratto* (1774); nos. 61–72 (about 1779); no. 73 in D, *La chasse* (1782); nos. 74–81 (1781–84); nos. 82–87, *Paris Symphonies*; no. 82 in C, *The Bear*, no. 83 in G minor, *The Hen*, no. 84 in E♭, no. 85 in B♭, *La reine*, no. 86 in D, no. 87 in A (1785–86); no. 88 in G, no. 89 in F, no. 90 in C, no. 91 in E♭ (1787–88); no. 92 in G, *The Oxford* (1789); nos. 93–104, *London Symphonies* no. 93 in D, no. 94 in G, *The Surprise*, no. 95 in C minor, no. 96 in D, *The Miracle*, no. 97 in C, no. 98 in B♭, no. 99 in E♭, no. 100 in G, *The Military*, no. 101 in D, *The Clock*, no. 102 in B♭, no. 103 in E♭, *The Drumroll*, no. 104 in D, *The London* (1791–95).

Henze, Hans Werner (1926–)

German composer whose immense and stylistically restless output is marked by literary sensibility and seductive use of orchestral coloration, as in the opera *Elegy for Young Lovers* (1959–61), and the later opera *The Sea Betrayed* (1992). Although he is influenced by **Schoenberg**, Henze is not strictly a 12-note composer. Following the student unrest of 1968 he suddenly renounced the wealthy musical establishment in favour of a militantly socialist stance in works such as the abrasive *Voices* (1973), austere settings of 22 revolutionary texts in often magical sonorities. In recent years Henze has returned to the musical past, and has become increasingly lyrical and elaborate: his reconstruction of **Monteverdi's** *Il ritorno di Ulisse* was staged at Salzburg in 1985. His works include many ballets, nine symphonies, concertos, and instrumental works.

❝I have taken the decision that in my work I will embody all the difficulties and all the problems of contemporary bourgeois music, and that I will, however, try to transform these into something usable, into something that the masses can understand. ❞

Hans **Henze**, *Music and Politics*

Heseltine, Philip (Arnold) or Warlock, Peter (1894–1930)

A dual personality: Heseltine (the original name) was a sensitive critic and writer of elegant songs, while Warlock was a beer-swilling beef eater who produced caricatures of Elizabethan music. Works include the orchestral suite *Capriol* (1926) based on 16th-century dances, and the song cycle *The Curlew* (1920–22). His music reflects the extreme mood swings of his personality; he died by suicide.

❝He who has heard the cry of a curlew on a lone and desolate moor has heard the music of this richly gifted personality. ❞

Eric **Fenby** on Warlock, in *Delius as I Knew Him*

hexachord

Not a chord in the true sense, but a group of six individual notes. Introduced in the 11th century as a method of sight-singing, a series of overlapping scalar hexachords embraced the entire compass of notes. In the 20th century the term has been redefined by composers using the twelve-tone system, particularly **Schoenberg** and **Webern**, as being half of a twelve-tone row.

Hildegard, Saint (1098–1179)

German abbess and musician, also known as Hildegard of Bingen, whose music for the church shows some departures from traditional plainsong style. She wrote music to her own poetry from 1140, collected in the 1150s as *Symphonia armonie celestium revelationum* (77 poems based on the liturgical calendar).

Hindemith, Paul (1895–1963)

Theatrically astute and politically aware German composer of the operas *Cardillac* (1926) and *Mathis the Painter* (1933–35). In 1939 he emigrated to the USA, where he taught at Yale and promoted a measured **Neo-Classical** idiom of self-evident contrapuntal mastery but matter-of-fact tone, exemplified in *Ludus tonalis* for piano (1942). In later life he revised many of his compositions to conform to a personal theory of tonality. His works include the *Kammermusik*

> As a teacher in Berlin (1927–33), Hindemith encouraged the development of a functional modern repertoire (Gebrauchsmusik) for home and school.

nos. 1–7 (1922–27), *Der Schwanendreher*, viola concerto after folksongs (1935), *Trauermusik* for viola and strings (1936), *Nobilissima visione*, suite from the ballet (1938), and *Symphonic Metamorphosis on Themes of Carl Maria von Weber* (1943).

Holliger, Heinz (1939–)

Swiss oboist and composer who combined avant-garde techniques with a lyric expressionist style in works such as *Sevensong* (1967) for amplified oboe, voices, and orchestra. He has given first performances of works written for him by **Berio**, **Henze**, and **Stockhausen**. His *Scardanelli-Zyklus* (1975–85) is among the most important instrumental works of the late 20th century.

Holloway, Robin (Greville) (1943–)

English composer who is influenced by German **Romanticism**, reworking material from **Bach** and **Schumann** in various works. He studied at Cambridge, and was later appointed lecturer there. His works include the opera *Clarissa* (1968–76; first performance 1990); *Scenes from Schumann*, 7 paraphrases for orchestra (1970) and *Fantasy-Pieces* (on Schumann's *Liederkreis*) for 13 players (1971), and 3 concertos for orchestra.

Holmboe, Vagn (1909–1996)
Denmark's most distinguished composer after Nielsen, Holmboe wrote 12 symphonies, 20 string quartets, 13 chamber concertos, and many other pieces, including the *Requiem for Nietzsche* (1963–64). His output also includes the opera *Fanden og Borgmesteren* (1940), the ballet *Den galsind-ede Tyrk*, and three violin sonatas.

Holst, Gustav us Theodore von (1874–1934)
English composer of distant Swedish descent. He wrote operas, including *Sávitri* (1908) and *At the Boar's Head* (1924); ballets; choral works, including *Hymns from the Rig Veda* (1908–12) and *The Hymn of Jesus* (1917); orchestral suites, including *The Planets* (1914–16); and songs. He was a life-long friend of Ralph **Vaughan Williams**, with whom he shared an enthusiasm for English folk music. His musical style, although tonal and drawing on folk song, tends to the severe and monotonous. His daughter Imogen was also a composer and became his biographer.

homme armé, l'
(French 'the armed man') Name of an old French secular song, the tune of which was often used by composers of the 15th and 16th centuries as *can-tus firmus* for their Masses, which were then designated by that name.

Honegger, Arthur (1892–1955)
Swiss composer who joined 'Les Six' and became known for his symphonic depiction of a steam train in *Pacific 231*. But the real Honegger was a **Neo-Classicist** who wrote dramatic oratorios *King David* (1921) and *Joan of Arc at the Stake* (1938). His masterly First Symphony was written for strings alone with a trumpet appearing only in the finale. He was eclectic in tastes: he enjoyed jazz and wrote the scores for Gance's silent movie classics *The Wheel* (1923) and *Napoléon* (1927).

> ❦ There is no doubt that the first requirement for a composer is to be dead. ❧
>
> Arthur **Honegger**, *I Am a Composer*

Hovhanessian, Alan (1911–)

US composer much influenced by Armenian, Indian, and other oriental music. A prolific composer, he destroyed a great deal of his work in 1940. His output nonetheless incorporates 10 operas, 63 symphonies (1939–88), *And God Created Whales* (1970) including a taped part for humpbacked whale, two *Armenian Rhapsodies* for strings, 23 concertos (1936–80), and chamber music including 5 string quartets (1936–76).

Huber, Klaus (1924–)

Swiss composer who combines avant-garde techniques with a strong religious awareness. He studied with Willy Burkhard at the Zürich Conservatory and with Blacher in Berlin. From 1950 he taught violin in Zürich and from 1960 music history at the Lucerne Conservatory. His pupils include Brian **Ferneyhough**. He has written the cantata *Des Engels Anredung an die Seele* (1957), *Tempora*, a violin concerto (1970), and *Spes contra spem* for voice, narrator, and orchestra (1988).

Hummel, Johann Nepomuk (1778–1837)

Austrian composer who followed in the steps of **Mozart** (his teacher). He was known as a conservative in his lifetime, clinging to a decaying tradition in the face of growing **Romanticism**. In addition to his keyboard works, which include seven concertos, he wrote choral and chamber works and operas. He was employed at the court of Weimar (1819–22, and from 1833 to his death), undertaking extensive concert tours in between and spending much time in London. He was a friend of **Beethoven** and was the original dedicatee of **Schubert's** last three piano sonatas.

hymn

Song in praise of a deity. Early examples include ancient Greek Orphic hymns, Old Testament psalms, and extracts from the New Testament (such as the 'Ave Maria'). The earliest sources of modern hymn melodies can be traced to the 11th and 12th centuries, and the earliest polyphonic settings date from the late 14th century. Gospel music and **carols** are forms of Christian hymn singing.

Ibert, Jacques François Antoine (1890–1962)

French composer of generally light music including seven often witty operas. However, his music always reflects its subject matter; in his symphonic poem *La Ballade de la geôle de Reading* (1922) he captures the horror of Oscar Wilde's poem.

idée fixe

Berlioz's term for a theme (in the *Fantastic Symphony*) which recurs in varying forms in the course of a composition as an allusion to some definite idea.

Indy, (Paul Marie Théodore) Vincent d' (1851–1931)

Composer best known for his *Symphonie sur un chant montagnard français* (*Symphonie cévenole*) for piano and orchestra (1886). He studied under **Franck**, and was one of the founders of the *Schola Cantorum*. His works also include operas (*Fervaal* 1897), symphonies, tone poems (*Istar* 1896), and chamber music. He helped the conductor Lamoureux introduce **Wagner's** music to Paris (*Lohengrin*, 1887) and revived works by **Rameau**, **Gluck**, and **Monteverdi** (*Poppea* in his own edition). His pupils included **Varèse**.

in nomine

An instrumental piece of the later 16th century for **viols** or keyboard, similar to the fancy or **fantasia**, but based on the plainsong melody 'Gloria tibi Trinitas', an **antiphon** for Trinity Sunday. It was used by **Taverner** as the **cantus firmus** of his Mass *Gloria tibi Trinitas*.

intermedii or *intermezzi*

In 15th- and 16th-century Italy, musical or dramatic interludes played between the acts of a play or during the intervals of a banquet. The musical *intermedii* consisted of instrumental pieces played out of sight of the audience. The dramatic *intermedii* were stage spectacles performed by singers, dancers, and actors in costume. In their combination of music and drama, *intermedii* can be regarded as an important forerunner of **opera**. The court of 15th-century Ferrara was particularly important in their development.

interval
The pitch difference between two notes, for example a fifth (counting the first and last notes up the diatonic **scale**).

intonation
The means by which a performer maintains correct **tuning**. Pitch accuracy requires continuous slight adjustments in those instruments for which it is feasible. The term is also applied to a range of theoretical concepts, ranging from tone quality, to the collective intervallic and harmonic characteristics of an entire work.

Ippolitov-Ivanov, Mikhail Mikhaylovich (1859–1935)
Russian composer whose most famous work, the orchestral *Caucasian Sketches*, shows a strong influence of Georgian folk music (about which he wrote a book). He studied under **Rimsky-Korsakov** at the St Petersburg Conservatory. In 1884 he was appointed conductor of the Imperial Opera at Tiflis, and later directed the Moscow Conservatory (1906–22). He composed seven operas, as well as choral works, and orchestral, chamber, and instrumental music. His memoirs were published as *Fifty Years of Russian Music* (1934).

Ireland, John Nicholson (1879–1962)
English composer whose works include the mystic orchestral prelude *The Forgotten Rite* (1917) and a piano concerto (1930). His first important compositions were two violin sonatas, and these established his reputation at once. His best-known subsequent works are a piano sonata, and the symphonic rhapsody *Mai-Dun* (1921). His song cycles are distinguished by his sensitive choice of words, and by the lyrical beauty and sincerity of their music.

Isaac, Henricus (*c*. 1450–1517)
Prolific Flemish composer of songs and instrumental music; he wrote a *Choralis Constantinus* consisting of 58 liturgical offices for the whole year. His wide travel is reflected in the various national influences in his music. He was a major contemporary of **Josquin Desprez** and **Obrecht**.

Ives, Charles Edward (1874–1954)

US composer who experimented with atonality, quarter tones, clashing time signatures, and quotations from popular music long before most other composers. He wrote five symphonies; chamber music, including the *Concord* sonata; and the orchestral works *Three Places in New England* (1903–14) and *The Unanswered Question* (1908). He composed in isolation, without much thought for the ease of performer or publisher, earning his living very successfully from his own insurance company. Ives stopped composing around 1920, but it was only after his death that his music was widely played and appreciated. The first performance of the *Concord* sonata in 1939 was greeted with acclaim, in spite of its complexities, but the Fourth Symphony was not performed until 11 years after Ives' death, under Stokowski.

Ives US composer Charles Ives.

 Every dissonance doesn't have to resolve itself if it doesn't happen to feel like it, any more than every horse should have its tail bobbed just because it's the prevailing fashion.

Ives, quoted in Wooldridge, *Charles Ives*

Janáček, Leoš (1854–1928)

Czech composer of highly original music influenced by Moravian folk music. His output includes operas (*Jenufa*, *The Cunning Little Vixen*, and *From the House of the Dead*), the *Glagolitic Mass*, the *Sinfonietta*, two string quartets, and effective piano music. His first mature work, the opera *Jenufa*, was begun in 1894 and staged at Brno in 1904. Although it was a success, wider recognition did not come until its production in Prague in 1916, which was followed by a production in Germany. His last decade saw a great burst of activity, with the composition of many new works that are full of exuberance and expressive power. Much of his astonishing later music, in particular the opera *Káta Kabanová* and the second string quartet *Intimate Letters*, was inspired by his unrequited love for Kamila Stösslová. Many scenes in his operas, as well as the song cycle *Diary of One Who Disappeared*, seem to have an epistolary basis; they are often brief vignettes in which the characters communicate with one another in a confiding, confessional manner.

> ❢ I proclaimed freedom in harmonic impressions long before Debussy, and really do not need French Impressionism. ❧
>
> Leoš **Janáček**, in a letter to Jan Mikota, 1926

Janequin, Clément (*c.* 1472–*c.* 1560)

French composer of chansons and psalms. He was choirmaster of Angers Cathedral and then lived in Paris from 1549. His songs of the 1520s–30s are witty and richly textured in imitative effects, for example 'La bataille de Marignan' (1515) incorporates the sounds of fighting.

Järnefelt, (Edvard) Armas (1869–1958)
Finnish composer chiefly known for his *Praeludium* (1907) and the lyrical *Berceuse* (1909) for small orchestra, from music for the drama *The Promised Land*. He often conducted works by Sibelius and gave the first Swedish performances of works by **Mahler** and **Schoenberg**.

Jenkins, John (1592–1678)
English composer and lutenist who composed in the traditional English style and in the new Italian fashion. He wrote a quantity of music for consorts of **viols**, which was popular with amateur players. He lived under the patronage of the nobility, especially Sir Hamon L'Estrange in Norfolk, and Lord North, to whose sons he taught music.

Jolas, Betsy (1926–)
French composer who has experimented with substituting voices for instruments, as in *Quatuor II* (1964). She has run new music on French radio and replaced **Messiaen** as head of the Paris Conservatory in 1974. Her works include the operas *Le pavillon au bord de la rivière* (1975), *Le cyclope* (1986), and *Schliemann* (1989); *Stances* for piano and orchestra (1978); and a number of instrumental works.

Josquin Desprez (1440–1521)
Franco-Flemish composer whose synthesis of Flemish **counterpoint** and Italian harmonic expression, acquired in the service of the Rome papal chapel (1484–1503), marks a peak in Renaissance vocal music. In addition to masses on secular as well as sacred themes, including the Mass *'L'Homme armé* (1504). He also wrote secular chansons such as 'The Cricket,' employing imitative vocal effects.

Kabalevsky, Dmitry Borisovich (1904–1987)

Russian composer who, along with Khrennikov, all too easily colluded with the Soviet regime in its denunciation of his betters, **Shostakovich**, **Prokofiev**, and **Myaskovsky**. While he was known in the West for a time for his keyboard and instrumental works (Horowitz played a piano sonata of his), his reputation in the USSR was based on dull socialist realist works, including the opera *The Taras Family* (1947).

Kagel, Mauricio (1931–)

Argentine composer prone to satire, off-beat humour, and theatrical absurdity. He studied in Buenos Aires, and settled in Cologne, Germany, in 1957. He has employed serial and **aleatoric techniques**, permutations of different languages, light effects, and aural distortions. But instead of being a modernist, his real influences include **Satie**, **Cage**, and the Dada movement. His works include *Ludwig van*, film (1970) and *Staatstheater*, a 'ballet for non-dancers', with instruments including chamber pot (1971).

Kalinnikov, Vasily Sergeyevich (1866–1901)

Russian composer admired by **Rachmaninov** and whose beautiful First Symphony suggests that his early death was a great loss. In 1884 he went to Moscow and, in spite of great poverty, obtained a musical education at the Philharmonic Society Music School. After conducting Italian opera for the 1893–94 season, he discovered he had tuberculosis and then lived mainly in the Crimea, composing.

kapellmeister

Chief conductor and chorus master, also resident composer for a private chapel, responsible for musical administration.

Karetnikov, Nikolay (1930–1994)

Russian composer who was obliged to compose and publish in secrecy, owing to his political and musical dissent. From the time of his Fourth

Symphony (1963) he worked on his opera *Til'Ulenshpigel* for 20 years. Recorded over five years with the co-operation of friends, it was dubbed the first *samizdat* opera and premiered in Germany in 1993.

Karlowicz, Mieczyslaw (1876–1909)

Polish composer associated with the Young Poland movement of **Szymanowski** and others. After studies in Warsaw, Berlin, and Leipzig, he settled in the Tatra mountains in 1908 and was killed in a climbing accident. His richly scored orchestral compositions reflect a number of influences including **Strauss** (without the kitsch) and **Skryabin** (of the middle period), and are richly rewarding. His works include the symphonic poems *Eternal Songs* (1907), *Stanisław i Anna Oswiecimowie* (1912), *An Episode during a Masquerade*, and a *Lithuanian Rhapsody*.

key

The diatonic scale around which a piece of music is written. For example, a passage in the key of C major uses mainly the notes of the C major scale, and harmonies related to that scale. Most music does not remain in one key, but moves to related keys by using a process known as modulation. This adds contrast and creates tension, which is relieved when the music returns to the 'home' key.

Khachaturian, Aram Ilich (1903–1978)

Armenian composer who lived in Russia for most of his life. His use of folk themes is shown in the ballets *Gayaneh* (1942), which includes the 'Sabre Dance', and *Spartacus* (1956). He studied the folksongs of Armenia and other regions, which influenced his compositions. He was successful with a pre-war symphony and piano concerto, but was denounced in a purge of 1948 and as a result turned to patriotic film and ballet music.

Knussen, (Stuart) Oliver (1952–)

Precocious English composer who conducted his first symphony in London aged 15. His Third Symphony took him six years to write and other works have also been marked by a slow gestation. He has written two successful children's operas *Where the Wild Things Are* (1983) and *Higglety Pigglety Pop!* (1990), and has been active as a conductor (of the London Sinfonietta). His accessible style has influenced a number of prominent British composers of a conventional bent, including **Adès** and **Benjamin**.

Koechlin, Charles Louis Eugène (1867–1950)

Eclectic Frenchman who wrote a series of symphonic works based on Kipling's *The Jungle Book*. His 300 works range from the Romantic, to the impressionistic, and jazz-influenced. Later in life he used the electronic ondes martenot in his Second Symphony (1944).

Koechlin wrote a *Seven Stars Symphony* with movements depicting Fairbanks, Garbo, Clara Bow, Dietrich, and Chaplin.

Kokkonen, Joonas (1921–)

Finnish composer influenced by **Bach**, **Sibelius**, and **Bartók** after **Neo-Classical** beginnings. He was professor of composition at the Sibelius Academy, Helsinki (1959–63). His works include the opera *The Last Temptations*, produced Helsinki 1975 and London 1979, and five symphonies (1960–82).

Korngold, Erich Wolfgang (1897–1957)

Austrian-born composer who began composing while still in his teens and achieved early recognition when his opera *Dead City* was premiered simultaneously in Hamburg and Cologne 1920. In 1934 he moved to Hollywood to become a composer for Warner Brothers. His film scores, in richly orchestrated and Romantic style, include *The Adventures of Robin Hood* (1938) and *Of Human Bondage* (1945).

> There was a review by Irving Kolodin which noted that Korngold's Violin Concerto had more corn than gold.
>
> Nicolas **Slonimsky** on Korngold in, *A Thing or Two About Music*

Krebs, Johann Ludwig (1713–1780)

German organist, harpsichordist, and composer. He was a pupil of J S **Bach** at Leipzig from 1726, and became organist at Zwickau, Zeitz, and Altenburg. His works include a Magnificat, settings of the Sanctus, and much keyboard music.

Kreisler, Fritz (1875–1962)

Austrian violinist, best known for his broad-toned and emotionally committed performances of the **Brahms** and **Beethoven** violin concertos. His compositions include a string quartet, the operetta *Apple Blossoms* 1919, and a number of violin solos.

18TH-CENTURY IMITATION

Kreisler composed and recorded pieces in the style of the 18th century that he at first tried to present as the work of 18th-century composers.

Krenek, Ernst (1900–1991)

Austrian-born US composer and theorist. Following early popular success with the jazz-influenced operas *Johnny Strikes Up* (1926) and *Life of Orestes* (1930), he supported himself as a critic while working on the ambitious twelve-tone opera *Charles V* (1938). He moved to teaching posts in the USA in 1939 but remained in contact with post-war developments in extended serialism and **aleatoric** music with *In Search of Time* (1957), and with **electronic music** in *Spiritus intelligentiae sanctus* (1956).

❝ To my knowledge I am the only composer of my generation who has thoroughly and consistently practised what is called serialism, and I have been blamed (a) for doing it at all, (b) for doing it too late, and (c) for still being at it. ❞

Ernst **Krenek**, *Horizons Circled*

Kuhnau, Johann (1660–1722)

German organist, composer, and writer on music, who was **Bach's** predecessor in the post of cantor at St Thomas's, Leipzig. His biblical sonatas for harpsichord are early examples of **programme music**. Other works include motets on hymn-tunes and other church music, and partitas and other pieces for harpsichord, including seven sonatas entitled *Frische Clavier-Früchte*.

Kurtág, György (1926–)

Hungarian composer who remained almost silent during the communist era. He later emerged with an austere, direct but disquieting voice in the mid-1980s with works such as *Messages of the Late Miss RV Troussova* for soprano and chamber ensemble (1980), *Scenes from a Novel* for soprano and ensemble (1981), and *Attila-Jószef Fragments* for soprano (1981). Early influences were **Bartók** and Kodály; later he employed a technique in which mosaics of sound are used to build a larger picture.

Lalo, (Victor Antoine) Edouard (1823–1892)

French composer whose Spanish ancestry and violin training are evident in the *Symphonie espagnole* (1873) for violin and orchestra. He wrote little until 1865, the year of his marriage to Mlle de Maligny, who sang his songs in public. Gradually his success grew both in the opera house and the concert room. His most popular work during his lifetime was the opera *Le roi d'Ys*.

Lambert, Constant (1905–1951)

Reacted against the prevalent English pastoralism with the jazz- and Stravinsky-influenced *Horoscope* and *The Rio Grande*. The son of the painter George Lambert, while still a student, Diaghilev commissioned the ballet *Romeo and Juliet* from him and produced it at Monte Carlo in 1926. He also became a conductor, was for a time critic to the journal *Referee*, and published a book of biting essays, *Music Ho! A Study of Music in Decline* (1934). He drifted into alcoholism and died young.

La Rue, Pierre de (c. 1460–1518)

Flemish composer and pupil of **Ockeghem**; by turns in the service of the court of Burgundy, Charles V, and Margaret of Austria. He wrote 31 Masses, 7 Magnificats, a Requiem, 38 motets, and numerous chansons.

Lassus, Orlande de (1532–1594)

Franco-Flemish composer, also known as Orlando di Lasso, he seems to have gone to Italy as a boy, serving in various noble households. In 1553 he was choirmaster at St John Lateran in Rome, after which he returned home to Antwerp, where in 1555 he published his first works. In 1556 he went to Munich and entered the service of the Duke of Bavaria. In 1574 he

> **RENAISSANCE MASTER**
>
> The abundance, variety, and polyphonic ingenuity of Lassus's music places this Flemish musician as one of the greatest composers of the Renaissance.

went to Rome to present Pope Gregory XIII with a volume of Masses and received the order of the Golden Spur. In spite of an offer from Dresden, he remained attached to the Bavarian court to the end. His Latin motets were collected and published in 1604 by his sons Ferdinand and Rudolph under the title *Magnum opus musicum*. He wrote more than 2,000 compositions, including about 60 Masses, 4 Passions, 101 Magnificats, a Requiem, and about 500 motets.

Lawes, William (1602–1645)
English composer who, with his brother Henry, studied with John Coperario (*c.* 1570–1626) and became a musician at Charles I's court.

Lawes joined the Royalist army during the Civil War and was killed by a shot during the Siege of Chester.

Leclair, Jean-Marie (1697–1764)
Originally a dancer and ballet master, he composed ballet music, an opera, *Scylla et Glaucus* (1746), and among the first French violin concertos. He met his death at the hand of an unknown murderer.

Leeuw, Ton de (1926–)
Experimental Dutch composer, also influenced by *musique concrète* as well as serialism. He studied composition in Paris with **Messiaen** and later became interested in musical folklore; in 1961 he toured India to collect material. His works include the TV opera *Alceste* (1963), two symphonies, *Ombres* for orchestra and percussion, and concertos for piano and string orchestra.

Lehár, Franz (1870–1948)
Hungarian composer of the operetta *The Merry Widow* (1905). His other operettas include *The Count of Luxembourg* (1909), *Gypsy Love* (1910), and *The Land of Smiles* (1929). He also composed songs, **marches**, and a violin concerto. His music shows the influence of the southern Slavonic folksong and he first tried to win fame as a composer of serious opera as, for example, in *Kukuska* (later renamed *Tatjana*) (1896); but it was in the field of operetta that he achieved real distinction.

Le Jeune, Claude or Claudin (*c.* 1530–1600)
Franco-Flemish composer who, having become a Huguenot, tried to escape from Paris during the siege of 1588. His manuscripts were saved from

seizure by the Catholic soldiers by his colleague Jacques Mauduit, himself a Catholic. Later he became chamber musician to the king. He was an exponent of *musique mesurée*, psalms set to rhymed versions in measured music. He also wrote madrigals and instrumental fantasies.

Lekeu, Guillaume (1870–1894)
Generally thought likely to become the leading Belgian composer had he not died at a very early age. He studied with **Franck** and **d'Indy** in Paris. His most memorable works are an Adagio for strings, a string quartet, a piano sonata, and other chamber works.

Leoncavallo, Ruggero (1858–1919)
He studied at the Naples Conservatory, after which he went to Bologna and was on the point of producing his first opera, *Chatterton*, there, but was swindled and found himself penniless. He later managed to travel widely as café pianist. He then began a trilogy on the Italian Renaissance, *Crepusculum*, with *I Medici*, but never produced the planned two following works, *Savonarola* and *Cesare Borgia*. In the meantime he made an enormous success

Leoncavallo played in restaurants, composing in his spare time, until the success of *I pagliacci* (1892).

with *I pagliacci* at Milan in 1892 and soon all over Italy. His other operas include *La Bohème* (1897, contemporary with **Puccini's** version) and *Zaza* (1900).

Lieberson, Peter (1946–)
US composer whose study of Buddhism (1976–81) inspired him to write his piano concerto of 1983. His other works include a *Tashi Quartet* (1979), *Drala* for orchestra (1986), and *Wind Messengers* for 13 instruments (1990).

lied (plural lieder)
(German 'song') Musical dramatization of a poem, usually for solo voice and piano; referring to Romantic songs of **Schubert**, **Schumann**, **Brahms**, and **Wolf**.

Ligeti, György Sándor (1923–)
Hungarian-born composer who developed a sometimes dense, at others naively sparse, polyphonic style in which melody and rhythm are

sometimes lost in blocks of sound. He achieved international prominence with *Atmosphères* (1961) and *Requiem* (1965), which achieved widespread fame as background music for Kubrick's film *2001*. Other works include an opera *Le grand macabre* (1978), and his numerous and ongoing études for the piano. He gradually moved to a style that he labelled 'transparent'; his later work has echoes of **Nancarrow** and is notable for its technical fluency.

Liszt, Franz (1811–1886)

Hungarian composer who was also an outstanding virtuoso of the piano (he was an established concert artist by the age of 12). His expressive, Romantic, and frequently wild works mostly involve the piano, but in later life he also wrote Masses and oratorios, and orchestral works. Much of his music is programmatic; he also originated the **symphonic poem**.

Liszt was taught by his father, then by **Czerny**. He producied an operetta, *Don Sanche*, in Paris at the age of 14. There he achieved great success and fame as a pianist, met **Chopin**, **Paganini**, and George Sand, and in 1833 began his liaison with the Countess d'Agoult. They went to live at Geneva in 1835, where a daughter, Blandine,

Liszt *Franz Liszt with his signature below, Hungarian composer revolutionary in his composition.*

was born, followed by another, Cosima, who became first **von Bülow's** and then **Wagner's** wife. He then paid visits to England (1840), Russia, Turkey, and Denmark. In 1846 he met Princess Caroline Sayn-Wittgenstein, the wife of a wealthy Russian landowner, who fell in love with him and in 1848 left with him for Weimar, where he was engaged as conductor and music director to the grand-ducal court for certain periods of the year.

In Weimar he settled down to write various works, some on a very large scale, having previously confined himself almost exclusively to piano music. His piano sonata of 1853, followed by the *Faust* and *Dante* symphonies, were revolutionary for their extension of **sonata form** in a cyclic process extending for several movements, and for their use of limited motifs that become transformed as a means of development. He had a profound influence on Wagner. He retired to Rome in 1861, and took minor orders in the Catholic church in 1865 becoming an abbé, and henceforward many of his works were of a sacred character. In his last piano works he adopted a totally new, modern style, which his contemporaries found incomprehensible.

LISZT'S INFLUENCE

Liszt was the most important figure of musical **Romanticism**, influencing not only his own age but also the following century.

---

liturgy
In the Christian church, any written, authorized version of a service for public worship, especially the Roman Catholic Mass. Its development over the centuries has had a direct impact on music and composition, because until the Renaissance the church had a near monopoly in the West on skilled musicians and composers.

Locke, Matthew (c. 1622–1677)
Englishman remembered for **masques** such as *Cupid and Death* (1653), and his music for the plays *Psyche* (1675). He was a vigorous and acrimonious defender of 'modern music', writing a pamphlet defending his church music in 1666 and in 1672 opening a controversy with Thomas Salmon. **Purcell** wrote an elegy on his death.

Loewe, (Johann) Carl (Gottfried) (1796–1869)
German composer. He is remembered chiefly for his songs and settings of narrative poems such as 'Archibald Douglas' and 'Tom the Rhymer'. He visited Vienna in 1844, London in 1847, Sweden and Norway in 1851, and France in 1857. In 1864 he suffered a six-week-long coma; he died after a similar attack. His works include operas, oratorios, and songs.

Lortzing, (Gustav) Albert (1801–1851)
His first stage work, *Ali Pascha von Janina*, was produced at Münster in 1828 and repeated at Cologne, Detmold, and Osnabrück. The first two

comic operas he wrote there were very successful, and so was his adaptation from Kotzebue, *Der Wildschütz*, in 1842. Other operas include *Zar und Zimmermann* (1837) and *Hans Sachs* (1840).

GERMANY'S G&S

Although not well known outside Germany, Lortzing's operas *Undine* and *Der Wildschütz* occupy a similar position in his homeland to that enjoyed by the works of Gilbert and Sullivan in Britain.

Lourié, Arthur Vincent (1892–1966)
Russian-born composer associated with the Russian futurists; he was Akhmatova's lover during the 1910s. Initially he composed in an impressionist manner somewhat influenced by **Skryabin**, but after a period of radical atonality (in *Sintezi*, 1914) he turned to a more refined, melodic style. After directing music in the Soviet Education Department he left Russia, settling first in France, then from 1941 in the USA. He was associated for a while with **Stravinsky** and is reported to have been one of only five people who attended **Bartók's** funeral.

Lully, Jean-Baptiste (1632–1687)
Composer of Italian origin in the court of Louis XIV. He was also a ballet dancer. In 1661 he became a French citizen and in 1662 Music Master to the Royal Family; he continued to enjoy royal protection, in spite of his open homosexuality, which at that time was punishable by death. His first opera, *Cadmus et Hermione*, appeared in 1673; he composed music for the ballet, and for Molière's plays, and established French opera with such works as *Alceste* (1674) and *Armide et Rénaud* (1686). His last complete opera was *Acis et Galatée* (1686); by this time he had transformed French operatic style, developing the French overture and introducing a declaimed recitative.

A FATAL WOUND

In 1687, while conducting a *Te Deum* in celebration of the king's recovery, Lully injured his foot with his conducting staff. As a result, he died of blood poisoning.

---

lute
Member of a family of plucked stringed musical instruments of the 14th–18th centuries, including the mandore, theorbo, and chitarrone. Lutes are pear-shaped with up to seven courses of strings (single or double), plucked with the fingers. Music for lutes is written in special notation called **tablature** and chords are played simultaneously, not arpeggiated as for guitar.

Lutosławski, Witold (1913–1994)
Polish composer and conductor greatly influential both within and beyond his native land. His output includes four symphonies, *Paroles tissées* (1965), dedicated to the singer Peter Pears, and *Chain I* for orchestra (1981). For 30 years he conducted most of the world's leading orchestras in his own compositions. His early major compositions, such as *Variations on a Theme of Paganini* (1941) for two pianos and *First Symphony* (1947), drew some criticism from the communist government. He, with **Penderecki** and **Gorecki**, was a leading light of the Polish avant garde, but his style is generally lightweight and undemanding.

Lutyens, (Agnes) Elizabeth (1906–1983)
English composer of expressive and tightly organized chamber and orchestral works. Her choral and vocal works include a setting of Austrian philosopher Wittgenstein's *Tractatus*. The youngest daughter of architect Edwin Lutyens, in a 1950s lecture she coined the term 'cowpat music' to describe the work of early 20th-century English pastorally-inclined composers. Her autobiography, *A Goldfish Bowl*, was published in 1973.

Luzzaschi, Luzzasco (c. 1545–1607)
Italian organist and composer whose madrigals are his best-known compositions. His skilfully composed five-part madrigals were his most popular works; the later ones show an increased use of homophony. Luzzaschi was a pupil of Cipriano de **Rore** at Ferrara and in 1561 became a singer at the Este court there. **Frescobaldi** was one of his organ pupils. He composed madrigals for the celebrated 'singing ladies' of Ferrara, a group of virtuoso singers who performed for private audiences. His *Madrigali per cantare, et sonare a 1–3 soprani* (1601) contains some of these pieces with their fully notated keyboard accompaniments, which were long kept secret.

Lyadov, Anatoly Konstantinovich (1855–1914)
Russian composer whose late orchestral works *Baba Yaga* (1904), *The*

Enchanted Lake (1909), and *Kikimora* (1909), are perfectly-spun, miniature examples of the nationalist folk poetic. He also wrote especially well for the piano. Famously indolent, his gift was essentially reclusive and small-scale; **Stravinsky** got ahead through Lyadov's disinterest in a commission from Diaghilev for the *Firebird*.

Lyapunov, Sergey Mikhaylovich (1859–1924)
Russian composer of fantastical, virtuoso piano works. A pupil of **Balakirev**, he continued his nationalist traditions but combined them with a Lisztian bravura and fire in his *12 Transcendental Studies*, many of which are based on Russian folksong. He also wrote orchestral works, of which the finest is undoubtedly the Second Symphony, written in Petrograd as the Russian Revolution took place. He later fled to Paris.

Lyatoshynsky, Borys Mykolayovych (1892–1968)
The most significant composer to emerge from the Ukraine. He was end-lessly in trouble with the Soviet authorities. In his early years he cultivated an impressionist, then harshly modernist style. This later developed into a highly personal, dramatic, and lyrical manner. His best works are the sec-ond and third symphonies, both of which can be counted as among the most succesful essays in the genre of the mid-20th century.

Lysenko, Mykola Vitaliyevych (1842–1912)
Ukrainian composer who, while researching ethnography, became inter-ested in folksong, which he began to collect. He is regarded as the initiator of the Ukrainian musical renaissance of the 20th century; a Kiev musical school bears his name. His many arrangements of folksong are particularly effective, while his opera *Taras Bulba*, left unfinished at his death, was com-pleted by Revutsky and hailed as a national masterpiece.

MacDowell, Edward Alexander (1860–1908)
First acclaimed US composer, influenced by **Grieg** and **Liszt**. His works include the *Indian Suite* (1896) and piano concertos and sonatas. He was at his best with short, lyrical piano pieces, such as 'To a Wild Rose' from *Woodland Sketches* (1896).

Machaut, Guillaume de (1300–1377)
French poet and composer whose *Messe de Nostre Dame* (c. 1360) is an early masterpiece of **ars nova**, exploiting unusual rhythmic complexities. Born in Champagne, he was in the service of John of Bohemia for 30 years and, later, of King John the Good of France. He gave the ballade and rondo forms a new individuality and ensured their lasting popularity.

MacMillan, James (1959–)
Scottish composer whose *The Confessions of Isobel Gowdie*, premiered at the London Promenade concerts in 1990, demonstrated his populist, emotional approach. He was composer-in-residence at Maxwell Davies's Magnus Festival in 1989, and has taught at the Royal Scottish Academy from 1990. His works include the opera *Inès de Castro* (1993), *Veni, Veni Emmanuel*, percussion concerto (1992), and *Epiclesis*, a trumpet concerto (1993).

McPhee, Colin (1901–1964)
Canadian-born composer whose studies with **Varèse** much influenced his own music, as did his research into Balinese music (1934–36). From 1934 to 1939 he spent much time in Bali and Mexico. He also wrote a number of books, including *Music in Bali* (1966).

McPhee's best-known work, *Tabuh-tabuhan* for two pianos and orchestra (1936), uses a combination of Balinese and Western orchestral instruments.

Maderna, Bruno (1920–1973)

One of the godfathers of the Italian avant garde (along with **Dallapiccola**, and later **Nono** and **Berio**), he encouraged the work of younger composers by conducting, and by setting up an electronic studio in Milan in 1954. His own compositions sometimes combine **aleatoric** and graphic techniques with an elegance of sound. They include a pioneering work for live and pre-recorded flute, *Musica su due dimensioni* (1952), numerous concertos, and *Hyperion* (1964), a 'mobile opera', consisting of a number of composed scenes that may be combined in several ways.

See also: *electronic music.*

maestro di cappella

Italian equivalent of **kapellmeister**.

Magnard, (Lucien Denis Gabriel) Albéric (1865–1914)

His masterpieces, the operas *Guercoeur* and *Berenice*, owe something in their structure to the example of **Wagner**, but also reveal an individual visionary lyricism. As the son of the editor of *Le Figaro*, he was comfortably off and never held any official posts. He published his works himself, and never took any trouble to have them performed, though some were brought out by enthusiastic friends. He also wrote four symphonies and several chamber works.

During the very first days of World War I Magnard shot two German soldiers from his window and was killed as a sniper. His house, including several of his manuscripts, was burnt down.

Mahler, Gustav (1860–1911)

Austrian composer and conductor whose epic symphonies express a world-weary **Romanticism** in visionary tableaux, often incorporating folk music and pastoral imagery. He composed 11 large-scale symphonies (counting *The Song of the Earth* of 1909), many with voices, including the second

❝A symphony must be like the world, it must embrace everything. ❞

Gustav **Mahler**, a remark to Sibelius, Helsinki, 1907

Resurrection (1884–96), the eighth, *The Symphony of a Thousand,* and a tenth left unfinished at his death. He also composed orchestral lieder (songs) including *Kindertotenlieder* (1901–04).

Mahler's conducting career began in the summer of 1880 in Hall, Upper Austria. Posts followed at theatres in Ljubljana in 1881 and Olmütz in 1882. While in Kassel (1883–85) he wrote the *Lieder eines fahrenden Gesellen* and began the First Symphony. Mahler was chief conductor of the Hamburg Opera (1891–97); in 1892 he took the company to London, for the first Covent Garden performances of **Wagner's** *Ring.* In December 1895 he led the Berlin first performance of his

Mahler *Austrian Composer Gustav Mahler.*

Resurrection symphony, achieving his first success as a composer. In 1897 his baptism into the Catholic Church led to his appointment as director of the Vienna Court Opera. He succeeded Hans Richter as conductor of the Vienna Philharmonic Orchestra in 1898 but, largely as a result of his autocratic methods, he departed in 1901. During his years in Vienna he wrote his symphonies nos. 4–8 near a villa on the Wörthersee in Carinthia. On 1 January 1908 he made his debut as principal conductor of the New York Metropolitan Opera; but due to artistic and personal differences his tenure there was brief. In 1910 he led the triumphant Munich first performance of his Eighth Symphony, and the following year returned to Europe for the last time, mortally ill with a bacterial infection of the blood.

LATE RECOGNITION

Mahler's music took many years to gain acceptance – four of the symphonies were not heard in Britain until after 1945 – but he is now established as a founder of 20th-century music.

Malipiero, Gian Francesco (1882–1973)

Italian composer and editor of **Monteverdi** and **Vivaldi**. His own works, influenced by **Stravinsky** and **Debussy**, are often in a **Neo-Classical** style. He was professor of composition at Parma University (1921–23) and director of the Liceo Musicale Benedetto Marcello, Venice (1939–53). His works include the operas *Sette canzoni* (1919), *La favola del figlio cambiato* (libretto by Pirandello, 1934), and *Venere prigionera* (1955), 11 symphonies, and 6 piano concertos.

> Malipiero attended the first performance of Stravinsky's *The Rite of Spring*.

mandolin

Plucked string instrument with four to six pairs of strings (courses), tuned like a violin. It flourished 1600–1800 and takes its name from its almond-shaped body (Italian *mandorla* 'almond'). **Vivaldi** composed two concertos for the instrument.

Marais, Marin (1656–1728)

French virtuoso **viol** player and composer. He joined the royal band and the orchestra at the Paris Opéra, where he studied composition under **Lully** and co-operated with him in the performance of operas. In 1725 he retired to devote himself to gardening, but continued to teach. He added a seventh string to the bass viol, and wrote five collections of bass viol pieces (1686–1725).

march or (Italian) marcia

A piece originally intended to accompany marching soldiers, facilitating a regular rhythm. One of the earliest known forms of music, marches are usually in duple time, with a strongly marked beat and regular phrasing. The earliest examples of the march in art music are found in the work of **Lully** and **Couperin** in the 17th century. The march has been used ever since, as in **Mozart's** *The Magic Flute*, and **Beethoven's** *Eroica* symphony.

Marenzio, Luca (*c.* 1553–1599)

One of the most important of the Italian madrigalists, having written over 400 which were introduced into England through Nicholas Yonge's *Musica transalpina* in 1588. In Rome he served cardinal Cristoforo Madruzzo

(1574–78), when he became maestro di cappella to Cardinal d'Este. During this time he published many madrigals, and began to gain an international reputation as a composer. In 1588 he entered the service of Ferdinando de' Medici and in 1589 contributed two **intermedii** for wedding festivities in Florence.

Markevich, Igor (1912–1983)
Ukrainian-born teenage prodigy who was the last protegé and lover of Diaghilev. His parents emigrated and lived in Switzerland, but he went to Paris at the age of 15 and studied composition under Nadia **Boulanger**. His austere ballet *The Flight of Icarus* (1932) employs **microtones** and exotic elements, but he basically ceased composing after his later twenties. He became an Italian citizen during the war years. He later concentrated on conducting.

Marschner, Heinrich (August) (1795–1861)
Regarded as the most important German opera composer between **Weber** and **Wagner**. In 1823 he became assistant conductor to Weber and Francesco Morlacchi at Dresden. In 1827 he became conductor of the Leipzig theatre and from 1831 to 1859 court conductor at Hanover. He married four times. His main operas include *Der Kyffhäuserberg* (1822), *Lucretia, Der Vampyr* (1828), *Der Templer und die Jüdin* (after Walter Scott's *Ivanhoe*, 1829), *Des Falkners Braut* (1832), and *Austin, Sangeskönig Hiarne* (1863).

Martin, Frank (1890–1974)
Swiss composer whose works are characterized by delicate colouring in instrumentation and an expressive quality. Composing for both large- and small-scale forces, from orchestra to chamber music, his best known works are the operas *The Tempest* (1956) and *Monsieur de Pourceaugnac* (1962), and the Eight Preludes for piano.

Martinu, Bohuslav Jan (1890–1959)
Czech composer who settled in New York after the Nazi occupation of Czechoslovakia in 1939. His music is voluble, richly expressive, and has great vitality. His works include the opera *Julietta* (1937), symphonies, and chamber music. In 1922 he took composition lessons with **Suk** at the Prague Conservatory and studied with **Roussel** in Paris (1923–24). He wrote works influenced by jazz and **Neo-Classicism**. Operas with Czech subjects

followed during the 1930s, and after arriving in the USA as a refugee in 1941 he confined himself largely to instrumental music. He chose not to return to Czechoslovakia after the communist takeover in 1948, and lived in Switzerland from 1957.

Martín y Soler, Vicente (1754–1806)
Spanish composer who travelled widely, producing operas in Italy, Russia, and Vienna. He made his debut in Madrid in 1776, then went to Italy, producing operas successfully in Naples, Turin, and Venice. In Vienna (1785–88), he composed three operas on libretti by da Ponte, the most successful of which, *Una cosa rara* (1786), for a time eclipsed **Mozart's** *Marriage of Figaro*; Mozart quotes from it in the supper scene in *Don Giovanni*. From 1788 he lived in St Petersburg, in the service of the Russian court.

Marx, Joseph (1882–1964)
Austrian composer whose luscious harmonic language is optimally displayed in his *Romantic Concerto* for piano and orchestra. He studied in Vienna and in 1922 became director of the Academy of Music there. His other works include *Autumn Symphony* (1921), *Symphonic Night Music, Spring Music* for orchestra, and much chamber music.

Mascagni, Pietro (1863–1945)
Italian composer who, on gaining a place at the Milan Conservatory, but not wishing to apply himself to solid study, ran away with a travelling opera company. After many wanderings and a marriage that forced him to settle, he won the first prize in a competition with *Cavalleria rusticana* in 1889, and after its production in Rome the following year, he began to accumulate a great fortune, though his many later operas never repeated its success.

> ❝ It was a pity I wrote Cavalleria first: I was crowned before I was king. ❞
>
> Pietro **Mascagni**, quoted in Carner, *Giacomo Puccini*

masque
Court entertainment with a fantastic or mythological theme in which music, dance, and extravagant costumes and scenic design figured larger than plot.

Originating in Italy, the masque reached its height of popularity at the English court between 1600 and 1640, with the collaboration of Ben Jonson and Inigo Jones. Composers included **Campion**, Coperario, **Lawes**, **Byrd**, and **Purcell**.

Mass
The setting of the parts of the Christian Mass, the Kyrie, Gloria, Credo, Sanctus with Benedictus, and Agnus Dei. A notable example is **Bach's** *Mass in B Minor*. A *Requiem Mass* is a Mass for the dead and incorporates additional sections such as the Dies irae and In paradiso.

Massenet, Jules Emile Frédéric (1842–1912)
French opera composer who gave prominence to female roles. Notable works are *Manon* (1884), *Le Cid* (1885), and *Thaïs* (1894). His long and successful career included no fewer than 27 operas, mainly for the Paris Opéra and Opéra-Comique, and the Monte Carlo Opera. In *Werther* (1892), the lyrical impulse is balanced with a strong dramatic flair. Later operas such as *Cendrillon* (1895), *Grisélidis*, *Chérubin* (1902–03), and *Don Quichotte* (1908–09) have found recognition as a result of recent revivals.

Maxwell Davies, Peter
See *Davies, Peter Maxwell*

Medtner, Nikolay Karlovich (1880–1951)
Russian composer whose music is almost wholly centred on piano works (including three concertos and twelve sonatas) and songs, but he also wrote three sonatas and three nocturnes for violin and piano, and during the course of his life he produced a Piano Quintet. He studied piano at the Moscow Conservatory, and became professor there. He later retired to devote himself to composition. After the Revolution he taught at a school in Moscow and in 1921 went on a tour in the West, but did not return. He settled in Paris and later in London, where he died. As a keyboard composer he is as important, and in his way as characteristic as his contemporaries **Rachmaninoff** and **Skryabin**. His numerous songs are deeply felt and tasteful, with piano parts as important as those for the voice.

Méhul, Etienne Nicolas (1763–1817)
Euphrosine (1790) established him as an opera composer, after which he became one of the most notable composers of the French Revolution. He went to Paris in 1778, where **Gluck** encouraged him to write for the stage.

On the foundation of the Conservatory in 1795 he became one of its inspectors. His greatest success came with *Joseph* (1807).

melody

(Greek *melos* 'song') A recognizable series of notes played or sung one after the other; a tune. Melody is one of the three main elements of music, the others being **rhythm** and **harmony**. In Western music a melody is usually formed from the notes of a scale or **mode**. A melody, with or without **accompaniment**, may be a complete piece on its own. It is more often used as a theme within a longer piece of music.

Mendelssohn (-Bartholdy), (Jakob Ludwig) Felix (1809–1847)

German composer whose music has the lightness and charm of Classical music, applied to Romantic and descriptive subjects. Among his best-known works are *A Midsummer Night's Dream* (1827); the *Fingal's Cave* overture (1832), and five symphonies, which include the *Reformation* (1830), the *Italian* (1833), and the *Scottish* (1842). Aged 9, he appeared at a public chamber concert, and before he was 13 he had written many works, including the piano quartet Op.1. In 1825 he wrote his first master-piece, the Octet for strings. In 1829 he conducted Bach's then-forgotten *St Matthew Passion* and paid the first of his ten visits to Britain, conducting the Philharmonic Society in London and taking a holiday in Scotland, where he gathered impressions for the *Hebrides* overture and the 'Scottish' symphony. After conducting a number of orchestras in the 1830s, he returned to Leipzig late in 1842 and founded the Conservatory there in November, opening it in April 1843. The death of his sister Fanny in the spring of 1847 greatly depressed him and he went to Switzerland too ill to do any work, returning to Leipzig in September completely exhausted.

Mendelssohn's music is most highly valued for its fusion of a Romantic, lyrical impulse with a sure sense of form. Much of his best music was writ-ten while he was in his teens or twenties; exhaustion through frail health and overwork conspired to prevent him from meeting his full potential, although such late works as the violin concerto and *Elijah* find Mendelssohn returning to his finest vein of inspiration.

❧ Art and life are not two different things. ❧

Felix **Mendelssohn**, in a letter

Mendelssohn (-Bartholdy), Fanny (Cäcilie) (1805–1847)

German pianist and composer who published very few of her 500 works, most of them piano pieces and lieder. But they have enjoyed a revival and her D minor piano trio of 1846 does not suffer from comparison with the early works of her brother Felix.

Menotti, Gian Carlo (1911–)

Italian-born US composer who created small-scale realist operas including *The Medium* (1946), *The Telephone* (1947), *The Consul* (1950), and *Amahl and the Night Visitors* (1951, the first opera to be written for television). He wrote libretti for his own operas and for **Barber's** *Vanessa* and *A Hand of Bridge*.

Merikanto, Aarre (1893–1958)

Finnish composer whose opera *Juha* (1922) has been successfully revived, suggesting an individual style that recalls **Janáček**. He studied with Reger at Leipzig and with Vasilenko at Moscow, later becoming professor at the Helsinki Conservatory. His other works include the ballet *The Abduction of Kylliki* (on a subject from the *Kalevala*); three symphonies (1916, 1918, 1953), and much more.

Messiaen, Olivier Eugène Prosper Charles (1908–1992)

French composer, organist, and teacher. His music is mystical in character, vividly coloured, and incorporates transcriptions of birdsong. The most important French composer after **Debussy**, he was also well known as an organist and teacher. Among his most succesful works are the *Quartet for the End of Time* (1941), the large-scale *Turangalîla Symphony* (1949), the *Vingt regards sur l'enfant Jésus* for piano, *Des canyons aux étoiles* (1974), and his opera *Saint François d'Assise* (first produced in 1983). He also wrote songs, and solo organ and piano pieces. As a

Messiaen *French composer Oliver Messiaen.*

teacher at the Paris Conservatoire from 1942 he influenced three generations of composers. His theories of melody, harmony, and rhythm, often drawing on medieval and oriental music, inspired **Boulez** and **Stockhausen**. He was born in Avignon, and spent most of his life in Paris, where he was appointed organist at La Trinité church in 1931. He was a devout Christian.

> ❝ Among the artistic hierarchy, the birds are probably the greatest musicians to inhabit our planet. ❞
>
> Oliver **Messiaen**, quoted in Sherlaw Johnson, *Messiaen*

metre
The time scale represented by the beat. Metre is regular, whereas rhythm is irregular. Metre can be simple as in 2/4, 4/8, and so on, where each beat divides into two sub-beats; compound metre as in 6/8, 9/8, 12/16, and so on, consists of sub-beats of 'compounded' units of three. The numerical sign for metre is a time signature, of which the upper number represents the number of beats in the bar, the lower number the type of beat, expressed as a fraction of a unit (semibreve). Hence 3/4 is three crotchet beats to the bar and 6/8 is two beats each of three quavers.

See also: *time signature.*

Meyerbeer, Giacomo (1791–1864)
German composer whose spectacular operas include *Robert le diable* (1831) and *Les Huguenots* (1836). He was at first trained as a pianist and had some lessons from Muzio **Clementi**. His first opera was produced at Munich in 1812 and the second at Stuttgart in 1813. He settled in Paris but wrote no new work between 1824 and 1831. In 1831 *Robert le Diable* made him sensationally fashionable; this opera, followed by *Les Huguenots* and *Le Prophète* established Meyerbeer as a master of the French grand opera, with ingredients including strong local colour, a sure sense of history, novel instrumental effects, and extended ballets. One of his most evocative operas, *L'africaine*, was left uncompleted at his death.

microtone
Any precisely determined division of the octave smaller than a semitone. Examples of quarter-tone divisions are heard in the violin solo parts of **Bartók's** *Second Violin Concerto*, and **Berg's** *Chamber Concerto*. Early

experiments were carried out by the Czech composer **Hába** and the Russian Wyschnegradsky. The Mexican Carrillo (1875–1965) composed in smaller divisions, and since 1984 **Stockhausen** has developed notations of up to 16ths of a tone for basset horn and flute, for example in *Xi* (1986) for basset horn. **Ferneyhough** and **Xenakis** have consistently applied microtones in most of their output.

Milhaud, Darius (1892–1974)
French composer and member of the group of composers known as 'Les Six', he was extremely prolific in a variety of styles and genres, influenced by jazz, the rhythms of Latin America, and even electronic composition. He is noted for his use of polytonality (the simultaneous existence of two or more keys), as in the *Saudades do Brasil* (1921) and *L'homme et son désir* (1918). A pastoral element also runs through many of his works, as in his first string quartet (1912) and six chamber symphonies (1917–22). His Jewish ancestry is evident in the cantata *Ani maamiu* written for the Festival of Israel (1973). Other works include the opera *Bolívar* (1943) and the ballet *La création du monde* (1923).

minimalism
Movement in abstract art (mostly sculpture) and music towards severely simplified composition. Minimal art developed in the USA in the 1950s in reaction to abstract expressionism, shunning its emotive approach in favour of impersonality and elemental, usually geometric, shapes. In music it manifested itself in large-scale statements, usually tonal and highly repetitive, based on few musical ideas. Major minimalist composers include **Adams**, **Reich**, and **Glass**.

Minnesinger
(German 'love-singer') A 12th- to 14th-century German lyric poet or musician. Their songs deal mainly with courtly love. Many were of noble birth, unlike the later Meistersingers (German 'master singers') who were from the middle classes. Dietmar von Aist, Heinrich von Morungen, and Walther von der Vogelweide were well known Minnesingers.

mode
A collection of five or more **pitches**, often notated as a **scale**, and identified with a particular emotion, ritual function, time, or season, to which music is composed or improvised.

modernism
In the arts, a general term used to describe the 20th century's conscious attempt to break with the artistic traditions of the 19th century; it is based on a concern with form and the exploration of technique as opposed to content and narrative. In music, the traditional concept of key was challenged by atonality.

Mompou, Federico (1893–1987)
Spanish pianist and composer whose evocative, often extremely spare and simple style is a perfect foil to the complexities of **Albéniz** and **Granados**. He studied at the Barcelona Conservatory and later in Paris with Isidore Philipp. He lived at Barcelona again 1914–21, then settled in Paris, returning to Barcelona 1941.

Monteverdi, Claudio Giovanni Antonio (1567–1643)
Italian composer who straddled the late Renaissance and early Baroque, and who made the most important contribution to the early development of the **opera** with *La favola d'Orfeo/The Legend of Orpheus* (1607) and *The Coronation of Poppea* (1642). He also wrote madrigals, motets, and sacred music, notably the *Vespers* (1610). He was in the service of the Duke of Mantua (*c*. 1591–1612), and was director of music at St Mark's, Venice, from 1613. He was the first to use an orchestra and to reveal the dramatic possibilities of the operatic form. He had probably heard **Peri's** *Euridice* at Florence in 1600 before he wrote *Orfeo* for the carnival at Mantua in 1607. *Orfeo* remains the earliest opera to be regularly performed today. His next opera, *Arianna*, now lost except for the famous 'Lament', made him widely famous. Meanwhile Monteverdi had written his first five books of madrigals, which are scarcely less important in the development of their species. He remained in

Monteverdi *Italian composer Claudio Monteversi.*

Mantua until his death, adding church music of great splendour to his previous output. In 1630 he took holy orders after escaping the plague at Venice. Two further operas survive from this period: *Il ritorno d'Ulisse in patria* (1641), and his last opera *L'incoronazione di Poppea* (1642), widely performed today in an increasing variety of editions. Monteverdi was a key figure in providing the impetus for change in which secular music and music for the general public became increasingly important.

MONTEVERDI'S VESPERS

In 1610 Monteverdi dedicated his collection of church music, the *Vespers*, to Pope Paul V. From the opening chorus it is evident that music is moving away for the first time from the private into the public domain.

Morley, Thomas (*c.* 1557–*c.* 1602)

English composer of consort music, madrigals, and airs including the lute song 'It was a Lover and his Lass' for Shakespeare's *As You Like It* (1599). He edited a collection of Italian madrigals *The Triumphs of Oriana* (1601). He was organist at St Paul's Cathedral, London.

> ❝ If therefore you will compose in this kind, you must possess yourself of an amorous humour ... so that you must in your music be wavering like the wind, sometimes wanton, sometimes drooping, sometimes grave and staid, otherwise effeminate. ❞
>
> Thomas **Morley**, *A Plain and Easy Introduction to Practical Music*

Mosolov, Aleksandr Vasilevich (1900–1973)

Russian pianist and composer once famous for his notorious *The Iron Foundry*, described as a 'mighty hymn to machine work'. Wth the rise of Stalin he got into trouble, and later ended up collecting folk music in central Asia and northern Russia. His works, which were initially aggressive and atonal, include two early Soviet chamber operas, *The Dam* and *The*

Hero (1928), six symphonies (1929–50), two piano concertos (1927, 1935 on Kyrgyz themes), and four gargantuan piano sonatas.

MOSOLOV'S TROUBLES

Mosolov was expelled from the Russian Composers' Union for purported involvement in drunken brawls. He was later arrested and sent to a labour camp in Siberia; only a letter from his former teacher Glière to the Russian Prime Minister saved him from probable death.

Moszkowski, Moritz (1854–1925)

Polish-born composer whose fanciful, sparkling, and effervescent *Etincelles* and *Etude in F* were championed by the pianist Vladimir Horowitz (1904–1989) as encores. He studied at Dresden and Berlin, and after a successful career as pianist and composer he retired to Paris in 1897. He died in poverty. His eloquent Piano Concerto in E has been recorded several times in recent years.

Mozart, (Johann Chrysostom) Wolfgang Amadeus (1756–1791)

Austrian composer who showed astonishing precocity as a child and was an adult virtuoso. He was trained by his father, Leopold Mozart (1719–1787). From an early age he composed prolifically, and his works include 27 piano concertos, 23 string quartets, 35 violin sonatas, and 41 symphonies. Together with the work of Haydn, Mozart's music marks the height of the **Classical era** in its supposed purity of melody and symmetricality of form.

Mozart's career began when he was taken on a number of tours (1762–79), visiting Vienna, the Rhineland, Holland, Paris, London, and Italy. He appeared at court at Versailles, and four sonatas for violin and harpsichord by Mozart were published in Paris. In Vienna he composed his first Mass (C minor, K139) and produced the opera *Bastien und Bastienne*. In September 1777 he embarked on a lengthy journey which took him via Mannheim to Paris, where his mother died in July 1778. The main object of this trip was to find suitable employment, but being unsuccessful Mozart returned in January 1779 to the uncongenial post of court organist at Salzburg. One of his finest instrumental works, the *Sinfonia concertante*

K364, was written later that year. His opera seria *Idomeneo* was produced in Munich in January 1781, but later the same year he gave up his post to settle in Vienna as a freelance, living by teaching and playing in concerts. His German opera *Die Entführung aus dem Serail* was produced in July 1782, and the next month he married Constanze Weber.

Mozart, Wolfgang Amadeus, *Austrian composer and child prodigy.*

At the height of his fame as a pianist, 1782–86, Mozart composed many concertos for his own use, but thereafter was increasingly plagued by financial worries, which his appointment in 1787 as court composer did little to ease. The first of three operas on libretti by the Italian poet Lorenzo da Ponte, *Le nozze di Figaro*, was produced in 1786, followed by *Don Giovanni* (1787) and *Così fan tutte* (1790). Mozart brought opera to new heights of musical ingenuity, dramatic truth, and brilliance of expression. For almost the first time, characters are recognizable human beings, rather than stock types.

In 1788 he wrote his last three symphonies, the summation of the Classical symphonic style. Assimilating all he had learned from **Haydn** and others, he took standard forms and gave them new meaning. After several lean years, 1791 was one of overwork, which must have contributed to his

❦ If any of us were to die and then wake hearing it we should know at once that (after all) we had got to the right place. ❧

Neville **Cardus** on the beginning of Mozart's *Piano Concerto no. 23* in A Major, in *Manchester Guardian* 1938

early death; in addition to the last piano concerto (K595), the Clarinet Concerto (K622), and several smaller works, he composed the operas *La Clemenza di Tito*, and *Die Zauberflöte*. The Requiem remained unfinished at Mozart's death, and was completed later by his pupil Süssmayr.

While Mozart was not a great innovator like **Beethoven**, he set creative standards in a wide variety of forms to which later composers could only aspire.

MOZART'S OPERAS

Mozarts operas include *Idomeneo* (1780), *Entführung aus dem Serail/The Abduction from the Seraglio* (1782), *Le Nozze di Figaro/The Marriage of Figaro* (1786), *Don Giovanni* (1787), *Così fan tutte/Thus Do All Women* (1790), and *Die Zauberflöte/The Magic Flute* (1791).

Murail, Tristan (1947–)

French composer who, with Gérard Grisey, founded the Groupe de l'itinéraire, promoting performances of music which combine electronic and traditional instruments. He studied with **Messiaen** at the Paris Conservatory. He has taught computer music at IRCAM in Paris and the conservatory there. His music is beautiful from a purely sonic standpoint; many of his harmonies are based on natural overtones and other acoustical phenomena. His works include *Désintégrations* for 17 players and tape (1983); *Sillages* for orchestra (1985); *Vues aeriennes* for horn, violin, cello, and piano (1988); *Les sept paroles du Christ en croix* for orchestra (1986–89), and *Le fou à pattes bleues* for flute and piano (1990).

musica ficta

(Latin 'feigned music'). In the Middle Ages, theory relating to those notes not normally present in a simple scale. B♭ was the first so-called nondiatonic note allowed, avoiding the tritone B–F, and other notes later became sharpened or flattened for similar reasons. Musica ficta was not always written using **accidentals** (sharp, flat, or natural signs); rather, it required precise knowledge by the performer of correct theory and practice.

Mussorgsky, Modest Petrovich (1839–1881)

Russian composer whose operatic masterpiece *Boris Godunov* (1869–72), touched a political nerve and employed realistic transcriptions of speech patterns. Many of his works, including *Pictures at an Exhibition* (1874) for piano, were 'revised' and orchestrated by others, including **Rimsky-Korsakov**, **Ravel**, and **Shostakovich**, and some have only recently been restored to their original harsh beauty. He joined a regiment in 1856 and he did not seriously think of a music career until he met the composers Dargomïzhsky and **Balakirev** in 1857 and began to study under the latter. *Boris Godunov* was initially rejected by the Imperial Opera and a second version was produced in 1874. It gained wide popularity in an

Mussorgsky *Russian composer.*

orchestration by Rimsky-Korsakov, but Mussorgsky's original is now more often preferred. He sank into ever more acute poverty and ruined his health with drink, but between 1872 and 1880 managed to complete most of his historical opera, *Khovanshchina.*

Myaskovsky, Nikolay Yakovlevich (1881–1950)

Russian composer who maintained his integrity throughout the Soviet repressions by sticking to the writing of symphonies. He studied with **Rimsky-Korsakov** and **Lyadov** at the St Petersburg Conservatory. From 1914–17 he fought on the Austrian front and was badly wounded (his Fifth Symphony was started in the trenches). During the Russian civil war his father was killed by a mob of peasants – this episode is symbolized in the massive Sixth Symphony through the ironic use of 'revolutionary' songs. Although he was denounced in 1948 with **Prokofiev** and others for 'formalism', his music is in a late-Romantic idiom; he employed a more complex style in 1910s and 20s with experimental harmonies somewhat similar to those of **Skryabin**.

Nancarrow, Conlon (1912–1997)

US composer, forced to leave the US, having been branded a communist after fighting the Fascists in the Spanish civil war, he settled in a suburb of Mexico City, where for about 50 years he produced a series of remarkable *Studies for Player Piano*. In these, he used one or sometimes two pianolas to perform rolls that he had punched with a purpose built machine. These works combine jazz and Mexican elements with canonic devices derived from mathematical formulae. The result, though, is highly human, often witty, and always deeply dramatic. He has been admired by two generations of musicians including **Ligeti,** whom he influenced.

nationalism

The adoption, particularly by 19th-century composers, of folk idioms with which an untrained audience could identify. Nationalism was encouraged by governments in the early 20th century for propaganda purposes in times of war and political tension. Composers of nationalist music include **Smetana, Sibelius, Grieg, Rimsky-Korsakov, Kodály**, and **Copland**.

Navarro, Juan (*c.* 1530–1580)

Spanish composer highly regarded as a polyphonist; his church music was popular in Spain, Portugal, and Mexico for some time. He visited Rome in 1590, where his nephew Fernando Navarro Salazar arranged for the publication of some of his church music, which includes psalms, hymns, and magnificats.

Neo-Classicism

A deliberate combination of Baroque or Classical styles with modern aesthetics; examples include **Prokofiev's** '*Classical*' Symphony (1916–17), and **Stravinsky's** ballet *Apollo* (1927–28).

❝ The 12-tone school tried to revive the spirit of the old forms, while Neo-Classicism presented replicas of their facades with interesting cracks added. ❞

Krenek, *Horizons Circled*

neumes
Signs in chant and plainsong (and in some medieval song-books) indicating the single notes or groups of notes to which each syllable was to be sung. Originally not set on staves, but merely marked above the words and showing neither precise length nor exact pitch, they served as reminders of tunes already known to the singers.

Nielsen, Carl August (1865–1931)
Danish composer whose output includes the **Neo-Classical** opera *Masquerade* (1906), a *Wind Quintet* (1922), six programmatic symphonies, concertos, numerous songs, and incidental music on Danish texts. He was one of the most remarkable late Romantic symphonists, combining traditional forms with a new and original approach to tonality; the First Symphony is an example of progressive tonality, ending in a different key to the starting one. Later symphonies developed a complex, rhythmically driven polyphony. The Third Symphony, *Espansiva,* is the first of these great works in which thematic formation is achieved within closely controlled forms. In the Fifth Symphony, chaos is threatened by a side drummer who is instructed to obliterate the rest of the orchestra; order is restored in a triumphant conclusion.

nocturne
Reflective character piece, often for piano, introduced by **Field** and adopted by **Chopin**.

Nono, Luigi (1924–1990)
Italian left-wing avant gardist. He wrote attenuated pointillist works such as *Il canto sospeso* (1955–56) for soloists, chorus, and orchestra, in which influences of **Webern** and **Gabrieli** are applied to issues of social conscience. After the opera *Intolleranza* his style became more richly expressionist, and his causes more overtly polemical. Nono's earlier output

included numerous orchestral works, but after *La fabbrica illuminata* (1964), he concentrated exclusively on the electronic-vocal medium. His later works were often extremely sparse in texture. His other works include *Incontri* for 24 instruments, the opera *Al gran sole carico d'amore* (1974), *Sofferte onde serene* (1976) for piano and tape, and *Stille ... an Diotima* for string quartet.

Norgård, Per (1932–)

Danish composer initially influenced by **Sibelius**; later he turned to 'infinite' serialism, pointillism, and graphic notation. He studied with Vagn Holmboe (1909–96) and Nadia **Boulanger**, and taught at Aarhus from 1965. His works include the operas *Gilgamesh* (1973), *Siddharta* (1983); four symphonies (1954–81); and seven string quartets (1958–93).

notation

System of signs and symbols for writing music, either for performers to read from, or to make a permanent record.

• Early systems of music notation were developed in China in the 3rd century BC, and later by the ancient Greeks for their dramas.

• A means of writing down plainsong called **neumes** appeared in Europe in the Middle Ages.

• The use of notes on a staff of horizontal lines first appeared in the 11th century, and was invented by an Italian monk, Guido **d'Arezzo**.

• Modern notation uses a staff of five lines, with a clef to show the **pitch** of the notes on it. Other signs and words can be added to the written music to show the **tempo**, **dynamics**, and various other comments regarding technique and expression.

Novák, Vitezslav (1870–1949)

Czech composer of shimmering, pastoral symphonic works in a late Romantic idiom. He made a career as a distinguished teacher of composition and in 1909 was appointed professor at the Prague Conservatory. After World War I, which restored his country's independence, he became professor of a 'Master School' and was its director (1919–22). His works, the first of which were published with the help of Brahms, include the opera *The Imp of Zvíkov* (1915), the cantata *The Storm*, and the symphonic poems *In the Tatras* (1902), *About the Eternal Longing*, and *Toman and the Wood Nymph.* He also wrote piano music and songs.

Nyman, Michael (1944–)

Populist English composer who has made much money with film scores for Peter Greenaway (*The Draughtman's Contract*, 1982) and Jane Campion (*The Piano*, 1993), and the chamber opera, *The Man Who Mistook His Wife for a Hat* (1989). Although in 1974 he published *Experimental Music – Cage and Beyond*, his own music has not followed experimental paths, but has drawn on a range of influences, including **minimalism**, rock and roll, and a certain indebtedness to **Handel**, whose music he has edited.

Obrecht, Jacob (*c.* 1450–1505)

Innovative Flemish composer who borrowed material from secular sources – often in the form of a fixed **cantus firmus** – and developed it in works such as the *Missa super Maria zart*. His mostly polyphonic sacred music (which prefigures that of **Josquin**) centred on the Mass; he also wrote motets and secular works. He worked as a Kapellmeister in Utrecht, Antwerp, and Bruges. He had already spent six months at the ducal court of Ferrara in 1487–88 and returned there in 1504 as head of Ercole d'Este's choir, only to die of plague the following year.

Obukhov, Nikolay (1892–1954)

Eccentric Russian composer who wrote part of his *Livre de la vie* in his own blood; its ritual performance was intended to accompany the resurrection of the last Tsar of Russia, Nikolay II. He was a pupil of Nikolay Tcherepnin and Steinberg at the St Petersburg Conservatory, and settled in Paris in 1918. He experimented with a 12-note system and with extended vocal techniques.

> ❝ Among the most curious products in all music. ❞
>
> **G Whitehead** on Obukhov, *The Wireless Imagination*

ocarina

Early musical instrument of the flute type, roughly pear-shaped with finger-holes, and with a protruding mouthpiece like a fish's fin, usually made of terracotta.

The ocarina was used by Ravel in his opera *Les enfants et les sortilèges*.

Offenbach, Jacques (1819–1880)

French composer of light opera. Among his works are *Orpheus in the Underworld* (1858), *La belle Hélène* (1864), and *The Tales of Hoffmann* (1880). Born in Cologne, he went to Paris early in his youth, studying at the

Conservatory and then playing in the orchestra of the Opéra-Comique. In 1850 he became conductor at the Théâtre Français. In 1853 he produced his first operettas and during a quarter of a century he turned

Offenbach's only large-scale opera, *The Tales of Hoffmann*, occupied him for many years, but he left it not quite finished at his death, and it was completed by Guiraud.

out nearly 100 light stage pieces. In 1855 he took over the management of the Théâtre Comte and renamed it the Bouffes Parisiens.

Ohana, Maurice (1914–1992)
Composer of Moroccan descent who incorporated north African elements into his dynamic and, at times, colourful music. He studied in Barcelona, Rome, and the Schola Cantorum in Paris. His works include the operas *Chanson de Toile* (1969) and *La celestine* (1987), ballets *Prométhée* (1956) and *Paso*, a guitar concerto, and much piano music.

Okeghem, Johannes (Jean d') (c. 1421–c. 1497)
Flemish composer of richly contrapuntal church music. His works include the **antiphon** *Alma Redemptoris Mater* and the ornate *Missa prolationum*, employing complex canonic imitation in multiple parts at different levels. He was court composer to Charles VII, Louis XI, and Charles VIII of France. He wrote ten Masses, including *Ecce ancilla Domini*, *L'homme armé*, and *Mi-mi*, motets, and French chansons.

opera
Dramatic musical work in which singing takes the place of speech. In opera the music accompanying the action has paramount importance, although dancing and spectacular staging may also play their parts. Opera originated in late 16th-century Florence when the musical declamation, lyrical monologues, and choruses of classical Greek drama were reproduced in current forms. **Monteverdi** was the first master of operatic form. Initially solely a court entertainment, opera soon became popular, and in 1637 the first public opera house was opened in Venice. It spread to other Italian towns, to Paris (about 1645), and then to Vienna and Germany. In the later 17th century the elaborate **aria**, designed to display the virtuosity of the singer, became predominant, overshadowing the dramatic element. The Italian tradition, which placed emphasis on vocal display and melodic suavity (**bel canto**), continued unbroken into the 19th century in the operas of **Rossini**, **Donizetti**, and **Bellini**.

In France opera was developed by **Lully** and **Rameau**, and in England by **Purcell**. A lessening of artificiality began when **Gluck** insisted on the pre-eminence of the dramatic over the purely vocal element. **Mozart** learned much from Gluck in writing his serious operas, but excelled in Italian comic opera. In works such as *The Magic Flute*, he laid the foundations of a purely German-language opera, using the German *Singspiel* as a basis. This line was continued by **Beethoven** in *Fidelio* and by the work of **Weber**, who introduced the Romantic style for the first time in opera.

It is in the Romantic operas of Weber and **Meyerbeer** that the work of **Wagner** has its roots. Wagner attempted to create, in his 'music-dramas', a new art form, and completely transformed the 19th-century conception of opera. In Italy, **Verdi** assimilated much of Wagner's techniques, without sacrificing the Italian virtues of vocal clarity and melody.

Comic opera (*opéra comique*), as represented in the works of André Grétry (1741–1813) and, later, **Auber**, became a popular genre in Paris. More serious artistic ideals were put into practice by **Berlioz** in *The Trojans*, but the merits of his work were largely unrecognized in his own time. **Bizet's** *Carmen* began a trend towards realism in opera; his lead was followed in Italy by **Mascagni**, **Leoncavallo**, and **Puccini**. National operatic styles were developed in Russia by **Glinka**, **Rimsky-Korsakov**, **Mussorgsky**, **Borodin**, and **Tchaikovsky**, and in Bohemia by **Smetana** and, later, **Janáček**.

In the 20th century the Second Viennese School produced an outstanding opera in **Berg's** *Wozzeck*, and the **Romanticism** of Wagner was revived by Richard **Strauss** in *Salome*. Later developments were seen in **Birtwistle's** *The Mask of Orpheus*, **Zimmermann's** *Die Soldaten* and **Stockhausen's** *Licht* cycle.

oratorio

Dramatic, nonscenic musical setting of religious texts, scored for orchestra, chorus, and solo voices. Though dramatic in form, oratorios are generally performed without scenery or costumes in a concert hall or church. The oratorio's formal origins lie in the *Laude spirituali* plays performed by St Philip Neri's Oratory in Rome in the 16th century. The first definitive oratorio was **Cavalieri's** *La rappresentazione di anima e di corpo*, first performed in 1600. The form reached perfection in such works as **J S Bach's** *Christmas Oratorio* (1734), and **Handel's** *Messiah* (1741).

The term is sometimes applied to secular music drama in which there is little or no stage action, as in **Stravinsky's** *Oedipus Rex* (1926–27), which is described as an opera-oratorio (1926–27) and **Messiaen's** *St François* *d'Assise* (1975–83). In the earliest oratorios there was often an element of ritual and spatial dramatization, and Bach himself introduced audience participation with the chorales of his *St Matthew Passion* (1727). In 1993 Jonathan Miller reintroduced simple actions to a London performance of Bach's *St John Passion* (1723) with telling effect.

orchestra

A large number of musicians playing together on different instruments. In Western music, an orchestra typically consists of bowed, stringed instruments of the violin family, and usually wind, brass, and percussion sections. The size and format may vary according to the requirements of composers. The term was originally used in Greek theatre for the semicircular space in front of the stage, and was adopted in 17th-century France to refer first to the space in front of the stage where musicians sat, and later to the musicians themselves. *Orchestration* is the rendering of a composition for orchestra and involves the choosing of which instruments should play which parts of the music. Some works were written at a piano, and then transferred to an orchestral score.

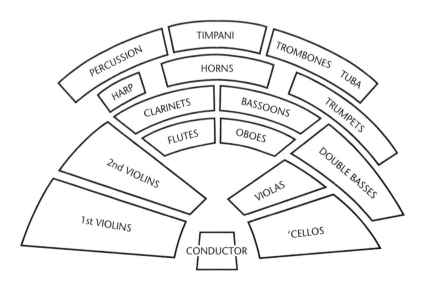

orchestra *The arrangement of an orchestra on a concert platform.*

organ
Keyboard wind instrument of ancient origin, in which sound is produced when a depressed key opens a valve, allowing compressed air to pass through a single pipe or a series of pipes. The number of pipes in total may vary, according to the size of the instrument. Apart from its continued use in serious compositions and for church music, the organ has been adapted for light entertainment. One note only is sounded by each pipe, but these are grouped into stops, each stop pertaining to a particular tone quality and register. The total number of stops are divided between various manuals, or keyboards, and they are usually called the great, swell, choir, solo, echo, and pedal organs, controlled by the player's hands and feet. Notable composers for the organ include **Buxtehude**, **Bach**, **Frescobaldi**, and later Widor (1844–1937), **Vierne**, **Messiaen**, and **Reger**.

ornamentation
Decoration of a melody by rhetorical flourishes or cascades of notes, indicated by special notational signs. Examples of ornament are the turn, a form of melodic pirouette around a note; the trill; the appoggiatura (and other **grace notes**), an upward or downward inflection; arpeggio, and the mordent, a form of accented trill. Until at least the early 19th century there are many repertories in which it was expected that the performer would add ornamental details.

ostinato
(Italian 'obstinate') Persistently repeated melodic or rhythmic figure conveying an ambiguous message of dynamic action unrelated to any movement. Ostinati play an important role in **Stravinsky's** *The Rite of Spring* (1913) and much other Russian music. In the 1960s, tape loop recycling of sound provided a starting point for the **minimalism** of **Riley** and **Reich**.

overture
Opening piece of a concert or opera, having the dual function of settling the audience and allowing the conductor and musicians to become acquainted with the **acoustic** of a concert auditorium.

Pachelbel, Johann (1653–1706)

German orgaist and composer. Although his only well-known work today
is the *Canon and Gigue* in D major for three violins and continuo, he was
a leading progressive composer of keyboard and religious works, and
influenced J S Bach. His works include 11 Magnificat settings, 94 organ
fugues on the Magnificat, and 6 sets of variations for harpsichord
Hexachordum Apollinis (1699).

Pachelbel *The title page of Hexachordum Apollinis by Johann Pachelbel , published by W
M Endter in Nürnberg, 1699. This work, consisting of six sets of variations for organ or
harpsichord, was Pachelbel's only publication during the last decade of his life.*

Paderewski, Ignacy Jan (1860–1941)

Pianist and composer who became prime minister of newly independent Poland in 1919. After his debut in Vienna in 1887 he became celebrated in Europe and the USA as an interpreter of the piano music of **Chopin** and as composer of the suave and exciting *Polish Fantasy* (1893) for piano and orchestra, and the Romantic *'Polonia'* Symphony (1903–09). During World War I he helped organize the Polish army in France. He resumed a musical career in 1922, was made president of the Polish National Council in Paris in 1940, and died in New York. He supervised a complete edition of Chopin's music.

> ❝ If I don't practise for one day, I know it; if I don't practise for two days, the critics know it; if I don't practise for three days, the audience knows it. ❞
>
> **Paderewski**, quoted in Shapiro, *An Encyclopedia of Quotations about Music*

Paganini, Niccolò (1782–1840)

Italian violinist and composer whose dissolute appearance, wild love life, and amazing powers of expression fostered rumours of his being in league with the devil. A prodigious technician, he drew on folk and gypsy idioms to create the modern repertoire of virtuoso techniques. His compositions include six concertos, and variations for violin and orchestra, sonatas for violin and guitar, and the famous 24 caprices for solo violin. In 1797 made his first professional tour, winning early acclaim for his technical virtuosity and flamboyant platform personality. After that he became increasingly famous, travelled widely, beginning with Vienna and Paris (1828–31), and in the latter year went to England for the first time. He exerted a profound influence on **Liszt**.

> Paganini's body was exhumed and reburied several times after his death by obsessed lovers.

Paik, Nam June (1932–)

Korean experimental composer whose work involves bizarre activities: in *Variations on a Theme of Saint-Saëns* the pianist plays 'The Swan' while the cellist immerses herself in an oil drum. After study with **Stockhausen** in Cologne he moved to New York in 1964, then to Los Angeles in 1970. In *Hommage à John Cage* (1959) two pianos are totally destroyed. Other works include *Opera Sextronique* (1967) and *Young Penis Symphony* (1970). The *Earthquake Symphony* of 1971 concludes with an appropriate finale.

Paisiello, Giovanni (1740–1816)
Italian composer whose opera *The Barber of Seville* (1782), written while he was serving in the Russian court, was very successful until it was displaced by **Rossini's** opera of the same name. With *Il ciarlone* (1764), he began his successful career as a composer of comic opera. Summoned to Paris as music director of Napoleon's household in 1802, he remained only a year before returning to his old post in Naples. Modern revivals of such operas as *Nina* (1789), and *Il ré Teodoro in Venezia* (1784) reveal a composer of real charm and vivacity.

Palestrina, Giovanni Pierluigi da (c. 1525–1594)
Italian composer canonized by Liszt and others in the 19th century. He wrote secular and sacred choral music, and is regarded as the outstanding exponent of Renaissance **counterpoint**. Apart from motets and madrigals, he also wrote 105 **Masses**. His technique has served as a tool for the instruction of counterpoint over two centuries. His clear but opulent writing has been eulogized and imitated by many, even in the 20th century.

PFITZNER'S OPERA

In his opera *Palestrina*, **Pfitzner** dramatized the myth that Palestrina wrote his *Missa Papae Marcelli* in response to the threat, issued by the Council of Trent, to ban music in churches due to its growing complexity, and in doing this saved the polyphonic school.

Panufnik, Andrzej (1914–1991)
Polish-born composer who settled in Britain. His music is based on the dramatic interplay of symbolic motifs. Panufnik was a pupil at the Warsaw Conservatory and received a diploma in 1936. Some of his music was destroyed in the bombardment of Warsaw. He became a British citizen in

1961 and conductor of the Birmingham Symphony Orchestra (1957–59). Much of his music, which includes orchestral, choral, and chamber works, is inspired by spiritual subjects.

Parry, (Charles) Hubert (Hastings) (1848–1918)
English composer remembered for his settings of Milton's 'Blest Pair of Sirens' and Blake's 'Jerusalem'. He did not make his mark until his Piano Concerto was played at the Crystal Palace in 1880, and his choral scenes from Shelley's *Prometheus Unbound* appeared at the Gloucester Festival the same year. Most of his music unfortunately combines a sub-Brahmsian academicism with Victorian piety, imperialist swagger, and provincial conservatism.

Pärt, Arvo (1935–)
Estonian composer who courted Communist condemnation with his adoption of serial techniques early in his career, but who later settled for **minimalist** sacred music. His *Nekrolog* (1960) for orchestra exemplifies his early manner and is dedicated to the victims of the Holocaust. Baroque models informed his minimalist work, the finest of which can be heard in the concerto grosso *Tabula rasa* (1977). He moved to West Berlin in 1982. Other works include *Cantus in Memory of Britten* for strings and glockenspiel (1977), *Arbos* for seven instruments (1977), *If Bach had been a Bee-Keeper*, two versions for harpsichord and ensemble (1978, 1980), and a *St John Passion* (1981).

Partch, Harry (1901–1974)
Self-taught US composer who experimented with microtonal scales and the construction of new instruments. His exotic, original, and hypnotic works include *Eight Hitch-hiker Inscriptions from a California Highway Railing; US Highball, a Musical Account of a Transcontinental Hobo Trip* for chorus and instruments (1944); *The Letter, a Depression Message from a Hobo Friend*; and *Water, Water*, an American ritual (1962).

PARTCH'S AESTHETIC

Partch travelled as a tramp during the Depression, and while working as an odd-job man formulated a new aesthetic embodied in his book *Genesis of a Music* (1949).

passacaglia

Spanish dance form in triple time that evolved into an instrumental form constructed over a ground bass (a cyclically repeating bass line). Dramatic tension is created by the juxtaposition of a developing melody and an unchanging background.

Passion music

Recitation of the gospel story of Christ's Passion sung by three singers with different vocal ranges, often with a choral and orchestral accompaniment.

- In the course of the 16th century the whole text was sung in a choral polyphonic setting.
- In the 17th century Lutheran composers introduced recitative, chorales, and instrumental accompaniment.
- In the early 18th century the inclusion of **arias** set to non-Biblical words turned the Lutheran Passion into an oratorio, indistinguishable in form from **opera**. **Bach's** two surviving Passions belong to this new category.

Penderecki, Krzysztof (1933–)

Polish composer whose early experimental and expressionist phase was demonstrated in the *Threnody for the Victims of Hiroshima* (1961) and the First Symphony (1973), both employing **cluster** effects with panache and abandon. He later turned to religious subjects and a more orthodox style, as in the *Magnificat* (1974) and the *Polish Requiem* (1980–83). His opera *The Black Mask* (1986) uncovered a vein of surreal humour.

percussion family

Perhaps the most numerous group of instruments, it comprises any from which sound is produced by hitting, shaking, or rattling. There are many different branches of the family, of which the most important are:

- drums, including the snare, tenor, and bass drum, congas, bongos, and timpani (or kettledrums), which can be tuned to particular **pitches**;
- metallic instruments, such as the triangle, cymbal, gong, and tam-tam (a large, untuned gong);
- tuned instruments, capable of playing specific pitches and often arranged in the manner of a piano keyboard, including the vibraphone, xylophone (made of wood), glockenspiel (German 'bell-play'), marimba, and tubular bells;

- and many miscellaneous items including castanets, maracas, and others often imported into the orchestra from the folk art of particular countries.

The first work written for percussion instruments alone was **Varèse's** *Ionisation* (1929–31).

Pergolesi, Giovanni Battista (1710–1736)

Italian composer of poor parents, thought to have been sent to study in Naples in 1725. His earliest works were sacred pieces, but he made his debut as a composer for the stage in 1731 with *La serva padrona*, a comic *intermezzo* performed between the acts of a serious opera. In 1732 he became maestro di cappella to the Prince of Stigliano at

Pergolesi's music is most often heard today through the pieces that **Stravinsky** selected for *Pulcinella*.

Naples. In February 1736 he retired on grounds of ill health to a monastery where he completed his last work, the *Stabat Mater*. Much music attributed to him is now known to be by other composers, but his output is nevertheless astonishing for a composer who suffered from ill-health and died young.

Peri, Jacopo (1561–1633)

An Italian composer who lived in Florence in the service of the Medici, his experimental melodic opera *Euridice* (1600) established the opera form and influenced **Monteverdi**. His *Dafne* (1597), believed to be the earliest opera, is now lost. He was a member of the **camerata**, with the composers **Caccini**, Corsi, and Galilei.

> ❝I shall consider myself to have done enough, having cleared the road for others who, by their merit, may go in my footsteps to that glory which it has not been granted me to reach.❞
>
> Jacopo, **Peri**, in the foreword to his opera *Euridice*

Petrassi, Goffredo (1904–)
Italian composer who made individual use of 12-note methods. He came under the influence of **Casella** and **Hindemith**, and in 1933 made his debut with his orchestral *Partita*. He continued by writing a series of brilliant concertos for orchestra; in the late 1950s he renewed his prominence with smaller instrumental works in an avant-garde idiom. His big choral works, *Psalm IX* (1934), *Coro di morti* (1940), and *Noche oscura* (1950), were also of importance.

Pfitzner, Hans (1869–1949)
German composer and conductor plagued by his possibly naive association with the Nazi Party. After the success of his opera *Palestrina* in 1917 he devoted himself to composition, but also wrote many essays attacking modernists, especially **Busoni**, and defending Romantic and Germanic ideals. His Violin Concerto (1923), however conservative, is an attractive work and has been performed by notable virtuosi. He wrote several operas, three symphonies, much chamber music, and 106 **lieder**.

Philips, Peter (1561–1628)
In his time he was probably the best-known English composer in northern Europe. His collections of madrigals and motets incorporate Italianate word painting and **polyphony**; they were reprinted many times in Antwerp. He left England in 1582, probably because he was a Roman Catholic, and settled in Antwerp in 1590, becoming a canon at the collegiate church of Soignies. Some of his keyboard music is preserved in the

In 1593, returning from a visit to hear **Sweelinck** play in Amsterdam, Philips was arrested on suspicion of being involved in a plot to assassinate Queen Elizabeth I.

Fitzwilliam Virginal Book. It belongs to the English tradition, with the most inventive pieces being based on madrigals

piano or pianoforte (originally fortepiano)
Stringed musical instrument played by felt-covered hammers activated from a keyboard. It is therefore a form of **percussion** instrument. It is capable of dynamic gradation between soft (Italian 'piano') and loud (Italian 'forte') tones, hence its name.

- The first piano was constructed in 1704 and introduced in 1709 by Cristofori, a harpsichord maker from Padua.

- Extensively developed during the 18th century, the piano attracted admiration among many composers, although it was not until 1768 that **Johann Christian Bach** gave one of the first public recitals on the instrument.

- Further improvements by makers such as Broadwood, Erard, and Graf, together with a rapid expansion of published music by **Haydn**, **Beethoven**, and **Schubert** led to the development of the powerfully resonant grand piano and the mass production of smaller upright pianos for the home.

- In the 19th century, the instrument's most notable exponents included **Liszt** and **Tausig**, while the 20th century has been dominated by figures such as **Busoni**, **Godowsky**, **Rachmaninov**, Rubinstein, Cortot, Sofronitsky, Richter, and, more recently, Brendel, Michelangeli, Gould, Ogdon, Pollini, and others.

Piccinni, Niccolò (1728–1800)
A significant figure in the development of both French and Italian opera. He produced his first opera in Naples in 1754. It was well received and was soon followed by other operas, both comic and serious. In 1776 he was invited to Paris, and wrote his first French opera, *Roland*, in 1778. The Revolution forced him back to Naples, where he was placed under close surveillance and lived in great poverty. He was eventually relieved by a gift from Napoleon. He wrote over 120 operas.

Pijper, Willem (1894–1947)
Dutch composer influenced by French impressionists and also by **Mahler**. Despite obvious difficulty in reconciling these trends, he became the most important Dutch composer of his generation. His works include the operatic cantata *Halewijn* (1934), three symphonies, concertos, chamber music, and songs.

Piston, Walter Hamor (1894–1976)
US composer and teacher who followed European **Neo-Classical** models, often favouring contrapuntal textures. His works include eight symphonies, a number of concertos, chamber music, and the orchestral suite *Three New England Sketches* (1959). He wrote a number of textbooks, including

Harmony (1941) and *Orchestration* (1955). He was well regarded as a teacher; his pupils included **Bernstein**.

pitch
How high or low a note is. This depends on the frequency of vibration of the sound and is measured in hertz (Hz), or cycles per second. It also means the standard to which instruments are tuned, nowadays using the A above middle C (A4 or a') with a frequency of 440Hz as a reference tone. This is often known as concert pitch. Absolute pitch (also called perfect pitch) is the ability to name any note heard, or to sing any note asked for. It is usually an ability that someone is born with, and is very difficult to acquire.

polyphony
Music combining two or more 'voices' or parts, each with an individual melody. A polyphony of widely separated groups is called **antiphony**.

Ponchielli, Amilcare (1834–1886)
Italian composer whose masterpiece, *La Gioconda*, based on Victor Hugo's *Angelo*, was produced at La Scala, Milan, in 1876. Its inspired melody and strong dramatic characterization established him as a worthy successor to **Verdi**. Ponchielli was born near Cremona and studied at the Milan Conservatory (1843–54) and produced his first opera, based on Manzoni's famous novel *I promessi sposi*, at Cremona in 1856. In 1881 he was appointed maestro di cappella at Bergamo Cathedral.

Poulenc, Francis Jean Marcel (1899–1963)
A self-taught composer of witty and irreverent music, he was a member of the group of French composers known as 'Les Six'. Among his many works are the operas *The Breasts of Tiresias* (1947) and *Dialogues of the Carmelites*. A commission from Diaghilev led to the ballet score *Les biches* (1923), influenced by the **Neo-Classical** brilliance of **Stravinsky** but also

❝ On the radio a lady has been caterwauling for a quarter of an hour some songs which may very well have been mine! ❞

Poulenc, *Diary of My Songs*

containing Poulenc's characteristic wit, charm, and melancholy. Similar traits are found in his great series of songs (1919–60), settings of poems by Apollinaire, Ronsard, Eluard, Colette, and Vilmorin. He wrote popular concertos for organ, two pianos, and harpsichord.

Pousseur, Henri (1929–)

Eclectic Belgian composer, initially influenced by Berio and **Stockhausen**, he engaged in post-Webernian serialism (one of his earliest works being *Quintet in Memory of Webern*) and then made use of open forms where the performer has freedom to decide the order of the musical material (for example *Mobile* for two pianos and *Caractères* for piano solo). He also wrote electronic works, such as the eloquent and witty *Trois visages de Liège*, and later developed a more personal style in works such as *Nuits des nuits* for orchestra (1985), and *Leçons d'enfer*, chamber opera (1991).

prelude

Composition intended as the preface to further music, especially preceding a **fugue**, forming the opening piece of a **suite**, or setting the mood for a stage work, as in **Wagner's** *Lohengrin*. As used by **Chopin**, **Skryabin**, and many others, a prelude is a short self-contained piano work.

programme music

Instrumental music that interprets a story, depicts a scene or painting, or illustrates a literary or philosophical idea. The term was first used by **Liszt** in the mid-19th century, but there had been a great deal of descriptive music before then. Examples include **Vivaldi's** *Four Seasons* concertos and **Beethoven's** *Pastoral* symphony. Nowadays, however, it is applied to any purely instrumental music based on a literary, pictorial, historical, biographical, autobiographical, or any other extra-musical subject, as opposed to *absolute music* with a purely abstract meaning. The programmatic element can be as vague as simply having a descriptive title given to it by the composer to set the mood, or a much more detailed depiction of a scene or story. Often, however, it is impossible to distinguish between the depiction of a scene and the composer's reaction to it.

Prokofiev, Sergey Sergeyevich (1891–1953)

Russian composer famous for operas such as *The Love for Three Oranges* (1921) and the ballet *Romeo and Juliet* (1935). He also wrote seven symphonies including the *Classical*; piano and violin concertos; songs and cantatas; and *Peter and the Wolf* (1936) for children, to his own libretto after a Russian folk tale. Prokofiev was essentially a classicist in his use of form, but his extensive and varied output

Ironically, after years of subjection to Stalinist oppression, he died on the same day as Stalin.

demonstrates great lyricism, humour, and skill. His earlier compositions are distinguished by their hard, modernist brilliance; his later works show a mellowing and maturity of style. In 1918 he left Russia, living in Britain, France, Japan, and the USA before returning to Russia. The opera *The Love for Three Oranges* was produced at Chicago in 1921, and the next year he went to live in Paris and became connected with Diaghilev, who produced several of his works. The visionary opera *The Fiery Angel* was completed in 1923 but not staged until 1955. Limited opportunities in the West impelled him to return to Russia. In 1936 he settled in Moscow; like many other Soviet composers, he was severely criticized in 1948 and was induced to simplify his style; however, much of the resulting music, such as the score for *Alexander Nevsky*, can be counted among his most powerful.

❝I have to hear the Russian language echoing in my ear, I have to speak to people so that they give me back what I lack here; their songs, my songs.❞

Prokofiev, quoted in Wolfgang Stahr, *Notes on Piano Concertos*

Puccini, Giacomo (Antonio Domenico Michele Secondo Maria) (1858–1924)

Italian composer with a strong gift for melody and dramatic effect. His operas combine exotic plots with elements of *verismo* (realism). They include *Manon Lescaut* (1893), *La Bohème* (1896), *Tosca* (1900), *Madame Butterfly* (1904), and the unfinished *Turandot* (1926). Born in Lucca, he was the fifth in a line of musicians and had his first great success with *Manon Lescaut* at Turin in 1893; *La Bohème* was produced in the same city in 1896. His first *verismo* opera, *Tosca* (1898–99), confirmed his stature: the combination of natural melody, a sure dramatic sense, and unerring aptness of orchestral colouring have made it his most enduring piece. His final work, *Turandot* (1920–26), unites some of the elements that most fired his imagination: physical passion, cruelty, strong sentiment, and oriental flavour. Puccini was the dominant figure in Italian music in his time; his operas combine the sensuous melody of **Verdi** with the richness of modern impressionist harmony.

PRIVATE SCANDAL

Puccini's successes made him immensely wealthy and he bought an estate near Lucca, where he lived with Elvira Bonturi, who had left her husband for him, but whom he was unable to marry until much later, when she became a widow. Their life together was marked by scandal in 1909 when their servant committed suicide after Elvira accused her of having a sexual relationship with Puccini.

Purcell, Henry (c. 1659–1695)

Regarded by many as the finest English composer. His music balances high formality with melodic expression of controlled intensity, for example, the opera *Dido and Aeneas* (1689) and music for Dryden's *King Arthur* (1691) and for *The Fairy Queen* (1692). He wrote more than 500 works, ranging from secular operas and incidental music for plays to cantatas and church music. Born at Westminster, he became a chorister at the Chapel Royal, and subsequently was a pupil of Dr John Blow. In 1677 he was appointed composer to the Chapel Royal, and in 1679 organist at Westminster Abbey. As composer to the king, Purcell set odes or anthems to music.

❛ Here lies Henry Purcell esquire, who left life and is gone to that blessed place where only his harmony can be exceeded. ❜

Purcell's epitaph in Westminster Abbey

Quantz, Johann Joachim (1697–1773)

German flautist who composed 300 flute concertos, but is best remembered for writing the treatise *On Playing the Transverse Flute* (1752). He improved the flute's adaptability by adding the second key and devising a sliding tuning mechanism.

Quilter, Roger Cuthbert (1877–1953)

English composer who wrote settings for the songs of Shakespeare and Tennyson, including 'Now Sleeps the Crimson Petal' (1904), and others, as well as incidental music, such as *A Children's Overture* (1920), and chamber works. He was a representative of what **Lutyens** called the 'cowpat school'.

quotations

Short passages in musical works taken from other music by the same composer or by another.

Examples of auto-quotations include:

- Brahms, *Regenlied* in the finale of the G major violin sonata;
- Mozart, 'Non più andrai' from *Figaro* in the second-act finale of *Don Giovanni;*
- Prokofiev, March from *The Love for Three Oranges* in the ballet *Cinderella;*
- Schumann, opening of *Papillons* in 'Florestan' from *Carnaval;*
- Shostakovich, themes from his tenth symphony and first cello concerto in the eighth string quartet (1960).

Examples of quotations from a different composer's work include:

- Bartók, the Nazi march theme from Shostakovich's Seventh Symphony in *Concerto for Orchestra;*
- Beethoven, 'Notte e giorno faticar' from Mozart's *Don Giovanni* in his *Diabelli Variations;*
- Berg, themes from Wagner's *Tristan* and Zemlinsky's *Lyric Symphony* in *Lyric Suite* for string quartet; Bach chorale *Es ist genug* in the violin

concerto;

- Debussy, theme from Wagner's *Tristan* in *Golliwogg's Cake-Walk* (*Children's Corner*);
- Rimsky-Korsakov, themes from Mozart's *Requiem* in the opera *Mozart and Salieri*; and
- Shostakovich, overture from Rossini's *William Tell* and the fate motif from Wagner's *Ring* in the 15th Symphony.

There are also numerous examples of quotations from earlier works in the music of contemporary composers including **Kagel**, **Berio**, and **Zimmermann**.

Rachmaninov, Sergey Vasilevich (1873–1943)

Russian composer, conductor, and pianist who settled in the USA after the 1917 Revolution. His music is rooted in 19th-century practices, and although melodious and emotionally direct it adheres to Classical principles of form. His work includes operas, such as *Francesca da Rimini* (1906), three symphonies, four piano concertos, piano pieces, and songs. He studied the piano with Zverev; among his classmates were Goldenweiser and **Skryabin**. He then went to the Moscow Conservatory, writing the one-act opera *Aleko* while still a student, and the piano pieces Op.3, containing the popular C♯ minor prelude, at the age of 19. In 1895 he wrote his First Symphony, but its premiere was a disaster: he returned to composition slowly and with the help of a hypnotist, Dr Dahl, to whom his famous Second Piano Concerto was dedicated. In 1905 he became conductor of the Imperial Grand Opera at Moscow and in 1909 visited the USA for the first time, writing the Third Piano Concerto for the occasion and playing it himself. He had by this time become one of the finest pianists of the time and he remained pre-eminent in that respect through-out his life. Finding himself out of sympathy with the Revolution – he hailed from a noble background – in 1917 he left his country forever. He spent much of the rest of his life in the USA, mostly working as a touring pianist. He wrote only a few, highly concentrated works in the 25 years of exile. Rachmaninov's reputation with the public has always been secure, although his frequently dark and emotional music has received opprobrium from critics and academics.

> ❝ I feel like a ghost wandering in a world grown alien. I cannot cast out the old way of writing, and I cannot acquire the new. I have made intense efforts to feel the musical manner of today, but it will not come to me. ❞
>
> **Rachmaninov**, quoted in Ewen, *American Composers*

Raff, (Joseph) Joachim (1822–1882)

Swiss composer best known for his **programme** symphonies *Im Walde* and *Voices of Spring*, suggesting alpine imagery tinged by German **Romanticism**. He settled at Weimar in 1850 to be near **Liszt** and in 1856 he went to Wiesbaden, where he wrote incidental music for plays and married an actress. His other works include operas, orchestral works, and much chamber music.

ragtime

American form of syncopated dance music of African-American origin, it influenced many composers including **Stravinsky**, who wrote an eponymous work for 11 instruments in 1918.

Rameau, Jean-Philippe (1683–1764)

French organist and composer whose *Treatise on Harmony* (1722) established rules for harmonic progression. His varied works include keyboard and vocal music and many operas, such as *Castor and Pollux* (1737).

Rautavaara, Einojuhani (1938–)

Leading Finnish composer who embraces a wide variety of idioms, including **Neo-Classicism**, serialism, and jazz. He studied at the Sibelius Academy in Helsinki, and with **Sessions** and **Copland** at Tanglewood. He wrote the operas *The Mine* (1963), *Apollo and Marsyas* (1973), *Marjatta the Lowly Maiden* (1977), *Thomas* (1985), and *Vincent* (based on the life of Van Gogh, 1990). Other works include seven symphonies, and concertos for cello, piano, and violin.

Ravel, (Joseph) Maurice (1875–1937)

French composer whose work is characterized by its sensuousness, exotic harmonies, and dazzling orchestral effects. His most famous works include the *Pavane pour une infante défunte* (1899), the ballet *Daphnis et Chloë* (1912), and *Boléro* (1928). Ravel's mother was of Basque descent; that this lineage affected his writing can be seen in the graceful but dark *Alborada del grazioso* (1918) and the *Rapsodie espagnole* (1907). In 1905 the rejection by the Paris Conservatory of his Prix de Rome submission provoked a scandal which led to the resignation of the director. Two of his finest works, the string quartet (1903) and the piano pieces *Miroirs* (1905), date from the same period. In 1908 he set a new standard in French piano writing with *Gaspard de la nuit*. During the next ten years he wrote some of his best works, but his first great public success came in 1912, when Diaghilev produced *Daphnis et Chloé*. His last large-scale works were the piano concerto in G and concerto for piano left hand. He made a great reputation and a comfortable living without ever holding an official musical post. A car accident in 1933 marked the beginning of a long illness, and he died after a brain operation.

Rawsthorne, Alan (1905–1971)
English composer who devoted all his time to composition but produced a comparatively small number of distinctive and highly finished works. His output includes three string quartets (1940, 1954, 1965) and sonatas for violin, viola (1953), and cello (1949).

Rebikov, Vladimir Ivanovich (1866–1920)
One of the most advanced, if by no means most important, Russian composer of his generation, using many unconventional devices (including whole-tone scales) and evolving an idiom of his own. He formulated a manner of setting words to music using the exact rhythms of speech that predates Janáček's efforts in this direction.

Some of Rebikov's stage works are described as 'musico-psychological' or 'musicopsychgolographic' dramas, among them his opera *The Christmas Tree* (1903).

recitative
A sort of speech-like singing, or sung narration, used especially to convey dialogue or to advance the plot in opera or oratorio. It is partly modelled on the rhythms and inflections of natural speech. It is usually sparingly accompanied by harpsichord, organ or other **continuo** instrument.

recorder
A range of woodwind instruments that flourished in consort ensembles in the Renaissance and Baroque eras, along with viol consorts, as an instrumental medium for **polyphonic** music. A consort (group of performers) may include a sopranino, soprano, alto, tenor, bass, and great bass. The revival of popular interest in recorder playing after 1920, largely through the efforts of Arnold Dolmetsch, led to its wide adoption as a musical instrument for schools.

Reger, (Johann Baptist Joseph) Max(imilian) (1873–1916)

German composer and organist whose works embody a particular blend of contrapuntal ingenuity and Romantic sentimentality. They include *Four Symphonic Poems* (1913), sonatas, concertos, character pieces, and orchestral variations and **fugues** on themes by **Beethoven**, **Mozart**, and **Bach**. In 1901 he went to Munich in the hope of making his way as a composer, but posing as a progressive while being in reality a conservative, he made enemies all round and had some success only with his piano playing. In 1907 he settled at Leipzig as professor at the Conservatory, a post he held for the rest of his life. A master of fugue, with the ability to control tightly the form and harmonic direction of his compositions, Reger is sometimes regarded as the greatest **organ** composer since J S Bach.

> ❝ I am sitting in the smallest room of my house. I have your review before me. In a moment it will be behind me. ❞
>
> **Reger**, letter to a critic in response to his review in *Münchener Neueste Nachrichten*, 7 February 1906

Reich, Steve (1936–)

US composer whose **minimalist** music employs simple patterns superimposed and modified to highlight constantly changing melodies and rhythms; examples are *Phase Patterns* for four electronic organs (1970), *Music for Mallet Instruments, Voices, and Organ* (1973), and *Music for Percussion and Keyboards* (1984).

Reicha, Antonín (1770–1836)

Czech-born French composer whose compositions include eight operas, two symphonies, three concertos, and much piano and chamber music. He spent much of his life in Paris and became professor at the Conservatory in 1818, where his pupils included **Berlioz**, **Franck**, and **Gounod**.

Reicha experimented with orchestral innovations but only his more conventional works were published in his lifetime.

Reimann, Aribert (1936–)
German composer inspired by literature; his best-known work is the opera *Lear* (1978). His early compositions use serial technique, but he renounced this kind of composition in 1967, turning to literary sources for a musical starting point, including Shakespeare, Kafka (*Das Schloss*), Euripides (*Troades*), Byron, Poe, and Plath.

Reinecke, Carl (Heinrich Carsten) (1824–1910)
German composer whose works combine elegance of Classical forms with Romantic wistfulness and expression. He was professor of composition at the Leipzig Conservatory from 1860. He wrote fairy-tale cantatas for female voices *Schneewittchen*, *Dornröschen*, *Aschenbrödel*, and three symphonies (1870–95), four piano concertos (1879–1900), and much else.

Respighi, Ottorino (1879–1936)
Italian composer of *Fountains of Rome* (1917) and *The Pines of Rome* (1924, incorporating the recorded song of a nightingale), operas, and chamber music. He was a student of **Rimsky-Korsakov**.

rest
A silence, or the notation indicating a silence.

| Breve | Semibreve | Minim | Crotchet | Quaver | Semiquaver | Demisemiquaver |

rest *The symbols for various rests. For the crotchet, modern notation favours the left-hand one of the two alternatives.*

Revueltas, Silvestre (1899–1940)
Mexican violinist and composer whose music has great vigour and rhythmic power. He gave recitals of modern music with **Chávez** as pianist, and joined the Orquesta Sinfónica at Mexico City as assistant conductor (1929–35). He also became professor at the Conservatory there.

Revueltas's *Sensemaya* is an orchestral depiction of a snake-killing ritual.

Reynolds, Roger (1934–)

US composer of unremittingly modern music. He makes use of electronics, synthesized sounds, and graphic notation. He won a Pulitzer Prize in 1989 for *Whispers out of Time*. He teaches at the University of San Diego. His other works include *Threshold* (1967) for orchestra; *Between* for chamber orchestra and electronics (1968); and *Archipelago* for chamber orchestra and computer (1982).

rhapsody

A type of instrumental **fantasia**, often based on folk melodies, such as **Liszt's** *Hungarian Rhapsodies* (1853–85).

Rihm, Wolfgang (1952–)

German composer of a vast quantity of Neo-Expressionist modern music. He studied in Karlsruhe and with **Stockhausen** and Wolfgang Fortner (1907–1987). Among his numerous works are the operas *Faust and Yorick* (1976), *Harlekin* (1977), *Jacob Lenz* (1979), *Die Hamletmaschine* (1986), *Oedipus* (1987), and *Die Eroberung von Mexico* (1992).

Riley, Terry (1935–)

US composer and saxophonist belonging to the **minimalist** school. His works involve repeated patterns and series, and contain freedom for improvisation. He studied at Berkeley, California, and since 1970 has been influenced by Indian music. His best known pieces include *Poppy Nogood and the Phantom Band* for saxophone, tape, and electronics (1968) and *A Rainbow in Curved Air* (1970).

Rimsky-Korsakov, Nikolay Andreyevich (1844–1908)

Russian composer who, with **Balakirev**, founded the Russian national school of composition. His operas include *The Maid of Pskov* (1873), *The Snow Maiden* (1882), *Mozart and Salieri* (1898), and *The Golden Cockerel* (1907), a satirical attack on monarchy that was initially banned. He wrote

❝ Rimsky was ... deeply and unshowingly generous, and unkind only to admirers of Tchaikovsky. ❞

Stravinsky, *Memories and Commentaries*

an influential text on orchestration that served as the basis of the often colourful palette achieved by later Russian composers. Other works include the symphonic poem *Sadko* (1867), the **programme** symphony *Antar* (1869), and the symphonic suite *Sheherazade* (1888).

Rodrigo, Joaquín (1901–1999)
Spanish composer who filled his works with Spanish folklore and ambience, as in the well-known *Concierto de Aranjuez* (1939) or the *Concerto heroico* (1943). He always composed in a conservative, lucid **Neo-Classical** style that is less adventurous than de **Falla** but nevertheless as effective and colourful.

romance
A song of a 'romantic' nature, usually moderate in tempo and emotional in style. There is no prescribed form, but it is as a rule fairly short and in the character of a song.

Romanticism
A term applied to music (and literature and art) of the approximate period 1815–1905, characterized by preoccupation with subjective emotion expressed primarily through melody, often accompanied by the use of folk idioms, and by the cult of the musician as visionary artist and hero (virtuoso). Often linked with nationalistic feelings, the Romantic movement reached its height in the late 19th century.

- The reaction against 18th-century Classical values first appears in imagery of untamed natural forces, in the hero figure of **Mozart's** *Don Giovanni* (1787).

- The essentially private emotional world of **Schubert's** and **Schumann's** **lieder** was rapidly transformed into the national mythic heroism of **Wagner** and **Verdi**, and experienced in the flesh in such virtuoso figures as **Paganini** and **Liszt**.

- Towards the end of the 19th century, however, the heroic ideal was increasingly challenged by intimations of fallibility, as in the antihero of **Mussorgsky**'s nationalist opera *Boris Godunov* (1874).

- By the early 20th century, Romanticism became expansive and elegiac in the work of **Mahler**, **Rachmaninov**, and **Sibelius**.

Rore, Cipriano de (c. 1516–1565)
Flemish composer who spent much of his life in Italy, where he was a

prolific composer of madrigals and sacred music. He wrote 125 madrigals, most of which are contained in the ten books he published 1542–46. His works made a strong impression on **Monteverdi**. He left Venice about 1550 to enter the service of Ercole II d'Este at Ferrara. In 1563 he succeeded **Willaert** as maestro di cappella of St Mark's, Venice.

Roslavets, Nikolay Andreyevich (1881–1944)

Russian composer who developed his own type of serial composition around 1914. His style was initially avant garde (as in his settings of Russian futurist poetry), but in the 1920s he formulated a type of Classicism in works such as his Violin Concerto (1925). He wrote a few orchestral works, much chamber music, songs, and piano pieces.

His music was banned in the 1930s by Stalinist ideologues, but has been revived since 1990.

Rossini, Gioacchino Antonio (1792–1868)

Italian composer whose first success was the opera *Tancredi* (1813). In 1816 his comic opera *The Barber of Seville* was produced in Rome. He was the most successful opera composer of his time, producing 20 operas in the period 1815–23. He also created (with **Donizetti** and **Bellini**) the 19th-century Italian operatic style. After *William Tell* (1829), Rossini gave up writing opera and his later years were spent in Bologna and Paris. Among the works of this period are the *Stabat Mater* (1842) and the piano music collectively entitled *Sins of my Old Age*. For many years Rossini's comic operas have overshadowed his serious works, but recent productions have helped to produce a more balanced view of his output. His works include the operas *L'italiana in Algeri* (1813), *La cenerentola* (1817), *La gazza ladra* (1817), *Mosè in Egitto*

Rossini *Italian composer Gioacchino Rossini.*

(1818), *Semiramide* (1823), *Il viaggio a Reims* (1825), and *Le comte Ory* (1828).

❝ I composed the overture to *Otello* in a little room in the Barbaja palace wherein the baldest and fiercest of directors had forcibly locked me with a lone plate of spaghetti and the threat that I would not be allowed to leave the room alive until I had written the last note. ❞

Rossini, letter

Roussel, Albert (1869–1937)

French composer known for *The Spider's Banquet* (1912), in which the hungry arachnid is depicted with appropriate scoring. His naval service in the East had a lasting impression on Roussel, colouring his finest work, the opéra-ballet *Padmâvatî* with Indian melodic patterns. Ballet and choral singing are found also in *La naissance de la lyre*, an evocation of ancient Greece. Other characteristics of Roussel's varying style appear in his Third Symphony, which includes **polytonality** and vital rhythmic patterns.

Rubbra, Edmund (1901–1986)

English composer who specialized in contrapuntal writing, as exemplified in his study *Counterpoint* (1960). His compositions include 11 symphonies, chamber music, and songs. In 1948 he became a Roman Catholic, and his later music shows the influence of Catholic mysticism.

Rubinstein, Anton Grigoriyevich (1829–1894)

Russian pianist and composer. One of the great virtuosos of his day, he did not join the Russian nationalist movement of his contemporaries but followed a European style. His compositions include five piano concertos and six symphonies, including the *Ocean* (no. 2); he also wrote 18 operas (of which the best known is *The Demon* 1871). Born in the Ukraine, he appeared in public at the age of nine and studied with **Liszt**. In 1858 he was appointed imperial music director at St Petersburg, founding the Conservatory there in 1862.

Ruders, Poul (1949–)

Danish composer of medieval-inspired **minimalist** works which occasionally surprise with crashing atonalities. He achieved some popularity for this unique and unlikely blend of idioms. His works include *Wind-Drumming* for wind quintet and four percussion (1979); two violin concertos (1981, 1991); two string quartets (1971, 1979); *Manhattan Abstractions* (for the New York Philharmonic Orchestra, 1982); and *Break Dance* for piano and ensemble (1984).

Ruggles, Carl (1876–1971)

US composer and an associate, during the 1920s and 30s, of the US experimentalist composers **Ives**, **Varèse**, and **Cowell**, trying to forge a new direction in music. His instrumental forms were, however, more conservative than those of other composers, as in his best-known work *Sun-Treader* (1932) for orchestra, which, typically, employs visionary, atonal harmonies in dense, **polyphonic** textures.

Rzewski, Frederic (Anthony) (1938–)

US composer and pianist whose works include *Spacecraft* (1967), *Symphony for Several performers* (1968), *Coming Together* for speaker and instruments (1972), and *Machine* for two pianos (1984).

Rzewski's piano variations on a Chilean revolutionary song 'The People United will Never be Defeated' exemplify his left-wing sympathies, his highly-charged **minimalism**, and his direct manner of expression.

Saariaho, Kaija (1952–)

Finnish composer of surreal, beautifully-scored instrumental works initially intricate but latterly more sparse, many of which employ computers and electronics. She studied with **Ferneyhough** and Huber at Freiburg, and has spent time in the USA; Her works include *Verblendungen* for orchestra (1984). A *Graal Theatre* for violin and orchestra (1994); *Nymphea* (1987) for string quartet; and the installation *La dame à la licorne* (1993).

Saint-Saëns, (Charles) Camille (1835–1921)

Prolific French composer who wrote many lyrical concertos, the symphonic poem *Danse macabre* (1875), the opera *Samson et Dalila* (1877), and the uncharacteristically informal *The Carnival of the Animals* (1886), his most popular work. He began to compose at the age of five. He promoted performances of **Liszt's** symphonic poems. One of his most frequently performed works, the first cello concerto in A minor, was composed in 1872; it displays the composer's familiar and conservative French Romantic style together with melodic inventiveness. His appealing third violin concerto in B minor followed in 1890. Saint-Saëns recognized that its success with the public would lead to neglect of his more important compositions and banned its performance during his lifetime.

Salieri, Antonio (1750–1825)

Italian composer who taught **Beethoven**, **Schubert**, **Hummel**, and **Liszt**, and was the musical rival of **Mozart** at the emperor's court in Vienna. Orphaned at 15, he went to Vienna and became court composer and conductor of the Italian opera. His opera *Europa riconosciuta* was produced at the opening of La Scala, Milan, in

It has been suggested, without proof, that Salieri poisoned Mozart.

1774. Recent revivals of operas such as *Les Danaides* show Salieri to be a resourceful and entertaining composer.

Sallinen, Aulis (1935–)

Finnish composer best known for the strong characterization and sustained dramatic intensity of his operas, which include *The Horseman* (1975), *The Red Line* (1978), *The King goes forth to France* (1984), and *Kullervo* (1992). He has also written six symphonies (1971–90).

Sarasate (y Navascuéz), Pablo (Martín Melitón) (1844–1908)

Spanish violinist and composer who had a remarkable career as a virtuoso all over Europe and the USA. **Bruch, Saint-Saëns, Lalo,** and **Wieniawski** dedicated concertos to him. His own works, which include fantasies, four books of Spanish Dances, and other pieces for violin, are highly acrobatic.

Satie, Erik (Alfred Leslie) (1866–1925)

French composer of Scottish descent, mostly famous for his piano pieces, such as the three *Gymnopédies* (1888), that are precise and tinged with melancholy, and often parody Romantic expression with surreal commentary. His aesthetic of ironic simplicity, demonstrated in the *Messe des pauvres* (1895), acted as a nation-alist antidote to the excesses of German **Romanticism**. Mentor of the group of composers 'Les Six', he promoted the concept of *musique d'ameublement* ('furni-ture music'), anticipating the impact of radio. A commission from Diaghilev led to the ballet *Parade* (1917), with instrumenta-tion for siren, typewriter, and steamship whistle, and he invented a new style of film music for René Clair's *Entr'acte* (1924). He made a precarious living by playing at cafés, but through his friendship with **Debussy**, in about 1890 he came into contact with intellectual circles.

Satie *French composer Erik Satie.*

scale

Sequence of **pitches**, in ascending or descending order, that comprise a particular **key** in its minor or major form. The 'degrees' of major or minor scales are known as the tonic, supertonic, mediant, subdominant, dominant, submediant, and leading note. The so-called melodic minor scale is slightly different in its ascending and descending versions. Other scales include the whole-tone (with six notes per octave), and the pentatonic, which is commonly used in folk music from the USA to the Celtic nations to China. A scale defines, to a certain extent, the **intonation** of a work.

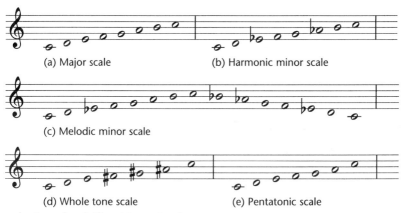

(a) Major scale   (b) Harmonic minor scale

(c) Melodic minor scale

(d) Whole tone scale   (e) Pentatonic scale

scale *Examples of different types of scale.*

Scarlatti, (Giuseppe) Domenico (1685–1757)

Italian composer and eldest son of the opera composer Alessandro Scarlatti (1660–1725). Domenico wrote over 500 sonatas for harpsichord – short pieces in binary form demonstrating the new freedoms of keyboard composition and inspired by Spanish musical idioms. Born in Naples, he initially composed operas; after visiting Venice and spending time in Rome

❝This son of mine is an eagle whose wings are grown; he ought not to stay idle in the nest and I ought not to hinder his flight.❞

Alessandro **Scarlatti** on Domenico, to Ferdinand de Medici, 1705

he went to Lisbon in the service of the Portuguese court. In 1729 he followed the Portuguese princess Maria Barbara to Madrid. It was for her that he wrote most of his harpsichord music, which exhibits an original approach to harmony and frequently demands great virtuosity. Scarlatti was the most celebrated harpsichordist of his time, and his music provided the foundation for modern piano technique.

Scelsi, Giacinto (1905–1988)

Italian aristocratic composer who, under the influence of a visit to Tibet, developed a highly original and sparse aesthetic, not to be confused with **minimalism**, seen in works such as *Four Pieces, Each One on a Single Note*. His transcendental approach has won him many admirers; his music

> Scelsi was reclusive by nature, refusing interviews and threatening to kill anyone who tried to photograph him. He also re-dated works to confuse historians.

exudes an inner intensity that is rarely matched. He also pioneered unusual techniques including the use of two bows by a cellist.

Scheidt, Samuel (1587–1654)

German composer whose influential *Tabulatura nova* for the organ (published in 1624) was printed in modern score, not in the old German **tablature**. He studied under **Sweelinck** at Amsterdam and became court organist at Brandenburg. His other works include *Cantiones sacrae* for eight voices (1620); sacred concertos for two–twelve voices with instruments; and *Liebliche Krafft-Blümlein* for two voices and instruments.

scherzo

(Italian 'joke') A lively piece, usually in rapid triple (3/4) time; often used for the third movement of a symphony, sonata, or quartet as a later substitute for the statelier minuet and trio. Originally skittish, the genre took on darker overtones in the work of **Chopin**.

Schillinger, Joseph (1895–1943)

Russian-born composer and theoretician who settled, in 1929, in the USA. He published a number of books on his system, and also several compositions, including the *First Airphonic Suite* for theremin (an early electronic musical instrument) and orchestra.

> Schillinger evolved a quasi-mathematical method of composition; among his many pupils was **Gershwin**.

Schmidt, Franz (1874–1939)
Austrian composer largely unaffected by 20th-century innovations; his four symphonies and the biblical oratorio *Das Buch mit sieben Siegeln* are most representative of his lyrical and serene post-Schubertian talent.

Schmitt, Florent (1870–1958)
French composer influenced by Richard **Strauss** and **Stravinsky**, but one who favoured impressionist colourings and harmonies. His most successful work was the ballet *La Tragédie de Salome* (revised as a symphonic poem in 1910).

Schnebel, Dieter (1930–)
German composer and theologian who questions the most basic concepts of music in works for reader (*mo-no*, 1969), and for conductor only (*Nostalgie*, 1969). Other pieces include *Webern-Variationen* (1972), *Wagner-Idyll* (1980), *Beethoven-Sinfonie* (1985), *Mahler-Momente* (1985) and *Sinfonie X* (1987–92), all for orchestra.

Schnittke, Alfred Garriyevich (1934–1998)
Russian composer of German descent who combined the influences of **Shostakovich** with Western avant-garde tendencies such as serialism, improvisation, and **aleatoric technique**. He has been described as a 'poly-stylist' for his frequent use of quotation and collage. Among his many works are *... pianissimo ...* (1969) for orchestra, the oratorio *Nagasaki* (1958), several symphonies, and *Lovesong* (1981) for 48 voices. His music often plays on the dichotomy between reality and illusion. He was one of the most important 'underground' composers of the later Soviet era.

Schoeck, Othmar (1886–1957)
Switzerland's first major composer, Schoeck cultivated a lush and lyrical post-Romanticism. He excelled in vocal music of all kinds, and wrote many fine song cycles (*Notturno*, 1933, and *Lebendig Begraben*, 1947) as well as several operas, including *Venus* (1922) and *Massimilla Doni* (1937). His music was successfully performed in Germany during the Nazi era.

Schoenberg, Arnold (Franz Walter) (1874–1951)
Austro-Hungarian composer who revolutionized 20th-century music but who was, at heart, a conservative who worshipped **Brahms**. After Romantic early works such as *Verklärte Nacht* (1899) and *Gurrelieder* (1900–11), he experimented with atonality producing *Pierrot Lunaire* (1912) and

Erwartung. He then developed the vastly influential twelve-tone system of musical composition. After 1918, Schoenberg wrote several **Neo-Classical** works for chamber ensembles. The twelve-tone system was further developed by his pupils **Berg** and **Webern**. Driven from Germany by the Nazis, Schoenberg settled in the USA in 1933, where he wrote works such as the opera *Moses und Aron* (1932–51).

> ❦ The introduction of my method of composing with twelve notes does not facilitate composing; on the contrary, it makes it more difficult. ❦
>
> **Schoenberg**, *Style and Idea*

Schreker, Franz (1878–1934)
Austrian composer, conductor, and teacher. He conducted the first performance of **Schoenberg's** *Gurrelieder* in 1913 and his own works were late Romantic in expression and popular in the 1920s; he directed the Berlin Academy of Music from 1920 until he was forced by the Nazis to resign in 1933. His output includes the operas *Der ferne Klang* (1912) and *Irrelohe* (1924), and a still-performed Chamber symphony for 23 solo instruments (1917).

Schubert, Franz Peter (1797–1828)
Austrian composer who established the German **lied**, writing over 600 examples, as well as excelling in instrumental works. He straddled the eras of **Classicism** and **Romanticism**. At 17 he became assistant teacher in his father's school, but disliked teaching; his first opera, *Des Teufels Lustschloss*, was written in the same year. Like all his stage works, it was unsuccessful, but he also composed at this time his first great song, 'Gretchen am

Schubert *Austrian composer, who wrote over 600 lieders, Franz Schubert*

Spinnrade'. The following year he wrote almost 150 songs. In 1816 he left the school and joined his friend Schober, gathering a circle of literary and artistic rather than musical friends

In 1814 Schubert allegedly sold his overcoat in order to buy a ticket for the revival of **Beethoven's** opera *Fidelio*.

around him. In 1817 he met the singer Michael Vogl, who took a great interest in his songs. By 1820 he had written some of his finest instrumental works, including the fourth and fifth symphonies, and the *Trout Quintet*.

Schubert's reputation slowly grew beyond his own circle, but publishers failed to recognize him until his friends had 20 songs published at their own expense in 1821. Most of his large works remained unpublished during his lifetime. His mastery of instrumental writing is demonstrated in the 'Unfinished' Symphony and 'Wanderer' Fantasy for piano of 1822. His Ninth Symphony of 1825 is one of the most carefully crafted and consistently inspired works of its kind ever written. He lived in Vienna all his life, except for some summer excursions and two visits to Hungary as domestic musician to the Esterházy family

Schubert wrote over 20 operas, 9 symphonies, 5 masses, 15 string quartets, 2 piano trios, much other chamber music, at least 20 piano sonatas, and over 600 songs in about 15 years.

on their country estate at Zséliz. He never held an official appointment and failed to stabilize his financial position, but earned enough casually to lead a modest if Bohemian existence. His industry was phenomenal. He died from typhoid, his condition having been weakened by syphilis.

Schulhoff, Erwin (1894–1942)
Czech pianist and composer. As a Communist in Nazi-ruled Czechoslovakia, he sought refuge in Soviet citizenship, but after the 1941 invasion of Russia he was arrested, and died in a concentration camp. Recent performances of works by this Czech composer, such as the opera *Flammen* (1928), suggest a powerful assimilation of a wide range of contemporary influences, including jazz and microtonality.

Schumann, Clara Josephine (1819–1896)
German pianist and composer who, early in life, wrote an accomplished Piano Concerto (1835–36), before her marriage to Robert **Schumann** in

1840. During his life and after his death she was devoted to popularizing his work, appearing frequently in European concert halls. Highly regarded as a pianist across Europe, she gave her own first concert in Leipzig in 1830. In 1878 she became chief piano professor at the Hoch Conservatory in Frankfurt.

Schumann, Robert (Alexander) (1810–1856)

German composer whose songs and short piano pieces portray states of emotion with great economy. Among his compositions are four symphonies, a violin concerto, a piano concerto, sonatas, and song cycles such as *Dichterliebe/Poet's Love* (1840). In 1828 he met Friedrich Wieck, from whom he took piano lessons, and first met Wieck's daughter Clara. In 1832 he permanently injured his hand with a contrivance he had invented for finger-development and thus had to give up a pianist's career. With a circle of young intellectuals (calling themselves the 'Davidsbündler') he founded the *Neue Zeitschrift für Musik* in 1834, the most comprehensive and innovative German musical journal. Some of his feelings for Clara were expressed in the C major Fantasy for piano, but Clara's father violently opposed a match and in 1839 they took legal proceedings against him; he failed to yield, but they married on 12 September 1840, the day before she came of age. The most prolific period of Schumann's life followed: the 'Spring' symphony of 1841 seems to symbolize artistic growth and the same fervent, vital impulse informs the song cycles *Dichterliebe* and *Liederkreis*. The first, rhapsodic movement of the Piano Concerto also dates from this time, the last two movements were added in 1845.

In 1843 Schumann suffered from mental exhaustion; he had a more serious breakdown after a tour in Russia. In spite of his personal problems Schumann completed in 1850 the most exuberant and accomplished of all his orchestral works, the 'Rhenish' Symphony, which celebrates the flowing of the Rhine and Cologne cathedral. Signs of a mental collapse grew more and more alarming, and in February 1854 he threw himself into the Rhine. On being rescued he was sent at his own request to a private asylum where he died more than two years later.

Schumann's works of all genres tend towards the lyrical qualities found most obviously in his songs; although the spontaneity and naturalness of his piano music and **lieder** have rightly been praised, his chamber and **orchestral** music shows similar qualities, although on a larger scale. One of his most attractive features is the essentially private nature of his genius.

Schütz, Heinrich (1585–1672)

German early Baroque composer and important precursor of J S **Bach**. He was musical director to the Elector of Saxony from 1614. His works include *The Seven Words of Christ* (c. 1660), *Musicalische Exequien* (1636), and the *German Magnificat* (1671). He increased the range and scope of instrumental and choral **polyphony**. He studied as a choirboy under Giovanni **Gabrieli** in Venice (1609–12). Back in Germany, he did much to establish the fashion for Italian music, but he set his own works to German or Latin words, notably the 26 *Psalmen Davids* of 1619. In 1627 he wrote the first German opera, *Dafne*. Schütz united the lyric and dramatic elements of Venetian vocal style with German polyphony.

Schwertsik, Kurt (1935–)

Austrian composer who has reacted against the contemporary avant garde. In 1978 he began teaching at the Vienna Conservatory. His works include the operas *Der lange Weg zur grossen Mauer* (1975) and *Das Märchen von Fanferlieschen Schönefusschen* (1982); and *Verwandlungsmusik* for orchestra (1983).

Sciarrino, Salvatore (1947–)

Italian composer known for his brilliant operas, which take an irreverent view of the conventions of the genre, filtering familiar myths through a surreal sensibility; these include *Amore e Psyche* (1973), *Aspern* (1978), *Vanitas* (1981), *Lohengrin 'azione invisible'* (1983), and *Perseo e Andromeda* (1991). His instrumental music is now widely performed; gesturally and harmonically beautiful, it is often concerned with peripheral ingredients of expression such as trills, harmonics, and **grace notes**.

Sculthorpe, Peter (1929–)

Composer who has reflected his fascination with the culture and landscape of his native Australia. His works often have a searing, primitive intensity. He first became known when the Kronos Quartet's recording of his Eighth Quartet sold 25,000 copies.

Seiber, Mátyás (1905–1960)

Hungarian-born composer who settled in London in 1935 and taught many British composers including Hugh **Wood**. He was also active as a conductor and cellist. Influences in his music range from **Bartók** and **Schoenberg** to jazz. Although he is best known for his cantata *Ulysses* (1947), based on a chapter from James Joyce's novel, his chamber works are very effective.

Senfl, Ludwig (c. 1486–c. 1542)

Swiss composer who made imaginative arrangements of traditional German melodies, ranging from chordal harmonization to canons, and is regarded as the most important German-speaking composer of motets and songs during the Reformation. He studied under **Isaac** in Vienna and worked with

Senfl was in correspondence with Martin Luther.

him copying a large amount of music published as part of Isaac's *Choralis constantinus*, a task Senfl completed around 1520.

Sessions, Roger Huntington (1896–1985)

US composer whose modernist style secured a US platform for serious German influences, including **Hindemith** and **Schoenberg**, and offered an alternative to the lightweight, fashionable modernism of Milhaud and Paris. An able symphonist, his works include *The Black Maskers* (1923), eight symphonies, and a *Concerto for Orchestra* (1971).

Séverac, (Joseph Marie) Déodat de (1873–1921)

French composer of delicate, fragrant works evoking his native south of France. He avoided officialdom and devoted himself entirely to composition. His works include the opera *Le cœur du moulin* (1909), the ballet *La fête des vendanges*, a string quintet, piano works, and 19 song settings of Verlaine, Maeterlinck, and Poe.

Shebalin, Vissarion Yakovlevich (1902–1963)

Russian composer who was director of the Moscow Conservatory (1942–58), but was sacked after being denounced by Stalinists. His pupils included **Denisov**. His works include the opera *The Taming of the Shrew* (1957), five symphonies (1925–62), and nine string quartets (1923–63).

Shostakovich considered Shebalin the finest teacher in Russia.

Shostakovich, Dmitry Dmitriyevich (1906–1975)

Russian composer whose expressive and sometimes highly dramatic music was not always to official Soviet taste. He wrote 15 symphonies, chamber and film music, ballets, and operas, the latter including *Lady Macbeth of the Mtsensk District* (1934), which sparked off the first serious suppression of music in the USSR, being described as 'muddle instead of music'. His symphonies are among the greatest of the 20th century. Shostakovich was born in St Petersburg, entered the conservatory there in 1919 and studied with **Glazunov**; he left in 1925, having already written his First Symphony, which dates from that year. First performed in 1926 and subsequently throughout Europe, it quickly established his reputation internationally. *The Nose*, an opera based on Gogol, was typical of his early work with its atonal harmony and insistent rhythms. Shostakovich was initially shattered by official

Shostakovich *Russian composer Dmitry Shostakovich.*

denunciation, but his popular Fifth Symphony was labelled by a party hack (and probably not the composer himself) as 'a Soviet artist's creative reply to just criticism'. The deliberately empty bombast of the finale contained much coded criticism of the Soviet machine that went unnoticed for decades. Similar subterfuge is found in the first movement of the Seventh Symphony, arising from the siege of Leningrad: the banal march theme suggests Stalinist oppression as much as it does invading Nazis. In his later years the dichotomy between 'official', Soviet Shostakovich and the 'real' grew; the 13th Symphony set poems by Yevtushenko hinting at Soviet disregard of the Holocaust and was promptly banned. Shostakovich's reputation has grown after his death; his influence, especially on Russian music, is still detectable.

Sibelius, Jean Julius Christian (1865–1957)

The most distinguished Finnish composer, he moved from nationalism – with the symphonic poems such as *En saga* (1893) – to a deeply personal style culminating in the Seventh Symphony (1924). This work is a summation of the composer's career, beyond which it was difficult to develop. The conventional four movements are linked thematically into a single unit, creating an awe-inspiring structure as each idea unfolds and develops over a huge span. In 1940 he abruptly ceased composing and spent the rest of his life as a recluse, apparently gardening. Restoration of many works to their original state has helped to dispel his conservative image and reveal unexpectedly radical features. In 1889 he had a string quartet and a suite for string orchestra performed in public. After study in Germany, he became a passionate nationalist, studying the 'Kalevala' and other Finnish literature for subjects for his works. Sibelius captured popular feeling of protest against foreign, particularly Russian, oppression. Further nationalist sentiments were aroused by *Finlandia* (1899), which became an unofficial national anthem. An annual grant was voted to Sibelius by the Finnish government in 1897 and increased in 1926, and he was thus enabled to devote himself entirely to composition without having to fill any official or administrative post. The Second Symphony followed in 1902 and is a wholly individual work, building massive paragraphs of sound from short phrases, and moving inevitably towards a triumphant finale. In Britain he became much better known after the performance of the Fourth Symphony at the Birmingham Festival in 1912; composed the previous year, it seems to exemplify the view expressed by Sibelius to **Mahler** that a symphony's justification is the 'profound logic creating a connection between all the motifs'.

> ❝ Pay no attention to what the critics say; there has never been a statue set up in honour of a critic. ❞
>
> **Sibelius**, attributed remark

Simpson, Robert (Wilfred Levick) (1921–)
English composer and music critic active in the BBC. He wrote on music, especially that of Bruckner, Nielsen, and **Sibelius**. His music displays tonal stability and an emphasis on organic unity, influenced by **Beethoven** and Bruckner. His output includes 11 symphonies and 15 string quartets.

Sinding, Christian August (1856–1941)
Norwegian composer chiefly remembered for the once popular piano piece *The Rustle of Spring* (1896). His works also include songs and four symphonies.

Skalkottas, Nikos (1904–1949)

Greek composer who adopted **Schoenberg's** twelve-note method. Skalkottas was Greece's first composer of international stature; only after his death did his vast output begin to be performed. He spent 12 years in Germany, where he studied composition with Schoenberg and **Weill**. In 1933 he returned to Greece and spent the remainder of his life as an obscure orchestral player, composing in his spare time.

Skryabin (or Scriabin), Aleksandr Nikolayevich (1872–1915)

Russian composer of piano music and influential, orchestral works including the *Poem of Ecstasy* (1895–08) and *Prometheus* (1909–11). Initially influenced by **Chopin**, his early works are often delicate but do not shy away from virtuosity. Later, he experimented with harmony and form to create a 'principle' by which he wrote his later, luminous, and crystalline piano sonatas 5–10 in which the attainment of a spiritual ecstasy is seen as a form of passage to godliness and enlightenment. He was a fine pianist and was also associated with many writers of the Russian symbolist movement.

Skryabin *Leonid Pasternak's sketch of Skryabin at the piano, 1909.*

> ❝ I was once a Chopinist, then a Wagnerist, now I am only a Scriabinist. ❞
>
> **Skryabin**, quoted in Bowers, *Scriabin*

Smetana, Bedřich (1824–1884)

Bohemian composer who established a Czech nationalist style in the opera *The Bartered Bride* (1866). He was educated in Germany, however, and all his life, in spite of his musical nationalism, spoke Czech like a foreigner. In 1848 he took part in the revolution against Austria and established a school of music for which **Liszt** supplied funds. He settled in the Czech capital in 1863; his work became Czech in character. The opera *The Brandenburgers in Bohemia* was a success in January 1866, although *The Bartered Bride*, with which he was to be most closely identified, was a failure in May. In 1872 he began composing his great cycle of symphonic poems, *Má Vlast/My Country* which is often performed in the Czech Republic at times of national celebration. In 1881 he had his last major success when his patriotic opera *Libuse* was premiered in Prague. In 1883 he became insane and in May 1884 was taken to an asylum, where he died.

FROM MY LIFE

In 1874 Smetana suddenly became totally deaf, and composed the string quartet *From my Life* depicting his love for his wife and children (all of whom had died by 1859). At the beginning of the last movement, the onset of his deafness is portrayed by a piercing high note on the violin.

Smyth, Ethel Mary (1858–1944)

English composer imprisoned as an advocate of women's suffrage. Her works include *Mass in D* (1893) and several operas. She was encouraged by the Wagnerian conductor Levi to write an opera; *Fantasio* was performed at Weimar in 1898 and was taken up three years later by the conductor Mottl in Karlsruhe. *The Wreckers* was completed in 1904 and premiered at Leipzig in 1906; its 1909 performance in London under Beecham almost caused the conductor to alter his unflattering opinion of

In 1911 when jailed at Holloway, Smyth led her fellow suffragettes in her song 'March of the Women', conducting them with a Government-issue toothbrush.

In his *Dodo* trilogy, novelist E F Benson modelled Edith Arbuthnot, who drank whisky for breakfast, on Ethel Smyth.

women composers. After World War I she turned increasingly to writing, producing ten entertaining volumes of memoirs, including the autobiographical *Female Pipings in Eden* (1933) and *What Happened Next* (1940).

Soler, Antonio (1729–1783)
Spanish composer of celebrated harpsichord sonatas, distinguished successors to those of Domenico **Scarlatti**, with whom he probably studied. He wrote church music as well as organ concerti and incidental music for plays; he was maestro de capella at Lérida Cathedral and entered the Escorial monastery in 1752, becoming organist and choirmaster there the following year. His treatise *Llave de la Modulación* was published in 1762.

solmization
The designation of the musical **scales** by means of syllables. The notes of the Greek tetrachords were already designated by syllables, but in the 11th century **Guido d'Arezzo** replaced Greek 'tetrachords' with **hexachords**. He used the Latin syllables ut, re, mi, fa, sol, and la for their six notes, si being added later for the seventh and ut being replaced by do in Italy and elsewhere, though still largely retained in France. These syllables were not immutably fixed to C, D, E, F, G, A, but could be transferred by mutation to other degrees of the scale.

sonata
(Italian 'sounded') An essay in instrumental composition for a solo player or a small ensemble and consisting of a single movement or series of movements. The name signifies that the work is not beholden to a text or existing dance form, but is self-sufficient. Sonata form consists of an opening 'exposition', in which two main themes are contrasted; a 'development' in which they are varied and explored; and a 'recapitulation' in which they are heard again in their original form.

song
A setting of words to music for one or more singers, with or without instrumental **accompaniment**. Song may be sacred, for example a psalm, motet, or cantata, or secular, for example a folksong or ballad. In verse song, the text changes in mood while the music remains the same; in **lied** and other forms of art song, the music changes in response to the emotional development of the text.

Sor, (Joseph) Fernando (Macari) (1778–1839)

Spanish guitarist and composer who wrote an important guitar tutor, published in 1830. He produced his first opera at the age of 19, then went to Paris and *c.* 1815 to London, where he played and taught the guitar, returning to Paris in 1823. He wrote the opera *Telemaco nell' isola di Calipso* (1797); eight ballets, including the once-popular *Cendrillon* (1822); and over 60 guitar pieces and studies.

Sorabji, Kaikhosru Shapurji (1892–1988)

Composer of Spanish-Sicilian and Parsi heritage who lived in England for much of his long life. Initially influenced by **Ravel**, **Busoni**, and **Szymanowski**, he started writing piano works that by the mid-1920s were unparalleled in their complexity and length. After the early 1930s he stopped playing his works in public and ceased to publish them, reckoning that the current musical climate was ill-suited to the appreciation of his particular temperament. But despite the fearsome reputation of his music, much of it is in fact accessible and very beautiful, especially his various **nocturnes** inspired by Sicily and Persia (such as *Villa Tasca* and *Djami*).

Opus clavicembalisticum, which Sorabji performed in Glasgow in 1930, lasts for over three hours and includes a **passacaglia** with 81 variations.

spinet

17th-century domestic keyboard instrument. It has a laterally tapered case with a single manual (keyboard) of up to a three-and-a-half octave range, having a plucking action and single strings. It was the precursor of the **harpsichord**.

Spohr, Ludwig (1784–1859)

German violinist and composer who travelled throughout Europe as a soloist and leader of orchestras; his music includes 15 violin concertos, chamber music, and nine symphonies. Spohr's music was widely performed during the 19th century, but today few of his works are played regularly. In 1813 and 1814 he wrote two of his most popular pieces, the nonet and octet; after producing his opera *Faust* in Prague, he travelled in Italy (1816–17) and then became conductor at the Frankfurt opera. He became court music director at Kassel in 1822 but was pensioned off against his will in 1857.

Spontini, Gaspare (Luigi Pacifico) (1774–1851)

Italian composer who produced several operas in Italy but had little success until 1807, when he produced *La vestale* in Paris. In 1820 he went to Berlin; his greatest success there was the opera *Agnes von Hohenstaufen* (1837). In recent years Spontini's operas have enjoyed a limited revival, with performances of *Fernand Cortez, Agnes von Hohenstaufen,* and *Olympie.*

> Spontini was hindered throughout his career by his quarrelsome personality, which led to his dismissal on more than one occasion.

Stamitz (lived 18th–early 19th centuries)

Bohemian family of musicians including:

- *Johann Wenzel Anton* (1717–1757), violinist and composer. Under his direction the Mannheim court orchestra became the most famous in Europe, called by Charles Burney 'an army of generals'. He was the founder of the Mannheim school of symphonists, which had a profound influence on **Mozart's** instrumental style. His works include 74 symphonies (58 extant), concertos, and chamber music.
- *Carl* (1745–1801), son and pupil of Johann, appeared as a virtuoso on the violin. His works include the operas *Der verliebte Vormund* (1787) and *Dardanus* (1800), and about 80 symphonies and sinfonies concertantes.
- *Anton* (1750–before 1809), son and pupil of Johann, wrote 12 symphonies, concertos for violin, viola, flute, and oboe, as well as chamber music.

Stanford, Charles Villiers (1852–1924)

Irish composer and teacher whose academicism resulted in the formal sterility of many otherwise interesting works by his pupils **Vaughan Williams**, **Holst**, and **Bridge**. Despite this, he has been described as a leading figure in the 19th-century renaissance of British music.

Stanley, John (1713–1786)

English composer and organist whose works, which include organ voluntaries and concertos for strings, influenced **Handel**. He succeeded **Boyce** as Master of the King's Musick, 1779. He was blind from the age of two, but later held various organist's appointments in London. In 1759 he helped continue Handel's oratorio concerts.

staff or stave
The five-line grid, reading from left to right, on which music is notated. The **pitch** range of the staff is indicated by a sign called a clef. **See also:** *clef.*

Stenhammar, (Karl) Wilhelm (Eugen) (1871–1927)
Swedish composer whose song *Sverige* made him a national hero. In other works, the influences of **Brahms** and **Wagner** are noticeable; he wrote the opera *Tirfing* (1898), incidental music to plays including Strindberg's *Ett römspel*, two symphonies (1903, 1915), serenade in F major for orchestra, and six string quartets (1894–1909). He was conductor of the royal orchestra at Stockholm.

Stevens, Bernard (1916–1983)
English composer who refused to write down to the masses with whom he wished to communicate. His *Symphony of Liberation* (1946) won a competition organized by the *Daily Express*; he was not, however, vigorously promoted as a result of this, partly because he was a committed socialist who often wrote in a twelve-tone idiom. He served in the army (1940–46) and was appointed professor of composition at the Royal College of Music in 1948. His pupils include Michael **Finnissy**, who has performed Stevens's piano works.

Stevenson, Ronald (1928–)
English composer and pianist resident in Scotland allied to the likes of **Alkan** and **Sorabji**. His first piano concerto, *Triptych* (1960), is based on themes from **Busoni's** *Doktor Faust*. His *Passacaglia on DSCH*, an 80-minute work for piano dedicated to **Shostakovich** (and based on his name), was championed by John Ogdon.

stile rappresentativo
(Italian 'representative style') Vocal style of declamatory, recitative-like dramatic music, which in the early 17th century tried to imitate human speech as closely as possible and thus endeavoured to represent dramatic action in a naturalistic way.

Stockhausen, Karlheinz (1928–)
German composer of initially avant-garde then eccentrically self-absorbed music. He has explored new musical sounds and compositional techniques since the 1950s. His major works include *Gesang der Jünglinge* (1956),

Kontakte (1960), and *Momente* (1960s). Since 1977 all his works have been part of *LICHT*, a cycle of seven 'operas' intended for performance on each evening of a week. He studied in Paris with **Messiaen** and also learned from the example of **Webern**, whose controlled brand of serialism inspired Stockhausen's brief venture into 'integral' serialism (in which all elements – including pitch, duration, and dynamics – are controlled by serial considerations). From 1953 he worked intensively at Cologne Radio's **electronic music** studio, influencing contemporaries such as **Berio** and **Boulez**. During the 1950s and 60s he was perhaps the most enterprising composer creating electronic music. In the later 1960s he experimented with a closely-knit group of intuitive performers, with works such as *From the Seven Days* (1968), which comprise a series of texts. He then reverted to traditional forms of notation in the early 1970s with the widely admired *Mantra* for two piano and electronics. His subsequent works all display an increasing interest in melody.

> ❝ What is modern today will be
> tradition tomorrow. ❞
>
> **Stockhausen**, *Notes on Telemusik*

Storace, Stephen (1762–1796)

English composer who wrote operas in Italian and English, including the Mozart-influenced *Gli equivoci* (1786) and the successful *The Pirates* (1792). After study in Naples, and a visit to Vienna, he returned to London with his sister, the soprano Anna Storace, and became composer to Sheridan's company at the Drury Lane Theatre.

Stradella, Alessandro (1644–1682)

Italian composer, singer, and violinist who taught singing in Venice, and wrote operas and oratorios. Of noble birth, he was probably educated privately. He never held any official posts, and most of what is known of his career seems to be based on legend rather than fact. In Flotow's opera *Alessandro Stradella* (1844), a composer avoids being murdered by a pair of bandits by singing to them of mercy.

Stradella had numerous love affairs, the last of which probably led to his assasination.

Strauss (lived 19th–early 20th centuries)

Austrian family of musicians including:

- *Johann (Baptist)* (1804–1849) wrote dances, especially waltzes, which had by that time become fashionable. By 1837 he had toured Europe. He added the quadrille to the music of the Viennese ballrooms, having picked it up in Paris, and made a great hit with the *Radetzky Marsch*.

- The most famous, *Johann* (1825–1899), son of Johann Baptist, was not allowed to follow his father's profession, and studied music secretly. In 1844 he appeared as conductor in the Heitzing suburb, and his father capitulated. After his father's death he amalgamated both their orchestras, toured in Austria, Poland, and Germany and in 1855–65 visited St Petersburg. In 1863 he became conductor of the court balls. In 1871 his first operetta had been produced at the Theater am der Wien and in 1874 he had his most enduring stage success with *Die Fledermaus*. His greatest popularity was achieved with such waltzes as *Tales from the Vienna Woods* (1868), *The Blue Danube* (1867), *Wiener Blut* (1870), *Roses from the South* (1880), *Frühlingsstimmen* (1883) and the *Emperor Waltz* (1885).

- *Josef* (1827–1870), another son of Johann Baptist, became an architect, but then formed his own band and wrote 283 dances for it. He died after a visit to Warsaw, where he injured his hand in a fall on the platform at his last concert.

- *Eduard* (1835–1916), composer and conductor, third son of Johann Baptist, also wrote dance music.

Strauss, Richard (Georg) (1864–1949)

German composer and conductor. He followed the German **Romantic** tradition but had a strongly personal style, characterized by his bold, colourful orchestration. Strauss began to compose at the age of six and at ten two works – the *Festival March* and the serenade for wind instruments – were published. In 1885 Strauss became conductor at Meiningen; his first truly characteristic piece, the First Horn Concerto, was written at this time. In 1889 he became assistant conductor at the Weimar Court Opera and gained his first major success with the tone poem *Don Juan*; the famous exuberant opening of the work seems to announce the young composer in all his confidence and technical assurance. Between 1895 and 1900 he composed some of his most popular and enduring tone poems, each one superbly orchestrated and with its own distinctive character: *Till Eulenspiegel* (1894–95), *Also sprach*

Zarathustra (1895–96), *Don Quixote* (1896–97), and *Ein Heldenleben* (1897–98). In 1905 his opera *Salome* was premiered at Dresden; in London it was to have trouble with the censors for its lurid treatment of a Biblical subject. Strauss further collaborated with librettist Hofmannstahl in *Elektra*, in which he was considered wild and dissonant. More general favour was found with *Der Rosenkavalier* (1911), a comedy set in 18th-century Vienna, with anachronistic waltzes. In 1919 his masterpiece, *Die Frau ohne Schatten*, was produced in Vienna; the rich allusiveness of the score was a fitting farewell to a world which had all but disappeared in World War I. After Hofmannsthal's death Strauss worked with Stefan Zweig on *Die schweigsame Frau*, which was withdrawn after its first production at Dresden in 1935 because Zweig, as a Jew, was boycotted by the Nazi party. Strauss resigned his presidency of the Reichs-Musikkammer and was under a cloud for a time, but had long been too important a figure in German music to be ignored. He wrote music for the 1936 Berlin Olympic Games and composed four further operas during the Nazi regime.

> ❦ I may not be a first-rate composer, but I am a first-rate second-rate composer! ❞
>
> **Strauss**, quoted in Del Mar, *Richard Strauss*

Stravinsky, Igor Fyodorovich (1882–1971)

Russian composer, later of French and US nationality. Along with **Schoenberg**, the most important composer of the early 20th century; he determined more than any other the course of music for the following 50 years. His father, Fyodor, was the leading bass at the St Petersburg Imperial Opera. In 1903 he met **Rimsky-Korsakov** and played him his early compositions, but did not become his pupil until 1907. The performance of the *Fantastic Scherzo* in 1909 attracted the attention of the impresario Diaghilev, who commissioned Stravinsky to write *The Firebird* for his Ballets Russes. It was produced in Paris in 1910, and Stravinsky began to be known in western Europe. *Petruskha* followed in 1911 and *The Rite of Spring* in 1913; both were produced in Paris, where the latter provoked a riot of protest and fanatical partisanship. *The Rite of Spring* established Stravinsky, with Schoenberg, as the leading avant-garde composer of his time. In the inter-war years many of his works were written in the spirit of **Neo-Classicism**, beginning most clearly with the ballet *Pulcinella* (1920), based on pieces attributed to **Pergolesi**, and continuing with the Concerto for piano and wind (1925). He settled in Hollywood in 1939, and the following year he conducted the Chicago Symphony Orchestra in his Symphony in C (1938–40). A meeting with Auden led to the summation of the Neo-Classical phase; the Hogarth-inspired opera *The Rake's Progress*, premiered at Venice in 1951. Stravinsky had meanwhile met the conductor Robert Craft and under his influence began to explore the music of the Second Viennese School but only after its chief proponent, Schoenberg, had died. The ballet *Agon* and the religious vocal works *Canticum sacrum* (1955) and *Threni* combine serial methods with Stravinsky's creative generosity. Later music was increasingly sparse, however. His *Requiem Canticles* of 1966 was performed at his funeral in Venice, a city he regarded as his spiritual home.

> ❝ The greatest crisis of my life as a composer was the loss of Russia, and its language not only of music but of words. ❞
>
> **Stravinsky**, *Themes and Conclusions*

suite
In **Baroque music**, a set of contrasting instrumental pieces based on **dance** forms, known by their French names as allemande, bourrée, gavotte, gigue, and so on. The term refers in more recent usage to a concert arrangement of set pieces from an extended **ballet** or stage composition, such as **Tchaikovsky's** *Nutcracker Suite*.

Suk, Josef (1874–1935)
Czech composer who studied in Prague with **Dvořák**, whose daughter he married in 1898, and who influenced his early works. Later, he developed a more modern style of his own. The *Asrael* symphony (1906) refers to the deaths of both his teacher and his wife. In 1892 he formed the Bohemian String Quartet, playing second violin. Along with Janáček, he was the most original Czech composer of the early 20th century.

Sullivan, Arthur Seymour (1842–1900)
English composer famous for operettas written in collaboration with the librettist William Gilbert, including *HMS Pinafore* (1878), *The Pirates of Penzance* (1879), and *The Mikado* (1885). Their partnership broke down in

1896. Sullivan also composed serious instrumental, choral, and operatic works – for example, the opera *Ivanhoe* (1890) – that he valued more highly than the operettas.

Svendsen, Johan (Severin) (1840–1911)
After a career as a virtuoso violinist, he took up composing. He was a friend of **Grieg**, who admired his work. He wrote two symphonies and other orchestral works, as well as chamber and vocal works, many of which incorporate Norwegian folk music. He was the greatest Scandinavian conductor of his period.

Sweelinck, Jan Pieterszoon (1562–1621)
Dutch composer who was the first to write an independent part for the pedals in **organ** works, a technique which reached its peak in **Bach's** organ compositions. He studied under his father, Pieter Sweelinck, and when he died Jan succeeded to his post of organist at the Old Church at Amsterdam. His music was influenced by the English virginalists and the Venetian organists. His works include three books of *Psalms of David* (1604–14), *Cantiones sacrae*, organ fantasias, toccatas, and chorale variations.

symphonic poem
Term originated by **Liszt** for his 13 one-movement orchestral works that interpret a story from literature or history, also used by many other composers. Richard **Strauss** preferred the term 'tone poem'.

symphony
Abstract musical composition for orchestra, traditionally in four separate but closely related movements. It developed from the smaller **sonata form**, the Italian overture, and the concerto grosso. **Haydn** established the mature form of the symphony, written in slow, minuet, and allegro movements. **Mozart** and **Beethoven** (who replaced the minuet with the scherzo) expanded the form, which has since been modified and dramatized as quasi **programme** music.

Szymanowski, Karol Maciej (1882–1937)
The most important Polish composer after **Chopin**. He wrote piano music, violin concertos, four symphonies, a *Stabat Mater*

Szymanowski is regarded as the founder of 20th-century Polish music.

(1926), and the opera *King Roger* (1918–24), in a richly glamorous idiom drawing on national folklore, German **Romanticism**, and French and Russian modernist styles. He learnt music privately as a child, and from 1906, after a spell at the Warsaw Conservatory, he lived in Berlin for a time and promoted Polish music. He created his own lyrical and exotic vision, particularly in the Third Symphony *Song of the Night.* More abstract works such as his piano sonatas embrace modern techniques within traditional forms. As an aristocrat he lost his property and was imprisoned in Russia, but escaped to Warsaw, where in 1926 he became direc-

Szymanowski *The most important Polish composer after Chopin, Karol Szymanowski.*

tor of the State Conservatory. His last years were marred by tuberculosis.

tablature
Old form of notation indicating finger positions on a graph representing the fingerboard and strings, and therefore specific only to the instrument to which it applies, for example, the lute or guitar.

Tailleferre, Germaine (1892–1983)
The only female member of 'Les Six'. Her works include the opera *Il était un petit navire* (1951), the ballet *Le marchand d'oiseaux* (1923), and several instrumental works.

Takemitsu, Toru (1930–1996)
The first Japanese composer to be known in the West, he was mainly self-taught and initially influenced by **Schoenberg, Messiaen,** and *musique concrète*. By the mid-1970s he had evolved an evocative, fragrant, Neo-Impressionist language that endeared his music to many disillusioned with mainstream modernism. Works of this ilk include *The Flock Descends to the Pentagonal Garden* (1985) and *Visions* for orchestra (1990).

Tallis, Thomas (*c.* 1505–1585)
With **Byrd**, the leading composer of the English Renaissance. A master of **counterpoint**, his works include *Tallis's Canon* ('Glory to thee my God this night') (1567), the **antiphonal** *Spem in alium non habui* (*c.* 1573) for 40 voices in various groupings, and a collection of 34 motets, *Cantiones sacrae* (1575), of which 16 are by Tallis and 18 by Byrd. Tallis held a post at Waltham Abbey before its dissolution in 1540, and in about 1543 became a Gentleman of the Chapel Royal. He was one of the earliest composers to write for the Anglican **liturgy** (1547–53) but some of his most ornate music, including the Mass *Puer natus est nobis*, dates from the brief Catholic reign of Mary Tudor (1553–58). He and Byrd were joint organists at the Chapel Royal. In his last years he and his wife Joan, whom he had married about 1552, lived at their own house at Greenwich.

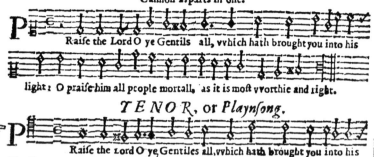

Tallis *Musical score of one of Thomas Tallis's works, c. 1700.*

Taneyev, Sergey Ivanovich (1856–1915)

Russian composer and teacher of **Rachmaninov**, **Skryabin**, **Medtner**, and many other Russian composers. He studied with **Tchaikovsky** and, after touring as a pianist, became director of the Moscow Conservatory in 1885. His works include the operatic trilogy *The Oresteia* (1895), cantatas and unaccompanied choral works, four symphonies, six string quartets and other chamber music, and about 50 songs; they are subtly highly structured and reflect his admiration for **Beethoven**. In 1875 he gave Moscow the first performance of Tchaikovsky's First Piano Concerto. He later concentrated on teaching **counterpoint** and **fugue**.

Tartini, Giuseppe (1692–1770)

Italian composer and leading exponent of violin technique. In 1728 he founded a school of violin playing in Padua.

Tartini composed numerous sonatas and concertos for strings, including the *Devil's Trill* sonata.

Tavener, John Kenneth (1944–)

English composer who embraced rock idioms and Celtic trappings, before becoming an adherent of the Orthodox faith. His undemanding music includes the dramatic cantata *The Whale* (1968) and *The Protecting Veil* (1987) for cello and strings, which became a best-selling recording.

Taverner, John (*c.* 1495–1545)

English organist and composer who wrote masses and motets in **polyphonic** style, showing great contrapuntal skill, but as a Protestant later renounced his art.

Taverner was imprisoned in 1528 for heresy, and, as an agent of Thomas Cromwell, assisted in the dissolution of the monasteries.

Tchaikovsky, Pyotr Ilich (1840–1893)

Russian composer whose strong sense of melody, personal expression, and brilliant orchestration are clear throughout his six symphonies, three piano concertos, a violin concerto, operas (including *Eugene Onegin* of 1879), ballets (including *The Nutcracker*, 1891–92), and chamber and vocal music. As a young man, he met **Balakirev**, and briefly became involved with the nationalist movement in music. He later successfully united western European influences with native Russian fervour and emotion, and was the first Russian composer to establish a reputation with Western audiences. In 1868 his fresh and spontaneous First Symphony *Winter Daydreams* was performed in Moscow; the Second Symphony, a distinctly nationalist work, was heard 1873. In 1876 he began a correspondence with Nadezhda von Meck, who admired his work and made him an allowance freeing him from financial anxiety; they never met. His first important ballet, *Swan Lake*, was premiered in 1877 at the Bolshoy. Also in 1877 he married Antonina Milyukova; but he was an undeclared homosexual and left her less than a month after the wedding, on the verge of mental collapse.

Tchaikovsky *Russian composer Pyotr Ilich Tchaikovsky.*

The first of his universally popular symphonies, the fourth in F minor, was premiered in 1878; its insistent 'fate' motive heralds a trilogy of works in which the tension between life affirmation and self-annihilation is dominant. His most brilliant and least introverted orchestral work, the Violin Concerto in D, was given at Vienna in 1881 and seven years later he composed the most powerful and fully integrated of the symphonies, the fifth in E minor. He completed the Sixth Symphony (*Pathétique*) in 1893; it was first performed at St Petersburg in October. Nine days later Tchaikovsky was dead; the cause of death is usually given as cholera, although it has recently been suggested that he took poison at the decree of a secret court of honour instituted to avert a scandal following allegations of a liaison between him and an aristocrat's nephew.

Tcherepnin, (also **Cherepnin**)

Russian family of musicians, many of whom have lived in France and the USA.

- *Nikolay Nikolayevich* (1873–1945) studied with **Rimsky-Korsakov** and wrote ballets for Diaghilev, including *Armida's Pavilion* (1908). Having appeared as a pianist, in 1901 he became conductor of the Believe Symphony Concerts. In 1908 he joined Diaghilev and conducted Russian opera and ballet in Paris and elsewhere, remaining with the Ballets Russes until 1914, when he returned to Petrograd, to become director of the Conservatory at Tiflis in 1918.

- His son *Aleksandr (Nikolayevich)* (1899–1977) wrote ballets and orchestral and chamber pieces in a **Neo-Classical** style. He was born at St Petersburg and studied under his father; he appeared as a boy pianist and began to publish his works, but in 1921 settled in Paris where he later taught. He settled in the USA in 1950.

- His son *Ivan* became a well-known composer, often employing electronic media.

Te Deum

A hymn based on the text *Te Deum laudamus* (Latin 'We praise Thee, O God'), possibly originating in the writings of St Ambrose or Bishop Nicetius of Remesiana. In the Roman Catholic **liturgy** it is sung at matins on feast days and on Sundays. In addition to its plainsong variant, composers including **Palestrina**, **Handel**, and **Berlioz** have set the *Te Deum*.

Telemann, Georg Philipp (1681–1767)

The best-known German composer of his time with a contemporary reputation much greater than J S **Bach's**. His prolific output of concertos for both new and old instruments, including violin, viola da gamba, recorder, flute, and bassoon, represents a fastidious investigation into the tonal resources of the Baroque orchestra, research which was noted by Bach. In Leipzig he founded a student *Collegium musicum* and was appointed organist of the New Church (St Matthew's) in 1704. In the service of the court at Eisenach (1708–12) he made the acquaintance of Bach in nearby Weimar. In 1721 he was appointed Cantor of the Johanneum in Hamburg, where he stayed for the rest of his life. He is famed for his huge output, although some of his instrumental music can sound routine and written to order.

> ❝ I have always aimed at facility. Music ought not to be an effort. ❞
>
> **Telemann**, quoted in Headington, *The Bodley Head History of Western Music*

tempo

(Italian 'time') The speed at which a piece should be played. One way of indicating tempo is by a *metronome marking*, which states the number of beats per minute; for example, 'crotchet = 60' means that there should be 60 crotchet beats to the minute. Before the invention of an accurate metronome, tempo was indicated by Italian words such as *allegro* (lively) or *lento* (slow). Rather than give precise metronome markings, composers use these Italian terms to describe general speed.

Thomas, (Charles Louis) Ambroise (1811–1896)

French composer. He wrote operas to please contemporary bourgeois Parisian taste; his most successful works emulate **Gounod**; they include *Mignon* (1866) and *Hamlet* (1868). He also wrote numerous cantatas, part songs, and choral pieces.

Thomson, Virgil (1896–1989)

US composer whose music is notable for a refined absence of emotion. That and his criticism for trenchant matter-of-factness were both at odds with the prevailing US musical culture. He is best known for his opera *Four Saints in Three Acts* (1927–33) to a libretto by Gertrude Stein, and the film scores *The Plow That Broke the Plains* (1936) and *Louisiana Story* (1948). The most important influences on his music were **Satie** and the **Neo-Classical Stravinsky**.

> ❝ The way to write American music is simple: all you have to do is be an American and then write any kind of music you wish. ❞
>
> **Thomson**, quoted in Machlis, *Introduction to Contemporary Music*

tie
A slur or curved line used in **notation** connecting two notes of the same **pitch** (or a group of such notes in a chord), usually over a bar line. It indicates that the second note is not to be reiterated, but played continuously as one long note.

timbre
(French 'tone') The tone colour, or quality of tone, of a particular sound. Different instruments playing a note at the same pitch have different sound qualities, and it is the timbre that enables the listener to distinguish the sound of, for example, a trumpet from that of a **violin**.

time signature
In musical notation, a numerical sign placed after the clef and key signature indicating the **metre** of the music. Consisting usually of two numbers, the upper number represents the number of beats in a bar, the lower number the type of beat, expressed as a fraction of a unit (semibreve). Hence 3/4 is three crotchet beats to the bar and 6/8 is two beats each of three quavers; alla breve represents 2/2, or two minim beats to a bar; C (common time) represents 4/4, four crotchet beats to a bar.

Tippett, Michael (Kemp) (1905–1998)
With **Britten**, he was the foremost English composer of his generation. His works include the operas *The Midsummer Marriage* (1952), *The Knot Garden* (1970), and *New Year* (1989); four symphonies; *Songs for Ariel*

(1962); and choral music including *The Mask of Time* (1982). His first major success came with the Concerto for Double String Orchestra (1939). Tippett's early lyrical exuberance reached its peak in the opera *The Midsummer Marriage* and the

During the war Tippett was a conscientious objector; his oratorio *A Child of our Time* (1941) was written in response to the persecution of the Jews by the Nazis.

associated piano concerto (1953–55). A sparer sound was achieved with the opera *King Priam* (1962), although by the time of *The Knot Garden* some reconciliation between his two earlier styles was achieved. His most significant later works are the Triple Concerto and the oratorio *The Mask of Time*. Tippett was highly self-critical, so that his works appeared in slow succession, but showed concentrated craftsmanship and originality.

toccata
(Italian 'touched') A display piece for keyboard instruments, especially the **organ**. Many such pieces were written to display finger technique, in particular.

Tomášek, Václav Jan Křtitel (1774–1850)
Bohemian composer whose pioneering 13 volumes of short lyric piano pieces were popular all over Europe and directly influenced **Schubert**. Tomášek's memoirs provide much information about the musical life of his time. He often visited Vienna, where he met **Beethoven** in 1814, and he played his settings of Goethe's poems to the poet at Eger. His other works include the opera *Seraphine* (1811), three Masses and other church music, three symphonies, two piano concertos (1805–06), and much chamber music.

tonality
In music, a sense of key orientation in relation to form, for example the step pattern of a dance as expressed by corresponding changes of direction from a tonic or 'home' key to a related key. Most popular and folk music worldwide recognizes an underlying tonality or reference pitch against which the movement of a melody can be clearly heard. The opposite of tonality is atonality.

Toovey, Andrew (1962–)
English composer of sometimes extremely violent, physical works. He studied with **Harvey**, and with **Feldman** at Dartington. He was director of

the ensemble Ixion from 1987, giving vital performances of music by Xenakis and **Cage**. He wrote several works connected with the poet Artaud, and has also been fascinated by the work of painters such as Guston and Riley. His works are generally reviled by the British establishment, a fact of which the composer is proud.

Torke, Michael (1961–)
US composer of lightweight, eclectic music incorporating **minimalism**, Neo-Romanticism, and popular idioms. He studied at the Eastman School in New York and with Jacob Druckman at Yale University. His works include the opera *The Directions* (1986) and ballet *Black and White* (1988), *Ecstatic Orange* (1986) and *Green* (1986) for orchestra, and *Adjustable Wrench* for chamber ensemble (1987).

transcription
The arrangement or reworking of a piece for a different combination of instruments or in a different style. **Liszt**, **Rachmaninov**, and **Godowsky** were famous for their transcriptions for piano.

transposition
The performance in a different key from that indicated in the printed music, or the appearance of a theme or motif in an alternative key. A transposing instrument is one for which music is usually written in one key and played in another, for example an instrument in B♭, such as a clarinet, sounds a tone lower than written.

trope
An interpolation into liturgical chants dating from the 8th or 9th centuries, probably of Byzantine origin. Tropes were at first purely musical **ornamentations** sung on syllables of certain words, especially 'Alleluia', but later they became so important that special words were written for them.

troubadour
Poet-musician of southern France in the 12th–13th centuries. The troubadours originated a type of lyric poetry devoted to themes of courtly love, the idealization of women, and to glorifying the chivalric ideals of the period. The *trouvères* were a similar class of poet-musicians active during the same period in northern France and England.

tuning

The adjusting of **pitch** in instruments to the correct **intonation**. For example, orchestral instruments tune to 'concert pitch', where A4 = 440Hz. Keyboard instruments are more difficult to adjust, often requiring a professional tuner.

Turina, Joaquín (1882–1949)

Composer who employed local Spanish colour in brilliant works such as *Danzas fantásticas* (1920). He also devoted much time to teaching and wrote a treatise expounding his aims, *Enciclopedia abreviada de música* (1917). Other works include the opera *Jardin de oriente* (1923), the *Sinfonía sevillana* (1920) and *Ritmos* for orchestra, and piano music.

Tye, Christopher (*c.* 1505–*c.* 1572)

English composer and poet whose Mass *The Western Wind* is regularly performed today. He also wrote a good deal of verse in his later years. He became a lay clerk at King's College, Cambridge, in 1537, and later held a post in Ely Cathedral before accepting the living at Doddington-cum-Marche in the Isle of Ely.

Ullmann, Viktor (1898–1944)

Austro-Hungarian composer imprisoned in Theresienstadt concentration camp, where he wrote a one-act opera, *Der Kaiser von Atlantis* (1943), about a tyrannical monarch who outlaws death; it was first performed at Amsterdam in 1975. In October 1944 he was transferred to Auschwitz, where he died. Other works include Variations and double fugue on a theme by **Schoenberg** (with whom he studied), two string quartets, and several piano sonatas.

unison

Music in which all musicians play or sing the same notes without **harmony**. Strictly, unison implies that all musicians sound the same **pitch** in the same octave, but it is also usual for the same pitch doubled at the octave.

Ustvolskaya, Galina (1919–)

Russian composer whose astringent music influenced **Shostakovich**, who proposed to her twice, but was turned down on both occasions. Employing the minimum of means, her music employs serialism and Russian traditions, but ultimately her style is completely independent. Her music is often religious in content and is often scored for unconventional chamber forces. She considers, however, that all of her music is symphonic, and dislikes being described as a 'woman composer'. After years of obscurity, her music is now widely heard.

Varèse, Edgard Victor Achille Charles (1883–1965)

Radical French composer who lived in the USA from 1916. There, he co-founded the New Symphony Orchestra in 1919 with harpist Carlos Salzédo to promote modern and pre-Classical music. Renouncing the values of tonality, he discovered new resources of expression in the percussion sonorities of *Ionisation* (1929–31), the swooping sound of two theremins in *Hyperprism* (1933–4), and the combination of taped and live instrumental sounds in *Déserts* (1950–54).

> ❦ There is no avant-garde: only
> some people a bit behind. ❦
>
> **Varèse**, attributed remark

variation

A form based on the repetition of a theme, each new version being elaborated or treated in a different manner. The theme is usually recognizable; it may be an original composition, a popular tune or – as a gesture of respect – the work of a fellow composer, such as **Brahms's** *Variations on a Theme by Haydn* (1873).

Vaughan Williams, Ralph (1872–1958)

English composer who evoked his native countryside – often by the use of folk themes – in works such as the orchestral *Fantasia on a Theme by Thomas Tallis* (1910), *The Lark Ascending*, and nine symphonies (1909–57). The son of a clergyman, in 1904 he joined the Folksong Society and studied old country tunes, collecting some in Norfolk. His first characteristic compositions, the *Wasps* overture, song cycle *On Wenlock Edge*, and *A Sea Symphony* (the first to employ a chorus throughout), appeared in 1909. His two best-known symphonies, numbers 4 and 5, were composed between 1934 and 1943; the angularity and fierce accents of the earlier work lead to the repose and serenity of its companion.

Although his compositions are usually classified as pastoral, he was conscious of contemporary musical developments and often employed a degree of dissonance in his later works.

Verdi, Giuseppe Fortunino Francesco (1813–1901)

Italian composer who took his native operatic style to new heights of dramatic expression. His music is essentially Italian in character, and owes little to **Wagnerian** influences, although in his late works (*Otello* and *Falstaff*) he developed a more continuous, orchestrally dominated texture. During the mid-1800s Verdi became a symbol of Italy's fight for independence from Austria, frequently finding himself in conflict with the Austrian authorities; they felt that his operas encouraged Italian nationalism.

The son of a grocer, in 1831 Verdi was sent to Milan with a scholarship, but was rejected over entrance age and studied privately instead. Meanwhile he had composed his first opera, *Oberto*, produced at La Scala in 1839. A second (comic) opera, *Un giorno di regno* 1840, was a failure but *Nabucco*, produced at La Scala in 1842, had a great success; the chorus of the Hebrew slaves was later to provide a rallying cry for the disaffected Italian people in their quest for freedom. He then went from strength to strength and his fame spread beyond Milan: *Ernani* was produced at Venice in 1844, *I due foscari* in Rome (1844), *Alzira* at Naples (1845), and *Macbeth* at Florence (1847). *Rigoletto*, the first of his masterpieces, was premiered at Venice in 1851; together with *Il trovatore* and *La traviata* (1853), it marks Verdi's emergence as a supreme melodist. At the same time he shows refinement of characterization and a radically improved awareness of orchestral timbre. The potentially sensitive subject of *Don Carlos*, dealing with Spanish oppression of the Netherlands, was performed in Paris in 1867; it is Verdi's most sombre and richly varied opera. *Aida* was performed at Cairo in 1871 and the Requiem followed three years later. *Otello* was produced at La Scala in 1887, and with its musical and dramatic unity marked Verdi's greatest public success. After a six-year break from composition, *Falstaff* was performed at the same theatre in 1893, though its unique subtlety was at first lost on audiences.

Verdi is the artistic successor of **Donizetti** and **Bellini**, but shows a far greater wealth of passionate feeling, craftsmanship, and power of enlightening pathos or tragedy. His lyricism was constant, but his last works show also a rare spirituality, a refinement, and a religious consciousness which place him among the foremost composers in the field of sacred, as well as of operatic, music.

VERDI'S OPERAS

- *Oberto, Conte di San Bonifacio* (1839)
- *Un giorno di regno* (1840)
- *Nabucco* (1842)
- *I Lombardi alla prima crociata* (1843)
- *Ernani* (1844)
- *I due Foscari* (1844)
- *Giovanna d'Arco* (1845)
- *Alzira* (1845)
- *Attila* (1845–46)
- *Macbeth* (1847)
- *I masnadieri* (1846–47)
- *Jérusalem* (French revised version of *I Lombardi*, 1847)
- *Il corsaro* (1848)
- *La battaglia di Legnano* (1849)
- *Luisa Miller* (1849)
- *Stiffelio* (1850)
- *Rigoletto* (1851)
- *Il trovatore* (1853)
- *La traviata* (1853)
- *Les Vêpres siciliennes* (1855)
- *Simon Boccanegra* (1857, revised 1881)
- *Aroldo* (revision of *Stiffelio*, 1857)
- *Un ballo in maschera* (1859)
- *La forza del destino* (1862)
- *Don Carlos* (1867, revised 1884)
- *Aida* (1871)
- *Otello* (1887)
- *Falstaff* (1893)

vespers
The seventh of the eight canonical hours in the Catholic church; the seventh Roman Catholic office (or non-Eucharistic service) of the day. It is also used by the Anglican Church to refer to evensong. **Monteverdi** and **Mozart** composed notable settings for this service.

vibrato
A rapid fluctuation of pitch for dynamic and expressive effect. It is distinct from a tremolo, which is a fluctuation in intensity of the same note.

Victoria, Tomás Luis de (1548–1611)
Spanish composer who wrote only sacred music, including 20 Masses, 52 motets, and many other liturgical pieces, and is noted for his expressive settings of the Mass (for example, *Ave regina caelorum*) and other Latin texts.

Vieuxtemps, Henry (1820–1881)
Belgian violinist and composer admired for his virtuosity in playing his own works and those of other composers. He is remembered for his seven violin concertos and several short pieces for violin. In 1828 he performed in Paris, and in 1833 he went on tour in Germany and Austria. In 1834 he first visited London, where he met **Paganini**, and the following year he studied composition with **Reicha** in Paris. He later taught at St Petersburg and Brussels.

Villa-Lobos, Heitor (1887–1959)
Brazilian composer who absorbed Russian and French influences to create Neo-Baroque works in Brazilian style, using native colours and rhythms. His gift for melody is displayed in the *Chôros* (serenades) series (1920–29), and the series of nine *Bachianas brasileiras* (1930–45), composed in the manner of **Bach**. His huge output includes guitar and piano solos, chamber

It is said that Villa-Lobos wrote so much music that sometimes he could not recognize his own work.

music, choral works, film scores, operas, and 12 symphonies. In 1929 he published a book on Brazilian folk music, *Alma de Brasil*.

viol
A Renaissance family of bowed six-stringed musical instruments with flat backs, fretted fingerboards, and narrow shoulders that flourished particularly in England about 1540–1700, before their role was taken by the violins. Normally performing as an ensemble or 'consort', their repertoire is a development of madrigal style with idiomatic decoration. The three principal instruments, treble, tenor, and bass, are played upright, resting on the leg (da gamba), and produce a transparent, harmonious sound.

violin family

Family of bowed stringed instruments developed in 17th-century Italy, which eventually superseded the viols and formed the basis of the modern **orchestra**. There are four instruments: violin, viola, cello (or violoncello), and the double bass, which is descended from the bass viol. The *violin* is the smallest and highest pitched of the violin family. The instrument was perfected in Italy by a group of makers including Amati, Stradivari, and Guarneri working in Cremona around 1670–1710. Today's violin has not changed in form since that time, but in the late 18th century aspects of the design were modified to produce a bigger sound and greater projection for the concert hall and to allow for evolving virtuoso expression. The *viola* is a bowed, stringed musical instrument, tuned one fifth lower than a violin. With its dark, vibrant tone, it is often used for music of reflective character. The *cello* is a common abbreviation for violoncello; it is tuned an octave lower than the viola. Its solo potential was recognized by **Bach**, and a concerto repertoire extends from Haydn to **Ligeti**.

violin family *The violin.*

Viotti, Giovanni Battista (1755– 1824)
Italian violinist and composer. The most important violinist of his day, encompassing both the earlier Italian tradition of **Corelli** and the beginnings of the 19th-century French Romantic school. He is best known for his 29 violin concertos. During a stay in Paris (1782–92), he was violinist to Marie Antoinette and founded an opera house. He settled in London, but was forced to leave for political reasons in 1798. He later withdrew from music and entered the wine trade.

virginal
Plucked stringed keyboard instrument of the 16th and 17th centuries, often called 'virginals' or 'a pair of virginals' in England, where the term was applied to any quilled keyboard instrument well into the 17th century. The virginal is rectangular or polygonal in shape and is distinguished from the **harpsichord** and **spinet** by its strings, which are set at right angles to the keys, rather than parallel with them.

Vivaldi, Antonio Lucio (1678–1741)
Italian **Baroque** composer and one of the most prolific of his day. He was particularly influential through his concertos, several of which were transcribed by **Bach**. He wrote 23 symphonies; 75 sonatas; over 400 concertos, including *The Four Seasons* (1725) for violin and orchestra; more than 40 operas; and much sacred music. His work was largely neglected until the 1930s.

Born in Venice, he entered the church in 1693 and was ordained priest in 1703 (being commonly known as *il prete rosso*, 'the red [-haired] priest'). He was associated with a girls'

> As a priest, Vivaldi came into conflict with Church authorities for keeping a mistress.

orphanage (1703–40), the Conservatorio dell' Ospedale della Pietà in Venice, for which he wrote oratorios and instrumental music, even sending manuscripts by post during his frequent absences. He toured Europe (1729–33), and returned to Venice in 1739, but his popularity was declining, and two years later he died in poverty in Vienna.

voice
The human voice is produced by forcing air from the lungs through the larynx and making the vocal cords vibrate. The **pitch** of the sound can be

altered by tightening or loosening the muscles of the larynx, and the sound is amplified and modified by the mouth and nasal cavities. There are several categories of singing voice, depending on how high or low the performer sings. Female singers are usually classified as either soprano (the highest voice) or contralto (often shortened to 'alto', the lowest female voice), but sometimes also as mezzo-soprano (a medium-high voice). Boys whose voices have not yet broken sing in a similar range as the female voices, but are referred to as trebles. The main categories of men's voices are countertenor (the higher male voice), tenor, baritone, and bass (the lowest).

COUNTERPOINT VOICE

The term 'voice' is also used to refer to the separate parts of a piece of music – even when they are played rather than sung. It is especially used when talking about the separate lines in **counterpoint**.

Volans, Kevin (1949–)

South African composer whose music combines **minimalist** techniques with native African idioms. The opera *The Man Who Strides the Wind* was performed at the 1993 Almeida Festival, London. He studied with **Kagel** and **Stockhausen** at Cologne. He was composer-in-residence at Princeton University in 1992. His works include *White Man Sleeps* for two harpsichords, viola da gamba, and percussion (1982), and four string quartets: no. 1 *White Man Sleeps* (1986), no. 2 *Hunting: Gathering* (1987), no. 3 *The Songlines* (1988), and no. 4 *The Ramanujan Notebook* (1990).

Wagner, (Wilhelm) Richard (1813–1883)

German composer who revolutionized opera, envisaging it as a wholly new art form in which musical, poetic, and scenic elements should be unified. In 1872 he founded the Festival Theatre in Bayreuth; his masterpiece *The Ring of the Nibelungs*, a sequence of four operas, was first performed there in 1876.

Wagner wrote poems and a tragedy at the age of about 13, and at 14 he heard **Beethoven's** works and tried to imitate them in compositions of his own. After writing two early operas – *Die Hochzeit* and *Die Feen* – he worked as a theatre conductor before going to Paris in January 1839. Although his time in Paris was spent in wretched poverty, he managed to finish *Rienzi* and *Der fliegende Holländer*, the second of which reveals for the first time Wagner's individual voice as a composer. *Tannhäuser* was finished April 1845 and produced in October. The lifelong theme of the conflict between sacred and profane love is most powerfully projected in this opera. More spiritual issues were portrayed in *Lohengrin* (1845–48).

In 1848 when the French Revolution occured, Wagner showed sympathy with liberal ideas and after the revolt at Dresden failed in May 1849 he was forced to escape arrest. He went to Switzerland, where he worked on the libretti and music for the *Ring*. The music of the first scene, set at the bottom of the River Rhine, demonstrates his genius for creating atmosphere. The *Ring* was interrupted for work on *Tristan und Isolde*, written under the influence of Mathilde Wesendonck, the wife of a friend with whom he had

Wagner *German composer who revolutionized opera, Richard Wagner.*

fallen in love. Wagner then went to Venice and later to Lucerne, where *Tristan* was finished in August 1859. Wagner's affair with Cosima von Bülow created a scandal that was exploited by his enemies, and soon after the production of *Tristan* in June 1865, Wagner was obliged to go into exile once more.

Tristan was an immensely influential work extending chromatic **harmony** to new heights. *Tristan's* antithesis is found in *Die Meistersinger von Nürnberg*, a partly autobiographical comedy in which a **Romantic** hero and a profound poet combine to confound their pedant enemies. Wagner planned a festival theatre to be erected by subscription at Bayreuth in Bavaria and the *Ring* was produced 13–17 August 1876, vindicating his genius as a composer and dramatist. The complex musical and moral strands of the *Ring* are brought together in the final opera, *Götterdämmerung*.

In Vienna Wagner was pursued by his creditors and threatened with imprisonment, but was fortuitously invited by Ludwig II of Bavaria to join his court as friend and artistic adviser.

Wagner's creative testament came with *Parsifal* in which his concept of the *Gesamtkunstwerk* ('complete art work') was further refined. By the time of his death Wagner's influence had already spread throughout the artistic world; his belief in a synthesis of all the arts represents the culmination of the Romantic philosophy.

Walton, William Turner (1902–1983)

English composer who, after the age of 16, was self-taught, though he later received advice from **Busoni** and others. He settled in London and was in close touch with the literary Sitwell family; their association led to *Façade*, for reciter and ensemble. Its 1923 premiere provoked uproar. **Hindemith** was the soloist in Walton's first widely successful work, the viola concerto of 1929, and two years later the aggressively mannered cantata *Belshazzar's Feast* was premiered at Leeds. In 1938 he went to the USA to confer with the violinist Jascha Heifetz (1901–1987) about the solo part of the violin concerto; as in the viola concerto and the First Symphony, the best of contemporary continental influences, including **Stravinsky**, **Poulenc**, and **Prokofiev** can be discerned here. A more ruminant, quasi-**Romantic** strain is evident in the post-war works, beginning with the opera *Troilus and Cressida* (1948–54) and continuing with the Cello Concerto.

Weber, Carl Maria Friedrich Ernst von (1786–1826)

German composer who established the **Romantic** school of opera with *Der Freischütz/The Marksman* (1821) and *Euryanthe* (1823). After an unsettled childhood, he succeeded in having his opera *Peter Schmoll und seine Nachbarn* produced at Augsburg in 1803. Weber settled at Stuttgart in 1807, but led a rather dissolute life there and incurred the displeasure of the king, his patron's elder brother. In 1810 he was banished from the kingdom on a trumped-up charge and went to Darmstadt, where he resumed his studies. His brilliant works for clarinet and orchestra (two concertos and a concertina) date from 1811. In 1816 he was appointed conductor of the Dresden court opera, where he did much to establish German opera in the face of the strong opposition. In 1821 his most famous opera, *Der Freischütz*, was produced in Berlin; it was immediately recognized throughout Germany as helping to establish a truly national style. *Euryanthe* followed in Vienna in 1823, and marked a major development with the way in which spoken dialogue, traditional in German opera, was replaced by continuously composed music. In 1824 Covent Garden commissioned an English opera from him, and he took English lessons to make a success of *Oberon*. In spite of his early death, Weber represents an important foundation of 19th-century German Romanticism. **Wagner** and **Mahler** were particularly indebted to him.

Webern, Anton (Friedrich Wilhelm von) (1883–1945)

Austrian composer of spare, enigmatic miniatures combining a lyrical poetic with severe structural rigour. A Renaissance musical scholar, he became a pupil of **Schoenberg**, whose twelve-tone system he interpreted as abstract design in works such as the *Concerto* (1931–34) and the *Second Cantata* (1941–43). His first major work was the **Passacaglia** for orchestra, written with an awareness of the example of **Mahler**; it was followed by the Five Movements for string quartet, which foreshadow Webern's later

TWELVE-TONE SYSTEM

It is more through his work than through Schoenberg's that the twelve-tone system later found so wide an acceptance: among composers who have been particularly influenced by Webern are Stravinsky (from the early 1950s), Stockhausen, and Boulez.

epigrammatic style. Song settings of Schoenberg's favourite poet, Stefan George, are Webern's first excursions into atonality. After World War I he settled near Vienna and devoted himself to teaching and composition. He first adopted Schoenberg's twelve-note method of composition in the *Three Traditional Rhymes* of 1925. In succeeding works, such as the String Trio and the Symphony, Webern adopted ever more rigidly controlled methods; he was also influenced there by the Renaissance composer Heinrich **Isaac**. His death was the result of a misunderstanding (he was shot by a US soldier). Although almost entirely unrecognized during his lifetime, Webern's music has proved very influential since his death: it introduced new concepts of sound, rhythm, and quasi-mathematical organization.

❝ Doomed to a total failure in a deaf world of ignorance and indifference, he inexorably kept on cutting out his diamonds, his dazzling diamonds, the mines of which he knew to perfection. ❞

Stravinsky on Webern, quoted in Kilnoder, *Anton Webern*

Weelkes, Thomas (*c.* 1576–1623)

English composer of ten Anglican services and around 40 anthems, including 'When David Heard'. He was also one of the most significant composers of madrigals. These demonstrate his intricate style, fine **counterpoint**, and brilliant imagery.

In 1601 he became organist and choirmaster at Chichester Cathedral, where during his turbulent career he received repeated reprimands for unruliness and drunkenness; he was dismissed in 1617.

Weill, Kurt Julian (1900–1950)

German composer (US citizen from 1943) who collaborated with Brecht on operas such as *The Threepenny Opera* (1928) and *The Rise and Fall of the City of Mahagonny* (1929), both of which attacked social corruption (*Mahagonny*, which satirized US frontier values, caused a riot at its premiere in Leipzig). He tried to evolve a new form of music theatre, using subjects with a contemporary relevance and the simplest musical means. In

1933 he left Germany, and from 1935 was in the USA, where he wrote a number of successful scores for Broadway, among them the anti-war musical *Johnny Johnson* (1936), *Knickerbocker Holiday* (1938) (including the famous 'September Song'), and *Street Scene* (1947), based on an Elmer Rice play set in the Depression.

> ❝ I write for today. I don't care about posterity. ❞
>
> **Weill**, quoted in Ewen, *American Composers*

Wert, Giaches de (1535–1596)

Flemish composer who was music director at the ducal court of Mantua from the early 1560s until 1595; he had a great influence on his successors, especially **Monteverdi**. He was a prolific composer, and wrote over 150 sacred vocal pieces, but his most celebrated compositions are his madrigals of which he published 16 books. Aged nine he entered the service of Count Alfonso Gonzaga as a member of the choir of the Novellara at Reggio. He began to publish madrigals towards the end of the 1550s, and about 1560 went into service at the ducal court of Mantua under Guglielmo Gonzaga. In 1567 he visited Venice with the court and later Ferrara under Alfonso (II) d'Este. About that time he suffered much from the intrigues of the Italian musicians, who disliked him as a foreigner. His madrigals were written for virtuoso court singers, particularly the *concerto delle donne* or 'singing ladies' of Ferrara. The texts used were often high-quality, the music was declamatory in style, and the three upper voices were frequently emphasised.

Wesley, Samuel Sebastian (1810–1876)

English organist and composer, the illegitimate son of the methodist Charles Wesley. In 1835 he became organist of Exeter Cathedral; he was organist of Winchester Cathedral 1849–65, and then, until his death, of Gloucester Cathedral. He became organ professor at the Royal Academy of Music in London in 1850. He continued his father's promotion of **Bach's** music and conducted the *St Matthew Passion* at Gloucester (Three Choirs Festival) in 1871. He wrote much sacred choral music that is still performed.

Wieniawski, Henryk (1835–1880)

Famous Polish violinist who composed spirited **Romantic** pieces for the violin, notably his second concerto in D minor. Wieniawski was sent to the

Paris Conservatory at the age of eight, and in 1846 made his first tour, in Poland and Russia. In 1860 he was appointed solo violinist to the Tsar, living in St Petersburg most of the time until 1872, when he toured the USA with Anton **Rubinstein**. In 1875 he succeeded **Vieuxtemps** as first violin professor at the Brussels Conservatory. Towards the end of his life he travelled again, in spite of serious ill-health that caused his sudden death in Russia.

Wilbye, John (1574–1638)
One of the first English composers to write madrigals and also one of the finest. Among his most characteristic works are the popular madrigals 'Draw on Sweet Night' and 'Sweet honey-sucking bees' (both 1609). Wilbye was patronized by the Cornwallis family at Brome Hall near Diss. Influenced by **Morley** and **Ferrabosco**, he published two books of madrigals (1598 and 1609), the second of which is generally regarded as one of the greatest English madrigal collections.

Willaert, Adrian (c. 1490–1562)
One of the most prolific and influential musicians of the mid-16th century, he was one of the earliest composers of madrigals, though his most important works are his motets. Of Flemish birth, in 1515 he became a singer in the household of Cardinal Ippolito d'Este. In 1527 he became maestro di cappella at St Mark's, Venice, where his pupils included Cipriano de **Rore** and Andrea

Willaert had a great influence on church music, broadening its character and achieving effect by a wide use of chromatic scales.

Gabrieli. His most important work is the collection of motets and madrigals *Musica nova*, published in 1559, though probably written much earlier.

Wolf, Hugo (Filipp Jakob) (1860–1903)
Austrian composer whose more than 250 **lieder** include the *Mörike-Lieder* (1888) and the two-volume *Italienisches Liederbuch* (1892–96). Wolf brought a new concentration and tragic eloquence to the art of lieder, seeking to enhance the dramatic and emotional potential of the poetry he set by establishing an equal partnership between singer and pianist. Among his other works are the opera *Der Corregidor/The Magistrate* (1895) and orchestral works such as *Italian Serenade* (1892). He often lived in great

poverty, but was befriended by various musical families; the conductors Franz Schalk and Felix Mottl took a professional interest in him. In 1881 he was engaged as second conductor at Salzburg under Carl Muck, but was found to be temperamentally so unfitted for the post that the engagement was terminated within three months. He was music critic for the Vienna *Salonblatt* (1884–87), but here again he offended many people by his irascibility and intolerance (which saw no fault in **Wagner** and no good in **Brahms**). Meanwhile his masterful song settings of Möricke and Eicherdorff won him wide recognition. However, he had contracted syphilis, and in 1897 became insane. He was sent to a sanatorium. Discharged as cured in 1898, he had a relapse after becoming involved in a quarrel with **Mahler** at the Vienna Opera, and was taken to an asylum in a hopeless condition at the end of the year, remaining there until his death.

> ❦ I sent him a song five years ago, and asked him to mark a cross in the score wherever he thought it was faulty ... Brahms sent it back unread, saying, "I don't want to make a cemetery of your composition." ❧
>
> **Wolf,** quoted in Lochner, *Fritz Kreisler*

Wolf-Ferrari, Ermanno (1876–1948)
Italian composer whose operas include *Susanna's Secret* (1909) and the realistic tragedy *The Jewels of the Madonna* (1911). He was sent to Rome to study art by his German father, who was a painter. However, he turned to music and studied with Josef Rheinberger (1839–1901) at Munich. In 1900 he brought out his first opera, after which his stage successes were frequently repeated. Many of his operas were first produced in Germany, including several that sought to evoke the spirit of 18th-century Venetian comedy. He was director of the Liceo Benedetto Marcello at Venice 1902–12.

Wolpe, Stefan (1902–1972)
US composer who studied with and **Schreker** and **Webern**, then went to Palestine and in 1938 settled in the USA. He cultivated an intense, **polyphonic**, and serial language; his pupils included **Feldman** and **Wuorinen**. His works include the operas *Schöne Geschichten* and *Zeus und*

Elida; ballet *The Man from Midian* (1942); symphony for 21 instruments (1956), Passacaglia and two Fugues for orchestra, and *Enactments* for 3 pianos.

Wood, Hugh (1932–)
English composer of lyrical but structurally rigorous works. He studied with **Seiber** and then taught at Morley College (1959–62) and Cambridge University (1976–99). His language incorporates elements of serialism, Classical form (in his Symphony, 1982, and several concertos), and a broad range of colour associated with composers such as **Messiaen**. He first came to notice with his *Scenes from Comus* for soprano, tenor, and orchestra, performed at the 1965 Promenade Concerts.

woodwind family
Instruments from which sound is produced by blowing into a tube, causing the air within to vibrate. Woodwind instruments include those, like the flute, originally made of wood but now more commonly of metal. The saxophone, made of metal, is also a woodwind instrument because it is related to the clarinet. The oboe, bassoon, flute, and clarinet make up the normal woodwind section of an orchestra. Woodwind instruments fall into two categories: reed instruments (such as the oboe, clarinet, and bassoon), in which air passes via an aperture controlled by a vibrating flexible reed or pair of reeds; and those without a reed, where air is simply blown into or across a tube (as with a flute). In both cases, different notes are obtained by changing the length of the tube by covering holes along it.

Wuorinen, Charles (1938–)
US composer, conductor, and pianist whose early works are tonal but he was later influenced by **Varèse**, Babbitt, and serial technique. He studied at Columbia University, and taught there 1964–71. His works include the **masque** *The Politics of Harmony* (1967), the 'burlesque' *The Whore of Babylon* (1975); three symphonies (1958–59), four chamber concertos (1957–59), *Evolutio transcripta* for orchestra (1961), two piano concertos (1966, 1974), and a concerto for amplified violin and orchestra (1971).

Xenakis, Iannis (1922–)

One of the most singular figures of the 20th century, this Romanian-born Greek composer was imprisoned by the Fascists in Greece and sentenced to death. He escaped to Paris where he practised as an engineering draughtsman for architect Le Corbusier. In compositions such as *Metastasis* (1953–54) he brings mathematical stochastic principles (for example, describing particle motion in fluids) to the composition of densely textured effects in which change is perceived globally. Other works, including a setting of the *Oresteia* (1965–56) for choir and ensemble, draw on Greek mythology. His later works are rhythmically more straightforward but nonetheless gripping; his piano concerto *Keqrops* (1987), concern-

Xankis *Romanian-born Greek composer Iannis Xenakis.*

ing the mythical king of Ancient Greece, half-man and half-beast, scored a hit at that year's Promenade Concerts. His ideas have exercised considerable influence on other composers. He published *Formalized Music: Thought and Mathematics in Composition* in 1972.

Young, La Monte (1935–)

US composer whose *Well-Tuned Piano* (1964) lasts over six hours and changes with each performance. The godfather of **minimalism**, his works are far more imaginative and spiritual in substance than those of his forebears; in fact, he shares the wild experimentalism of fellow-Americans **Cage**, **Nancarrow**, and **Partch**.

Other works include *The Tortoise Droning Selected Pitches from the Holy Numbers for the Two Black Tigers, the Green Tiger and the Hermit* (1964), and *The Tortoise Recalling the Drone of the Holy Numbers as they were Revealed in the Dreams of the Whirlwind and the Obsidian Gong, Illuminated by the Sawmill, the Green Sawtooth Ocelot and the High-Tension Line Stepdown Transformer* (both works staged with voice, gong, and strings, 1964).

Young lectured for a time on guerrilla warfare at the New York School for Social Research.

Ysaÿe, Eugène-Auguste (1858–1931)

One of the greatest and most individual virtuosos of his day, he toured as a soloist and conductor throughout Europe and America. Although he never studied composition formally, he mastered writing in a **Romantic** style and is one of Belgium's most important composers. In 1886 he formed the Ysaÿe Quartet, and premiered **Debussy's** quartet in 1893. Admired everywhere for his skill and musicianship, he often performed the Franck Sonata dedicated to him. He wrote the opera *Piére li Houîeu* in Walloon dialect (1931).

Yun, Isang (1917–1995)

Korean-born composer who lived in Berlin, where he taught at the Hochschule für Musik. His espousal of serial techniques led to withdrawal of works written before 1959. His works include the operas *Der Traum des Liu-Tung* (1965), *Sim Tjong* (1972), five symphonies, and chamber music.

zarzuela

Spanish music theatre combining song, dance, and speech. It originated as an amusement for royalty in the 17th century; the term comes from La Zarzuela, a royal country house in Spain where the first performances took place. Often satirical, zarzuela gained renewed popularity in the 20th century with the works of Frederico Tórroba (1891–1982).

Zelenka, Jan Dismas (1679–1745)

Bohemian composer who wrote unusual but lightweight orchestral works, trio sonatas, and solemn religious works including Magnificats in D (1725) and C (1727). He is best known today for his bold and adventurous instrumental music, including *Hippocondrie* (1723).

Zemlinsky, Alexander von (1871–1942)

Austrian composer and conductor who taught **Schoenberg**, (whose sister he married), and gave the first performance of his *Erwartung* in 1924. His personal ties with Schoenberg scarcely influenced his own music; he started composing in a Classical style and later was drawn to the progressive, late-**Romantic** style of **Mahler** and even **Schreker**. After time spent in Berlin, he emigrated to the USA. His works include the operas *Eine florentinische Tragödie, Der Zwerg* (both after Oscar Wilde, 1917, 1922), two symphonies (1892, 1897), *Die Seejungfrau* for orchestra (1903), *Lyric Symphony* for soprano, baritone, and orchestra (1923), and four string quartets (1895–1936).

Zimmermann, Bernd Alois (1918–1970)

German composer who studied philosophy at university but who developed a highly complex, modernist idiom in the early 1960s. His work often employs **quotation** from other composers' work. He committed suicide after failing to combat an unknown illness. Standing apart from the avant

Zimmermann's expressionist opera *Die Soldaten* employs film, electronics, jazz, and mime.

garde of the 1960s, his unique, humanist vision is heard at its best in works such as *Requiem for a Young Poet* (1969).

Zwilich, Ellen Taaffe (1939–)
US composer whose music is basically tonal in idiom, sometimes recalling **minimalist** or late **Romantic** precedents. Her First Symphony won a Pulitzer prize in 1983. She played the violin in the American Symphony Orchestra under Stokowski and studied with **Sessions** and **Carter**. Her other works include *Symbolom* for orchestra (1988), concertos for trombone (1988), flute (1990), oboe (1990), bassoon (1992), horn (1993), and trumpet (1994), and vocal and chamber music.

Appendix

Chronology of Important Compositions

1360	*Messe de Nostre Dame*	Machaut
1436	*Nuper rosarum flores*	Dufay
1502	First book of Masses	Josquin Desprez
1555	*Missa Papae Marcelli*	Palestrina
1573	*Spem in alium*	Tallis
1589	*Cantiones sacrae*, book 1	Byrd
1597	*Dafne*, opera	Peri
1607	*L'Orfeo favola pastorale*	Monteverdi
1611	*Parthenia* (collection of keyboard music)	Bull, Byrd, and Gibbons
1629	First *Sinfonia sacra*	Schütz
1642	*L'incoronazione di Poppea*	Monteverdi
1670	*Le bourgeois gentilhomme*	Lully
1689	*Dido and Aeneas*	Purcell
1708	*Gloria*	Vivaldi
1717	*Water Music*	Handel
1721	*Brandenburg Concertos*	Bach
1725	*The Four Seasons*	Vivaldi
1729	*St Matthew Passion*	Bach
1735	*Les indes galantes*	Rameau
1742	*Messiah*	Handel
1748	*Mass in B Minor*	Bach
1749	*Music for the Royal Fireworks*	Handel
1762	*Orfeo ed Eridice*	Gluck
1764	Symphonies 21–23	Haydn
1772	String quartets K155–156	Mozart
1783	*Linz* Symphony	Mozart
1785	*The Last Seven Words of our Saviour on the Cross*	Haydn
1786	*The Marriage of Figaro*	Mozart
1787	*Don Giovanni*	Mozart
1788	Last three symphonies	Mozart
1789	*Oxford* Symphony	Haydn
1791	*The Magic Flute*	Mozart
1798	*The Creation*	Haydn
1799	*Pathétique* Sonata	Beethoven
1801	*The Seasons*	Haydn
1804	The Third Symphony, *Eroica*	Beethoven
1805	*Fidelio*	Beethoven
1808	Fifth Symphony	Beethoven

1816	*The Barber of Seville*	Rossini
1821	*Der Freischütz*	Weber
1823	Ninth Symphony, *Choral*	Beethoven
1826	*A Midsummer Night's Dream*	Mendelssohn
1828	*Impromptus*	Schubert
1829	Piano Concerto no. 1	Chopin
1830	*Symphonie fantastique*	Berlioz
1831	*Norma*	Bellini
1832	*L'elisir d'amore*	Donizetti
1840	*Dichterliebe*	Schumann
1843	*The Flying Dutchman*	Wagner
1848	*Les préludes*	Liszt
1851	*Rigoletto*	Verdi
1853	*La traviata*	Verdi
1854	Piano Sonata	Liszt
1858	Piano Concerto no.1	Brahms
1863	*The Pearl Fishers*	Bizet
1865	*Tristan and Isolde*	Wagner
1867	*Night on a Bare Mountain*	Mussorgsky
1868	Piano Concerto	Grieg
1871	*Aida*	Verdi
1873	Third Symphony	Bruckner
1875	*Carmen*	Bizet
1876	First Symphony	Brahms
1877	*Swan Lake*	Tchaikovsky
1880	*In the Steppes of Central Asia*	Borodin
1882	*Parsifal*	Wagner
1884	First Symphony	Mahler
1886	*Carnival of the Animals*	Saint-Saëns
1887	Double Concerto	Brahms
1888	*Gymnopédies*	Satie
1890	Requiem	Fauré
1893	*New World* Symphony	Dvořák
1895	*Till Eulenspiegel*	Richard Strauss
1896	*La Bohème*	Puccini
1899	*Enigma Variations*	Elgar
1901	Second Piano Concerto	Rachmaninoff
1902	*Pelléas et Mélisande*	Debussy
1904	*Jenufa*	Janáček
1905	*La Mer*	Debussy
1908	*The Unanswered Question*	Ives
1909	*Prometheus*	Skryabin
1910	Ninth Symphony	Mahler
1912	*Pierrot lunaire*	Schoenberg
1913	*Rite of Spring*	Stravinsky
1916	*The Planets*	Holst
1919	*Die Frau ohne Schatten*	Richard Strauss

1921	*Classical* Symphony	Prokofiev
1924	*Rhapsody in Blue*	Gershwin
1925	*Wozzeck*	Berg
1926	*King Roger*	Szymanowski
1928	Symphony	Webern
1931	Second Piano Concerto	Bartók
1934	*The Lady Macbeth of the Mtsenk District*	Shostakovich
1935	First Symphony	Walton
1937	*Lulu*	Berg
1938	*Romeo and Juliet*	Prokofiev
1941	*Quartet to the End of Time*	Messiaen
1942	*Fanfare for the Common Man*	Copland
1944	*Concerto for Orchestra*	Bartók
1945	*Peter Grimes*	Britten
1946	First Piano Sonata	Boulez
1948	*Four Last Songs*	Richard Strauss
1951	*The Rake's Progress*	Stravinsky
1952	*4'33"*	Cage
1955	*Le marteau sans maître*	Boulez
1957	*West Side Story*	Bernstein
1958	*Poème eléctronique*	Varèse
1960	*Kontakte*	Stockhausen
1961	*War Requiem*	Britten
1962	*Pli selon pli*	Boulez
1965	*Die Soldaten*	Zimmermann
1966	*Oresteia*	Xenakis
1968	*Sinfonia*	Berio
1970	*Madam Press Died Last Week at 90*	Feldman
1972	*Tavener*	Davies
1973	*Clocks and Clouds*	Ligeti
1974	*Rituel in memoriam Bruno Maderna*	Boulez
1976	*Einstein on the Beach*	Glass
1977	*Symphony of Three Orchestras*	Carter
1978	*Le grand macabre*	Ligeti
1979	*Symphony of Sorrowful Songs*	Gorecki
1981	*Donnerstag aus Licht*	Stockhausen
1982	*The Mask of Time*	Tippett
1983	*The Desert Music*	Reich
1984	*Polish Requiem*	Penderecki
1986	*Carceri d'invenzione*	Ferneyhough
1987	*Nixon in China*	Adams
1991	*Gawain and the Green Knight*	Birtwistle
1996	*Asyla*	Adès
1997	*The Book of Elements*	Dillon
1998	*Vortex temporum*	Grisey
2000	*Recitativo oscuro*	Sciarrino

Appendix II – Italian Terms Commonly Used in Music

a cappella	'in a chapel'; music sung without instruments
accelerando	accelerating, getting faster
adagio	slowly
ad libitum	freely, optionally
al fine	until the end
allargando	getting broader
allegro	merry, lively
animato	animated
arco	with the bow, as opposed to plucked
assai	enough
attacca	'begin'; go onto the next part without waiting
bravura	'bravery'; with virtuoso sweep
brio	brilliance
caccia	'hunt'; music often imitating hunting horn
cantabile	in a singing manner
coda	'tail'; the end section of a piece
crescendo	getting louder; growing
da capo	from the beginning
divisi	'divided'; indicates when a number of instruments play separate parts
dolce	sweetly
forte, f	loud
giocoso	joyfully
glissando	sliding, between two pitches
lacrimoso	tearfully
largo	broadly
lento	slowly
maestoso	majestically
marcato	marked, accentuated
moto	movement, motion
muta	change (to a different instrument)
niente	nothing
ossia	otherwise
pesante	heavily
poco	a little
presto	quick
ritardando	slowing down
saltando	jumping
scherzando	jokingly
senza	without
sforzando	forcing, accented
simile	like, the same
solo	alone
sostenuto	sustained
sotto voce	'under the voice'; quietly
staccato	detached

stentando	labouring, dragging
stesso tempo	the same speed
strepitoso	noisy
stringendo	'tightening'; getting faster
subito	suddenly
tacet	silent
tempo giusto	'just' or the 'correct' speed
tenuto	held, sustained
tranquillo	tranquil, peacefully
tremolando	trembling; rapid repetition of a note
tutti	all, all together